The Jazz Process

The Jazz Process

Collaboration, Innovation, and Agility

Adrian Cho

✦✦Addison-Wesley

Upper Saddle River, NJ • Boston • Indianapolis • San Francisco
New York • Toronto • Montreal • London • Munich • Paris • Madrid
Cape Town • Sydney • Tokyo • Singapore • Mexico City

Editor-in-Chief
Mark Taub
Acquisitions Editor
Greg Doench
Managing Editor
Kristy Hart
Senior Project Editor
Lori Lyons
Copy Editor
Krista Hansing Editorial Services, Inc.
Indexer
Lisa Stumpf
Proofreader
Language Logistics, LLC
Publishing Coordinator
Michelle Housley
Cover Designer
Anne Jones
Compositor
Gloria Schurick
Graphics
Laura Robbins

Library of Congress Cataloging-in-Publication Data

Cho, Adrian.
    The jazz process : collaboration, innovation, and agility / Adrian Cho.
      p. cm.
    Includes index.
    ISBN-13: 978-0-321-63645-4 (pbk. : alk. paper)
    ISBN-10: 0-321-63645-7 (pbk. : alk. paper) 1. Teams in the workplace. 2. Diversity in the workplace. 3. Organizational effectiveness. 4. Communication. I. Title.
    HD66.C467 2010
    658.4'022—dc22

                        2010010507

Pearson Education, Inc.
Rights and Contracts Department
501 Boylston Street, Suite 900
Boston, MA 02116
Fax (617) 671 3447

ISBN-13: 978-0-321-63645-4
ISBN-10: 0-321-63645-7
Text printed in the United States on recycled paper at Courier in Stoughton, Massachusetts.
First printing June 2010

For Kira, Chief, and Adam,
who taught me the value of
tackling every task with gusto.

Table of Contents

List of Figures

Foreword

Group dynamics are an integral part of our daily work and private lives, whether we're driving a car and dealing with commuter traffic, working through computer code with a team of programmers, running a business, or performing with a jazz group on a concert stage. In *The Jazz Process*, Adrian Cho explains how high-performance experts from varied disciplines use certain underlying truths to reach agreements, solve complicated problems, and negotiate unexpected hurdles. The best teams do this on the fly, in real time, and in such a way that an uninformed observer might never notice the skill, dedication, and magic involved.

The 14 fundamental principles found in this book are essential to any collaborative venture. Following his own advice, Cho offers "just enough" description and analysis to make practical application of the principles easy and flexible. *The Jazz Process* provides a thorough diagnosis of top performance—how teams function, how stellar results are achieved, and how people can effectively work together on just about any project imaginable.

In my work and play as a musician, I can relate every principle here to my daily practice sessions, rehearsals, and performances. Cho's ideas about teamwork, trust, roles, and responsibilities can be applied to music and arts, as well as any other activity in which a high level of performance can translate to success.

When I perform with a group of jazz musicians, we are like a basketball team, passing the ball back and forth, waiting for the right moment to sink a basket. We are a business concern, and our business is jazz. Our work is not unlike a military squad on a secret mission or a group of politicians debating social issues and reaching agreements. I bring a complex combination of skill, preparedness, and intuition to every performance situation. By understanding the goal of a musical project and being keenly attuned to the other musicians, I help the group achieve the highest possible artistic success—or the most efficient *"return on time and energy invested,"* as Cho writes.

Music performance is all about agreement and teamwork. Successful performing musicians adhere to self-evident truths ingrained by countless hours of practice and performance. The agreements between experienced musicians are often unspoken, even when they appear and sound seamless.

I play many concerts where there is a clearly defined structure to the music—there are specific notes to be played in a certain way with a certain sound, rhythmic feeling, and interpretation. However, some of my favorite musical experiences involve freely improvised situations—a minimum of rules, a bare-bones structure, with more possibility for risks and rewards. When playing freely, there are still agreements. In improvised music, the structure might not be as formal as the detailed parts of written arrangements, but the balance between freedom and responsibility remains a common denominator.

Cho describes the concept of using "just enough rules." As applied to music, this means the right rules in the right amount, with the freedom to creatively break rules if the need arises. Musicians playing various styles must understand the rules, their individual roles, and the best team approach for a good outcome.

Whether playing in a highly structured situation or in a freer atmosphere, the best musicians strive toward one goal when they pick up their instruments: musical success. At first look and listen, the goal seems simple—the players should make no mistakes, and they should elicit a satisfying reaction from the audience. The basic task of playing a piece and having the audience applaud belies the complexity of the interaction between musicians as they perform.

Great musicians, like successful business people and top athletes, constantly balance individual contributions and elegant teamwork. The gems of individual performance are almost worthless without the team framework. In a jazz band, trust and respect among the musicians are indispensable. Deep listening and a passion for the task at hand are equally important.

Legendary jazz bassist Ron Carter once spoke to me about his work with drummer Tony Williams in the Miles Davis Quintet of the '60s, saying, *"The hook-up with Tony happened right away, from the first time we played. When we started developing the music rhythmically and harmonically, I trusted my judgment. If I said this was the top of the tune, that's where they took it to be. I just trusted that it was going to go where it was going to go. I was one person they would trust to play the top of the form or show where the top of the tune was. That's something I could always do, whatever was going on. They trusted that when I played one, if that wasn't their one, they would get to it on the next time around."*

Carter repeatedly refers to the element of trust between musicians. Team trust in a jazz group begins when a player offers something musically, and it's completed when another player supports that idea. Carter's experience verifies Cho's concept of "leading on demand." The best team players know instinctively when to lead or follow.

The basic performance principles that Cho describes transfer to diverse fields. In the business world, companies thrive or die by the use or abuse of these tenets. Sports teams win or lose games. Software developers invent the next big thing—or not.

"Companies all too often wonder why their employees are not more committed to their work, when, in fact, they should be asking themselves what they can do to achieve a higher level of commitment from their employees," writes Cho. I've found that a bandleader, soloist, or even an ensemble player known as an ace can inspire others to give more to a performance. Cho's premise of employing top talent increases the return on investment in any situation.

The level of commitment in a musical ensemble is palpable from the moment the musicians unpack their instruments. Miles Davis famously said he could tell if someone was a good player by *"His carriage…first. His carriage of the instrument. You can tell whether he plays or not by the way he carries his instrument, whether it means something to him or not."* [from "The Man with the Horn," interview by Cheryl McCall, *Musician Magazine*, 1982].

Davis appears regularly throughout *The Jazz Process* because he was a great musician and an even greater bandleader. He was an enigmatic and abrasive character, but his bands always seemed to give 110%, providing us with some of the best recordings in the history of jazz. Davis's groups were always at the forefront of musical developments, and the friction that they created defined new directions in music.

Friction is a force to understand and manage. Cho compares friction in business, sports, war, technology, and music. Bad friction can paralyze a group, lose a game, bankrupt the company, and send an army running in retreat. Good friction in the right amount is necessary for any activity to work well. Good friction makes the jazz band swing, cranks up the heat at a basketball game, and provides just the right level of competition to maintain a thriving economy.

Form, tempo, pulse, and groove are other elements that Cho describes as essential to the success of a team. When I moved to New York City in 1980 to pursue a career as a jazz musician, I often attended Monday night workshops with pianist Barry Harris. A master of the bebop style of jazz piano, Harris demanded a strict adherence to bebop jazz vocabulary—the melodies, rhythms, and stylistic nuances that make bebop sound unique. By mastering the vocabulary, students could successfully negotiate the structure and form of standard jazz songs.

Without strict attention to the basic underlying form, there is no freedom in the music. Tension and release in music occur when a player masters and controls the elements of form and stylistic vocabulary. To pass muster with Harris, we had to know the vocabulary, form, and have the right momentum when we played—the swing element, tempo, pulse, and rhythmic forward motion.

In a clever description of strategic approaches to warfare, basketball, business, and software development, Cho outlines the importance of form, tempo, pulse, and groove. Describing the optimal groove in a goal-oriented software development team, he shows how an organization can swing. The desire to maintain tempo and momentum that is so ingrained in a jazz musician's psyche is also the very thing that can lead a company to creatively reach goals on time. Business, bebop style.

In *The Jazz Process*, Cho lays out a clear path to achieving elegant teamwork, goal-oriented project completion, and winning results. Whatever your line of work or pleasure might be, I hope your team finds their groove.

John Goldsby
Bassist and author
www.johngoldsby.com
Cologne, Germany, March 2010

Preface

"Art is the desire of a man to express himself, to record the reactions of his personality to the world he lives in."
—Amy Lowell, nineteenth-century American poet

About This Book

This book is an artistic expression that captures some of my personal thoughts about the world in which we work and play. Although I didn't write this book with a thematic approach in mind, three themes emerged from the text in support of the concepts you'll find herein. Their presence is no surprise, as they are principles I value and have come to rely on over the years.

The first of these themes is **diversity**. I feel fortunate to have been exposed to a degree of diversity throughout my life. From a cultural perspective, I was born in Australia, where I spent the first 30 years of my life. My mother is Chinese, and my father was most likely Australian, although I can't be certain. In primary (elementary) school, I was the only child of Asian descent in a student body of approximately 600 students. Back then, Australia was less racially diverse than it is today. My reaction to the way other children treated me was to reject my Chinese ancestry. Fortunately, my attitude changed as I grew up, and I began to embrace the differences that come with diversity and to realize how those differences have enriched my life. In 2000, I moved to Ottawa, Canada, where I live with my wife, Deborah, an American Lutheran pastor. We live on the rural outskirts of Ottawa and share our home with a large family of cats and dogs. Career-wise, my interests have always been many and varied, but arts and technology were particularly important to me since an early age. I could never decide between the two and eventually developed parallel careers in the software industry and in music. I've long been fascinated by diversity in teams. In the arts, I am always looking for ways to bring together artists from multiple genres or disciplines. I like to form musical ensembles that include both classical and jazz musicians and perform works that span genres and challenge both musicians and audiences. I also like to stage productions that bring together artists from a variety of disciplines, including visual artists, actors, dancers, and musicians. In business, I enjoy the dynamics of cross-functional teams, and I'm often trying to find ways to integrate multiple disciplines.

Unification is another strong current in this book. It comes from the belief that although people are all different, many ties bind us together. More specifically, although we all work and play in a wide variety of domains, certain principles are universally applicable. We all deal collectively with many of the same fundamental problems; only our contexts differ. Jazz musicians must constantly collaborate, innovate, and manage change, and they have to do so in real time. The same is true of a basketball team, a squad of soldiers, and a team in business. Although it's natural to look toward fellow disciples when seeking solutions to the problems we encounter in our work, I've found that some of the best inspiration can come from people working in completely different disciplines. In this book, you'll find examples of excellence drawn not only from software development and music, but also from business, military operations, and sports. You'll also find the application of laws from the disciplines of sociology, psychology, physics, biology, and systems theory.

The final theme that plays out in this book is that of **execution**. I am always concerned by the glut of leadership, strategy and management education, and the dearth of focus on execution. It's not simply that there are so many more words and minutes given to the former, and it has nothing to do with management versus those who work in the trenches. One person's strategy is another person's execution. Middle management executes the strategy set by upper management. Even the most senior people in an organization execute on behalf of a board, and they in turn are answerable to shareholders. The problem is that many leaders do not give enough respect or consideration to the realities of executing strategies defined in isolation. The result is usually failure that leads to finger-pointing all around. The strategies that are most likely to succeed are those created collaboratively with input from all stakeholders. Execution is another one of those universally applicable principles that must permeate an organization at all levels so that it moves in concert like a symphony orchestra. Successful artistic leaders who help deliver great performances with minimal planning and rehearsal understand and/or give due consideration to execution. In jazz, ensembles often execute with no plan or rehearsal whatsoever.

Reading This Book

The Jazz Process provides a framework for improving collaboration, innovation, and agility by offering a method for execution and 14 best principles that act on that method. Many books begin with an overview and then drill down into the details, a kind of "top-down" approach. In contrast, I've chosen a linear approach, resulting in a more natural progression for discussing the subject matter, somewhat akin to telling a story. Consequently, you won't see the big picture until we've laid a foundation by discussing five principles for working. If you just can't wait and you would like to see a high-level view right now, take a peek at the listing of the principles of the jazz process in the figure on page 85 and the execution cycle illustrated in the figure on page 98 in the "The Essentials of Execution" section in Part II.

As a domain-agnostic view of the way in which high-performance teams succeed in the face of challenges, the *Jazz Process* is inherently abstract. To put it to work, you must translate its method for execution and its principles into concrete practices that work specifically for your team and its activities. You'll find many concrete examples to help you do that throughout this book. As you read through this book, you'll find it beneficial to ask yourself how you can put the *Jazz Process* to work for you. You can find out more about the *Jazz Process* and even participate in discussions at www.jazzprocess.com.

Acknowledgments

Over the years, I've worked with many people in both arts and business. Working with all these artists and business professionals has taught me a great deal and provided me with invaluable experience, regardless of the outcome of our various projects.

Especially notable are the wonderful musicians of the Impressions in Jazz Orchestra and the guest artists, including many dancers and actors, with whom we've had the good fortune to perform. Whether it's been free jazz explorations, swing dances, big band concerts, sacred music, theater shows, or genre-spanning presentations that push the envelope, this fabulous group of artists has enthusiastically taken on the challenges I have put before them. Their passion, musicianship, and, most of all, willingness to collaborate have enabled us to entertain and educate time and time again. You can find out more about this fabulous ensemble at www.impressionsinjazz.ca.

In business, I've been fortunate to work with an amazing software development team at IBM. The team began its life as Object Technology International under the reins of founder and CEO Dave Thomas, a free-thinking visionary with a deep understanding of execution and delivery. In later years, Brian Barry provided this team with invaluable leadership. The group continues to do amazing work as part of IBM's Rational division under the leadership of Dave Thomson. Over the years, this team has produced such ground-breaking, world-class products as ENVY™/Developer, VisualAge® for Java™, the Eclipse™ Platform and Java Development Tools, and, most recently, IBM's Jazz® technology and the first Jazz-based product, Rational® Team Concert™. If you're a software developer, you may have used one or more of these products or been influenced by the way the team that produced them has achieved its success. I should note that this team consists not only of software developers, but also businesspeople representing many different functions. This multidisciplined composition is similar to that of any effective product development team, and as you will soon read, it's vital to the success of such teams. You can find out more about IBM's Jazz-based projects at www.jazz.net.

Jazz is built on Eclipse open source software, software that is vitally important not only to IBM, but to countless other organizations and individuals across the planet. Under the auspices of the Eclipse Foundation and its executive director, Mike Milinkovich, the Eclipse ecosystem has continued to flourish. It is a vital part of thousands of software applications and a huge success story in the software industry, proving the benefits of openness, transparency, and decentralized leadership. You can find out more about Eclipse at www.eclipse.org.

Special thanks to Greg Doench at Pearson for believing that people would want to read this book and Lori Lyons for shepherding the book through the production process; Dave Thomson, Steve Kurlowecz, and Steve Stansel for helping me negotiate the IBM business and legal processes with speed; Erich Gamma, Scott Ambler, and Carol Yutkowitz for their feedback; Katherine Fick for her suggestions, encouragement, and humor; Karice McIntyre for her due diligence in the final iteration of proofreading; and, my dear wife, Pastor Deborah Ann Taylor, who supports me in everything I do and spent many hours editing my grammatical ramblings.

Finally, I must express how thrilled I was when jazz bassist John Goldsby agreed to write the foreword to this book. John is a world-class jazz musician, and I believe that much of his success comes from his deep knowledge of the jazz tradition and the dynamics of performing in both small and large ensembles. He has shared this knowledge over many years through his teaching and writing. Check out John's music and writing at his website, www.johngoldsby.com.

About the Author

Adrian Cho is well-qualified to draw parallels between the worlds of jazz, business, and software. A leader and innovative collaborator in the arts, he performs as a bassist and conductor and directs the Impressions in Jazz Orchestra, a unique, critically acclaimed symphonic jazz ensemble that brings together an impressive array of professional jazz and symphony musicians. Doug Fischer of the *Ottawa Citizen* labeled him "a musical missionary" while Melanie Scott of *WHERE Ottawa* described him as "one of our city's most adventurous musical renaissance men."

As a software development manager, he applies more than twenty years of experience to help teams deliver innovative solutions on time. Early in his career he consulted to a wide range of organizations, including retail and commercial banks and research and development labs at Fujitsu and IBM. For the past fifteen years he has helped to produce multiple class-leading and award-winning software engineering and team collaboration tools. At IBM he manages the global development of Rational Team Concert and Rational's Collaborative Application Lifecycle Management project. As a manager of intellectual property for more than ten years, he has played a key role in the Eclipse and Jazz initiatives of open innovation.

Dubbed "a cool guide to hot jazz" by Alex Hutchinson of the *Ottawa Citizen*, Adrian is a passionate educator who loves to write, speak, and perform. John Kelman of *All About Jazz* wrote, "Cho's intentions were clearly to educate as much as entertain, and he succeeded on both fronts." Adrian speaks and blogs regularly about high-performance teamwork at jazzprocess.com.

Introduction

Collaboration

Collaboration is the act of working together. The ability to collaborate with others is one of the most important skills a person can possess. No matter how inventive, creative, or productive you might be, as one person alone, you can achieve only so much.

The state of our planet would be radically different if we human beings did not possess the ability to collaborate. Forced labor is one of the oldest and crudest forms of collaboration, albeit one that is managed by duress. The Great Wall of China was built by millions of people, including soldiers, criminals, common people, and even children. Some estimates suggest that as many as three million people may have died as a result of the harsh working conditions they endured during the building of the wall. By comparison, the work force that built the great Egyptian pyramids was substantially smaller. It may have been as few as 20,000 to 30,000 workers strong, and possibly only a small proportion of that force may have been slaves. Regardless of the actual numbers, what's clear is that both the Egyptian pyramid builders and the Chinese wall builders were great organizers of labor. On a much smaller scale, our earliest ancestors would have cooperated to hunt and to protect themselves from predators. These accomplishments would not have been possible without our ability to work together.

The skills of collaboration are not unique to humans. Think about a pack of wolves hunting a moose, a colony of beavers building and maintaining a dam, or a group of humpback whales trapping fish in an amazing, innovative bubble net. Collaboration is present almost everywhere in our lives, both past and present, as well as in the world around us. Our natural tendency to work with others is so great that we have developed methods of mass collaboration, aided by technology, that enable us to harness the combined forces of multiple minds distributed across the planet. Projects such as the online encyclopedia Wikipedia are sustained by contributions from people across the globe. Open source software, powering most of the Internet servers across the planet and becoming ever more widely used, is built and maintained in much the same way.

The benefits of collaboration are obvious. By applying more people to a task, you can reduce the time taken to complete that task. This assumes that multiple people can undertake the task simultaneously. Collaboration is sometimes a necessity because some problems are so large or difficult that they are impossible to solve without a team. The larger stones in the pyramids at Giza are thought to weigh as much as two tons. Even with the aid of the pulley lifting machines employed by the pyramid builders, one person alone could not have moved even one of these stones. The combined efforts of multiple individuals, however, could move them.

A very simplistic theory of collaboration would conclude that if a team of one person can perform one unit of work within a set period, increasing the size of the team would, theoretically, produce proportionally more work in the same amount of time. In other words, ten people could produce ten units of work.

In reality, collaboration involves overhead that results in less work being produced than might be expected. For example, ten people might be able to produce the equivalent of only eight units of work in the time that one person could produce one unit of work. Figure I.1 illustrates this. Collaborative overhead increases as the size of a team increases, and at some stage, the law of diminishing returns leads one to conclude that it doesn't make sense to add any more people to a problem. One of the most obvious sources of collaborative overhead is **friction**. This is one of the many concepts we discuss in the pages that follow.

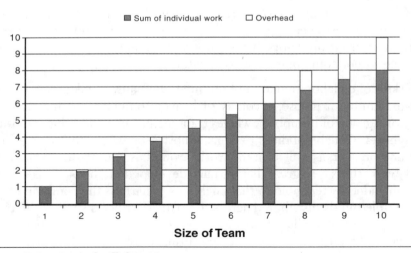

Figure I.1   *Cost of collaboration*

Synergy

In contrast to the overhead of collaboration is the principle of **synergy**, in which the combined efforts of many can be collectively greater than the sum of their individual efforts. This means that if we apply X number of people to a given task, we could theoretically accomplish *more than* X units of work within the same period of time. Figure I.2 illustrates the benefit of synergy combined with the overhead of collaborating. The benefit of synergy can partially or completely offset the overhead of collaboration.

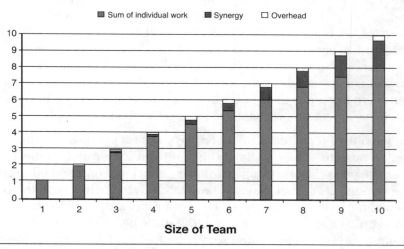

Figure I.2   *Benefit of synergy*

Synergy plays an important role in the political domain, where the outcome of an electoral or legislative decision depends on a total number of votes. Individual politicians might not draw enough votes to win a decision, but by forming alliances, they can aggregate votes and achieve their goals together. Many political partnerships—in fact, some of the most surprising and odd partnerships—have resulted from such a need. In the 2008 U.S. Presidential election, Republican John McCain chose Sarah Palin as his running mate, with the idea that she would inject energy and excitement into his campaign and win votes from the conservative, youth, and women's groups that McCain was having difficulty courting. Barack Obama chose Joe Biden for his foreign policy experience, seniority, and familiarity to long-time voters. These political examples demonstrate that synergy is often present when people combine complementary skills. Synergy is more likely to occur when the size of a team is limited, and a team is more likely to be effective when its composition is multidisciplined or cross-functional.

In the U.S. Army, a Special Forces Operational Detachment Alpha (ODA), or "A-team," consists of 12 soldiers. The team is led by a commander and a second-in-command, and the remaining ten positions are filled by an Operations Sergeant, an Assistant Operations and Intelligence Sergeant, and pairs of Weapons, Engineering, Medical, and Communications Sergeants. This doubling-up affords redundancy in case of personnel loss and allows the team to divide into smaller squads. Even with such duplication of skills, an A-team has a great deal of individual expertise. In comparison, regular army squads tend to have less individual expertise. A nine-soldier rifle squad consists of a squad leader and two fire teams, each with a team leader, one rifleman, one automatic rifleman, and a grenadier. Special Operations Forces (SOF) units such as those employed by the U.S. Army's Green Berets and Army Rangers, the Navy SEALs, Delta Force, and "hunter-killer" teams, whose very existence is classified, may be required to operate deep in enemy territory with limited or no support. In many cases, the government may deny their mission, or even their existence, if they are captured. They have a very real need to be as self-reliant as possible.

On a basketball team, each member plays a particular position and fulfills specific functions. The point guard is the team leader and often calls and sets up the plays. The shooting guard makes the long shots and often guards the opposing team's best player. The small forward scores near the basket and looks for rebounds and steals. The power forward, often the biggest and strongest player on the team, controls the space near the basket and is a key element in defense. The center, who is usually the tallest player, leverages his or her height when scoring, blocking shots, and grabbing rebounds.

In a jazz trio, each musician plays a specific role. The classic jazz trio includes piano, double bass (sometimes called acoustic bass, string bass, upright bass, or simply bass), and drums. Another common configuration is that of a drummer-less group employing a horn (such as a saxophone or trumpet), guitar or piano, and bass. In a piano trio, the piano plays a dual role as both the lead melodic instrument and the comping (short for *accompanying*) instrument that plays chordal harmony. The traditional role of the bass is to play the foundation of that harmony using roots of the chords. The primary role of the drums is to delineate the time and the groove. In the horn-guitar/piano-bass trio, the horn is the lead instrument, the guitar or piano comps, and the bass fulfills both its traditional role and that of the primary time-keeper.

A basketball team with only five players and a jazz trio with only three musicians have the same critical need for self-reliance as a Special Forces team. They both rely on a cross-functional approach to deliver the greatest performance possible with limited resources. Synergy is a natural outcome when each member of these teams plays to his or her strengths and successfully combines talents with those of the other ensemble members.

Performing

Synergy is present when any ensemble or company of artists gives a great performance. In an orchestra, the combined result of all the musicians and a conductor performing together is greater than the sum of all the individual participants working alone. Think about the powerful impact of a great orchestra performance, and then think what it would be like to hear each individual musician play his or her part in isolation from the rest. Each musician would play the same notes, whether playing individually or simultaneously, but the impact to listeners is much greater when the musicians perform together.

As in high-performance business teams, artistic ensembles are staffed with passionate and committed practitioners. They must leverage collective individual contributions if they are to deliver a performance (product) that will attract and retain customers. Their performances must be delivered on time with close to zero defects. This must be accomplished in real time while the ensemble is subjected to continuous scrutiny.

If a theater company is scheduled to present a performance, it can't just decide one day that it's not ready and postpone the performance when tickets have already been sold. As they say, "The show must go on." Timeliness of delivery is critical in many other jobs. Consider, for example, the clergy person who must be at worship each week to lead a service and deliver a sermon. Think about the tax accountant who must submit accurate and complete tax returns in time, to avoid costly penalty fees.

High-quality production of goods and services seems like an obvious goal. But just how good does the resulting product have to be? Let's say 99.9 percent is good enough. A large artistic ensemble, such as an orchestra, may have 100 musicians who each play 1,000 notes in the course of a performance. That's 100,000 total notes the ensemble plays. If only 99.9 percent of those notes are good, there are still 100 bad notes that could mar an otherwise perfect concert or recording take. The United States Postal Service delivered 667 million pieces of mail each day in 2008. If 99.9 percent was good enough, the USPS would have lost 667,000 packages daily!

Artistic performers must not only deliver their performance on time, but they must also deliver it in real time. A company of ballet dancers can't just stop in the middle of a performance to make a decision at its leisure. The same is true for a jazz ensemble, as well as for the driver of a fully loaded gas tanker who must suddenly decide what action to take to avoid an unexpected traffic obstruction.

Regardless of your line of work, thinking about your job as a series of performances offers advantages. Your personal goal should be to give the best individual performance you can while ensuring that your team gives the best collective performance it can. Figure I.3 illustrates an operating framework for collaborative performance. In this framework, the team concurrently executes in all four of the quadrants so that they are simultaneously contributing as individuals, working together as a cohesive unit, delivering a high-quality performance on time, and creating a unique offering. The central box is a special one that represents the team's efforts being maintained from one performance to another.

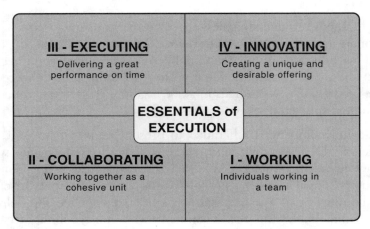

Figure I.3 *Operating framework for collaborative performance*

Learning from Jazz Performance

When jazz musicians perform, they create a unique style of music while confronting an equally unique set of challenges. They do not simply deliver a prepared product, but they must continuously create that product in the moment. In the movie *The Universal Mind of Bill Evans* (Carvell 1966), pianist Bill Evans says:

Jazz as we tend to look at it is a style, but I feel that jazz is not so much a style as a process of making music. It's the process of making one minute's music in one minute's time, whereas when you compose, you can make one minute's music and take three months to compose one minute's music.

Each jazz performance must be unique and innovative, and because the creative process occurs in real time, the musicians must constantly adapt to unpredictable changes. Even if they have never worked together, a group of skilled jazz musicians can collectively face these challenges and go on to deliver one great performance after another. As in any multidisciplined team, they do this by collectively integrating strong individual contributions from passionate and committed practitioners. In addition, they overcome their unique challenges and ensure success by employing best principles such as passionately committing themselves to the task at hand, following a set of simple rules that affords them autonomy but ensures that the music making doesn't simply degenerate into chaotic noise, acting transparently at all times, constantly listening and communicating, and taking measured risks.

Jazz can serve as an inspiration and example for anyone seeking to improve the skills of leadership, teamwork, innovation, and communication in today's knowledge-based economy. Although jazz musicians have been practicing the art of jazz performance for a hundred years, only about a decade ago did business management theorists begin to realize the relevance of jazz to their own discipline. The following words are often attributed to Warren Bennis, business professor and internationally acclaimed expert on management and leadership:

I used to think that running an organization was equivalent to conducting a symphony orchestra. But I don't think that's quite it; it's more like jazz. There is more improvisation. Someone once wrote that the sound of surprise is jazz, and if there's any one thing that we must try to get used to in this world, it's surprise and the unexpected. In this world of chaos, there's no other way of doing things. Truly, we are living in a world where the only thing that's constant is change.

In August 1996, management guru Peter Drucker was quoted as follows in *The Relentless Contrarian* (Schwartz and Kelly 1996):

The model for management that we have right now is the opera. The conductor of an opera has a very large number of different groups that he has to pull together. The soloists, the chorus, the ballet, the

orchestra, all have to come together—but they have a common score.
What we are increasingly talking about today are diversified groups
that have to write the score while they perform.

What you need now is a good jazz group.

In 1997, John Kao, former Harvard Business School professor and jazz pianist, published his book *Jamming: The Art and Discipline of Business Creativity* (Kao 1997). In later years, R. Keith Sawyer, a professor of psychology and education and also a jazz pianist, identified business and jazz connections as well.

When drawing analogies between jazz and business, people tend to focus on improvisation in jazz as a metaphor for innovation in business. This is an overly simplistic approach, as improvisation and innovation are not the same, and jazz musicians actually do both. To **innovate** is to create something new or unique. In a nonmusical context, to **improvise** is to make do or develop a solution to a problem with whatever time and resources you have available. As Evans points out, jazz musicians don't play every note from prepared music. They decide what notes to play when the performance is already underway. Often each note is chosen only milliseconds before it is sounded. Described by some people as "making it up as you go along," it is this process of real-time composition on which many people tend to focus in their attempts to describe the unique qualities of jazz. They miss two important points: First, the ability to compose in real time is based on years of training and experience. It's not as simple as choosing random notes in the spur of the moment. Second, and more important, although they may choose specific notes in the moment, the greater goal of a jazz musician is to create something unique. In other words, the musician aims to *innovate*. This quest for individual self-expression is most noticeable when a jazz musician performs an improvised solo in which he or she is featured and for which jazz audiences often applaud. In small-group jazz, the musicians are constantly innovating throughout a performance. When a pianist or guitarist comps a chordal accompaniment or a bassist walks a bass line, he or she is also creating something unique. The quest for innovation is balanced against the need to fulfill specific responsibilities, such as supporting the other musicians. With each musician continuously innovating, any jazz performance is sure to be unique. In fact, try as they might, jazz musicians rarely can successfully re-create a previous performance note for note.

Because most jazz performances are group efforts, it stands to reason that collective and simultaneous innovation is the genre's most notable feature.

In their paper *Jazz as a process of organizational innovation* (Bastien and Hostager 2001), David Bastien and Todd Hostager wrote:

> First, jazz is self-consciously spontaneous, creative, and expressive. It is fundamentally concerned with inventiveness as an expected mode of thought and behavior. Second, jazz is most typically a social process, involving a group of inventive musicians. Jazz enables individual musicians to coordinate the innovation process so that they achieve a credible and aesthetically pleasing collective outcome. The jazz process is built on the assumption that each individual musician is simultaneously and consciously adapting to the whole, supporting the other players, and mutually influencing the outcome. Jazz is thus a truly collective approach to the entire process of innovation, for it requires that the invention, adoption, and implementation of new musical ideas by individual musicians occurs within the context of a shared awareness of the group performance as it unfolds over time.

This collective and simultaneous innovation introduces substantial change and the potential for instability during the course of a jazz performance. Bastien and Hostager also observed this:

> As a collective approach to the process of innovation, jazz specifies a turbulent task environment for individual musicians, a complex field for interaction in which individuals are simultaneously required to invent new musical ideas and to adapt their playing to that of the collectivity. Turbulence in this environment not only results from the dynamic process of individual invention; turbulence also arises from the dynamic process of coordinating invention. Moreover, these dynamic processes are not independent of one another. The invention of musical ideas affects and is affected by the adoption and implementation of musical ideas. The inherent turbulence in this jazz process produces uncertainty for performers insofar as each musician cannot fully predict the behavior of the other musicians or, for that matter, the behavior of the collectivity.

This turbulence may require the musicians to improvise in order to deal with the unexpected. For example:

- The pianist may make a series of chord substitutions, replacing some of the expected chords with others that fit into the musical form but give it a different sound. The substitutions may be subtle enough that they fit with what the bassist intended to play. Or they may be more dramatic substitutions that require the bassist to complete the effect by outlining the alternative harmony. Such chord substitutions may, in turn, inspire the lead instrument to alter the melodic line. Such momentary deviations from an expected harmonic path can introduce tension, complexity, and interest in the music. Rarely charted ahead of time, they simply occur in the moment at the initiative of one musician, leaving others to improvise in response.

- A jazz band may perform a slow ballad, creating a mood of intensity and soulfulness. To take the music to a different place, the bassist may urge the band to shift into a "double-time feel" groove in which the tempo of the music appears to double. In actual fact, the navigation through the chord changes and the musical form continues at the same rate. The illusion is created by essentially doubling the number of notes played within a given space of time. For example, the bassist plays eight notes in the period where he or she would have played four notes. The other musicians must respond in kind. At some point, the band will likely shift back to the original slower groove. To prolong the double-time feel beyond a certain point only weakens the effect. The transition back to the original groove may be initiated by the bassist or by another musician.

These are just two examples of how jazz musicians are constantly improvising in response to changes in the music. It's important that they stay together, but equally important that they initiate forays into new territory to help create a unique and innovative performance. Improvisation in jazz may even come in response to one's own initiative. For example, in the course of attempting to craft a particularly innovative statement, a musician may fail to execute or may even lose his or her place in the musical form. The musician must then improvise a recovery, which may require participation of other musicians. They may, for example, play a musical fill or provide a clear musical sign to help the lost musician get back on track.

The skill of improvisation should be as highly prized in business as it is in jazz. More than ever, teams and organizations must be able to respond to the unexpected. Companies that can't react quickly may come under threat from even the least likely of competitors. In 1996, Larry Page and Sergey Brin, two Stanford University Ph.D. students, began work on a project nicknamed BackRub. Its purpose was to explore the mathematical properties of the World Wide Web, including the relationships between linked pages. Few would have predicted that such a project would develop into the force that is

Harmony in Jazz

Most music contains a harmonic element. Harmony is the sounding of multiple notes simultaneously. In music, harmonic structures are described by chords. These may be explicitly stated by an instrument capable of playing more than one sound at a time, such as a guitar or piano, or by multiple instruments working together, each sounding one note. Chords can also be implied by outlining them with just one note at a time or playing melodic passages that suggest the chords. Despite the general use of the term *harmony,* chords may not always sound harmonious. Many chords actually sound discordant and create tension in the music that can be resolved harmonically by transitioning to more concordant harmony.

Jazz harmony is typically more complex than classical harmony. Classical chords typically contain three or four notes while jazz chords may often have seven or eight notes, although they may not all be used in every instance. In a jazz ensemble, and especially in a small group, an important relationship exists between the bass and comping instrument, such as a guitar or piano. The bass outlines the harmony but tends to emphasize the roots or foundations of the chords, whereas the comping instrument intentionally avoids those roots, playing rootless chord voicings, giving the bassist the freedom to fulfill his or her role.

Most pieces of music contain a series of chord changes. Jazz musicians refer to these simply as changes. Certain chords or acceptable substitutions are expected at certain points in the music. To stay on the same page, all the musicians must play the changes, although they may each do so in different ways, depending on their instruments and their roles in the ensemble.

now Google. It took archrival Microsoft seven years to approach the then-fledgling company about a possible partnership or merger. By that time, Google had already been profitable for two years and was discussing a possible initial public offering (IPO) that would take place the following year. Who could have foreseen that Encyclopedia Britannica, first published in 1768, would be threatened almost 250 years later by Wikipedia, an online body of knowledge maintained by volunteers?

Jazz is not the only style of music in which improvisation plays an important role. As Derek Bailey points out in his book *Improvisation—Its Nature and Practice in Music* (Bailey 1992), improvisation is present in Indian, African, Turkish, and Polynesian music, as well as in baroque (especially organ), flamenco, rock, and blues. Vocal improvisation can be heard in myriad venues, from Presbyterian chapels to marketplaces in Cairo. The most extraordinary thing about the way jazz musicians perform is not that they improvise, but that they collaborate, lead, and execute with agility. The social practices and project management principles jazz musicians use have much to offer the world of business.

Not only business teams, however, are learning from jazz musicians. Many people may not be familiar with the intricacies of jazz performance, but they've probably witnessed countless sporting events in which improvisation, collaboration, and agility helped a team secure a victory. Great athletes have been doing this for years in team sports such as soccer, hockey, and basketball, but people have only recently identified parallels between the athletic and musical domains. In February 2009, the University of British Columbia hosted "Power Play: Improvisation and Sport," a previously unprecedented forum that convened athletes, artists, and researchers to discuss the thread of improvisation that weaves together the artistic and the athletic. Such a broad discussion on the subject may have occurred for the first time only recently, but at least one person has long known about the connection. Kareem Abdul-Jabbar, widely considered one of the greatest basketball players of all time, is also a big jazz fan. Abdul-Jabbar's father was a police officer and a jazz musician. Consequently, Abdul-Jabbar became a devout follower of the genre. He blogs about both basketball and jazz, and he wrote extensively on the topic in his must-read book *On the Shoulders of Giants: My Journey Through the Harlem Renaissance* (Simon & Schuster 2007).

It's not difficult to see how a basketball team can be likened to a swinging jazz quintet. Jazz journalist Larry Blumenfeld said in the article *Links Between Basketball and Jazz Run Deep* (Blumenfeld 2008):

> *Anyone with knowledge of both basketball and jazz recognizes natural affinities between the two pursuits: a marriage of form and improvisation, of individualism with teamwork; a primacy of rhythm (watch how basketball players dribble the ball before taking foul shots to re-establish a sense of tempo); and a requirement that players respond to one another's choices and to rapidly changing situations in real time.*

In the Internet newspaper *The Huffington Post* (2007), R. Keith Sawyer wrote this:

> *[T]he five members of a basketball team interact in an interdependent way that's a lot like jazz. You see this especially in pick-up games, because everything that slows down the professional game has been taken away—there are no free throws in streetball, for example.*

In basketball and in jazz, each player's action has an immediate effect on what can happen next. From second to second, the team's performance emerges from a chain reaction of individual acts. So much of what makes jazz great is the unique chemistry among individual players; there's no way that you could simply add up the quality of the bassist, drummer, pianist, and sax player, and predict what their group would sound like. Basketball players interact in a fluid, rapidly unfolding manner, and that's the way the most innovative businesses work today.

Scaling the Jazz Process

When I speak to audiences about the Jazz Process, I sometimes begin with three exercises.

First, I perform jazz as a trio with two other musicians.

Second, I ask ten volunteers from the audience to move silently in a straight line from one location to another and then return to their original position. Before the exercise begins, they are told the rules of engagement to which they must conform throughout the activity:

- Maintain a straight-line formation
- Face their heads and bodies forward
- Refrain from any verbal or nonverbal communication
- Execute all turns to the right (clockwise)
- Complete the exercise within 60 seconds

Third, I have the entire audience, which may be several hundred people, perform as a chorus by reading a given text together out loud.

I call these "exercises in music, dance, and theater," respectively. One of my goals in these impromptu performances is to demonstrate degrees of innovation or improvisation relative to the size of a team. As the size of the team increases in these exercises, the level of innovation decreases, as shown in Figure I.4. The jazz trio, for instance, is constantly improvising. In the dance exercise, the larger group of participants must conform to the rules, but they can vary their speed and even stop moving. Some room for self-expression exists, but not much. What about the even larger-scale theater exercise? If you've ever recited part of the liturgy as a member of a congregation during a worship service, then you've performed this exercise and you know that once the group begins to recite together, it is very hard to avoid conforming. Unless you simply refrain from participating, you must read along with the group. The size of the group makes it difficult to express yourself individually without appearing to be obviously nonconforming.

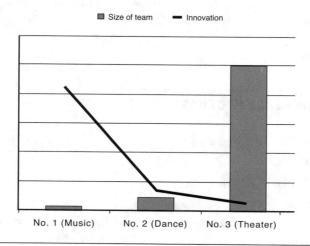

Figure I.4   *Innovation related to size of team for three different activities*

In the Drucker *Wired* article (Schwartz and Kelly 1996) I referenced earlier, I included only a subset of what he actually said. Consider now, the complete version of his words:

> *The model for management that we have right now is the opera. The conductor of an opera has a very large number of different groups that he has to pull together. The soloists, the chorus, the ballet, the orchestra, all have to come together—but they have a common score. What we are increasingly talking about today are diversified groups that have to write the score while they perform.*
>
> *What you need now is a good jazz group. And if you want to have a really good jazz group, how large can it be? How large can it be when you have people who improvise on their own and the group realizes that the trumpet player is now playing his solo and everybody needs to stop and support him? You can use seven to nine people—maximum. If you get more, you have to score.*

So how can you have a big company or a very big organization when you have to develop the score as you go along? Today you build different teams. Sounds beautiful. Yet nobody has really found a way to do it.

Drucker recognized that although a jazz band may be a good model for teams, the model may not necessarily scale. His critique certainly has some basis. After all, a typical jazz orchestra has no more than 18 members, and in that format, a lot of the music is scripted or precomposed. Most of the musicians, except perhaps the rhythm section (piano, guitar, bass, drums), have specific written parts, and only certain musicians get to improvise a solo as a feature for specific sections of a piece. This is typical of the music performed by orchestras or big bands of artists such as Benny Goodman or Duke Ellington. In some cases, even the individual solos were not improvised. When a piece was recorded, musicians would improvise in the recording studio. At live performances, fans would often demand to hear the solos performed exactly as on the record. This was especially true when people attended events primarily to dance and not just to listen, The irony is that, to do this, a musician would have to go back and listen to the recording and transcribe to paper or memory the exact notes that had been improvised in the studio.

Jazz groups in which all the musicians are improvising for almost the entire performance typically have no more than seven members, and quite often less. The basic configuration consists of a rhythm section (usually piano, bass, drums) and one or more lead instruments, such as saxophones, trumpets, trombones, and so on. This is small-group jazz typical of bands led by Louis Armstrong, Charlie Parker, Miles Davis, John Coltrane, Charles Mingus, Thelonious Monk, and countless other famous and lesser-known jazz musicians.

There are some exceptions, where larger groups of up to 20 musicians are mostly improvising, but they are typically performing a specific class of large-ensemble **free jazz**, and they are definitely a rarity. Examples include Michael Mantler's Jazz Composer's Orchestra from the late 1960s, William Parker's Little Huey Creative Music Orchestra, and the aptly named Instant Composers Pool (ICP) Orchestra. What's notable about free jazz, whether performed by large ensembles or smaller groups, is that the musicians perform with a great deal of musical freedom, adhering to only a minimal set of musical rules. These are rules that relate to musical elements such as melody, harmony, rhythm, form, dynamics, and so forth. It's analogous to abstract painting, in which an artist has the freedom to draw the observer away from conventional reality-based imagery. In the same way, free jazz musicians are free to draw listeners away from conventional melodies, harmonies, and so forth. However, if the musicians are seeking to produce a truly collaborative creative product that can attract and retain a wide audience, they must heed the rules of engagement, such as those described in this book, even more so than musicians playing more traditional jazz styles. If they fail to do this, their musical product can easily degenerate into meaningless, self-indulgent creativity that is of interest to only a very limited audience.

These descriptions of three basic styles of jazz—big band, small group, and free—demonstrate that not all jazz ensembles produce the same kind of music. Nor do they all use precisely the same performance process. Similarly, not all business teams produce the same kind of product or service, and their work processes also differ. Every situation is different, and each team has to do what makes the most sense for it at a specific point in time. Some teams give greater priority to agility, some to inventiveness and creativity, and others to efficiency or return on time and energy invested.

In theory, a thousand jazz musicians could perform together and produce an innovative performance that would garner the interest and appreciation of audiences. Although that may be intriguing, it's not really practical. What is interesting is identifying the practices that allow jazz musicians to be successful and distilling these into principles that can then be applied to large teams. In many cases, technology can be an enabler. Wikipedia and open source software projects, and indeed the entire Internet itself, harness the combined efforts of thousands upon thousands of individuals. They work as distributed, virtual teams, coming together and disbanding as required, improvising and innovating with agility, and in many (but not all) cases, delivering high-quality offerings consistently on time. While they may not realize it, the way in which they work has much in common with the way in which jazz musicians perform.

In recent years, jazz has inspired IBM, the information technology giant that has existed as long as jazz itself. In 2003, the company began to use the concept of **jamming** to innovate with huge numbers of people. Using what the company calls Jam technology, IBM hosted intranet-based online discussions that engaged 50,000 employees over a period of three days. The goal of this very ambitious exercise was to rewrite the company's core values. By all accounts, it was a hugely successful undertaking. Today, IBM encourages all its employees to act by those values in everything they do for the company. IBM has since used the Jam technology and process to conduct many other large-scale exercises in collaborative creativity. In July and September 2006, IBM ran InnovationJam with more than 150,000 participants from 104 countries. The contributors to InnovationJam included IBM employees and members of their families, universities, and IBM partners and customers. Conducted over two sessions, each lasting 72 hours, InnovationJam generated more than 46,000 ideas. In November 2006, IBM announced that it would invest $100 million to develop the ten best of those ideas. The Jam technology proved to be so successful that, in 2007, IBM launched a service to run Jams for other organizations.

In 2008, IBM released Rational Team Concert, the first of its next-generation software-development tools powered by its Jazz team collaboration software. Jazz supports many principles of jazz performance in a software development context, and IBM has riffed on the jazz theme in its promotion of Jazz-based products with catchphrases such as "Develop software like a band plays jazz." IBM's Jazz-based products are designed to support the collaborative efforts of thousands of people.

Recapitulation

- Collaboration is the act of working together. The ability to collaborate with others is one of the most important skills a person can possess. No matter how inventive, creative, or productive you might be, as one person alone, you can achieve only so much.

- When a team has synergy, it can achieve more than each of its individual team members would if they each worked alone. Synergy is more likely to occur when the size of a team is limited, and a team is more likely to be effective when its composition is multidisciplined or cross-functional.

- Thinking about your job as a series of performances can be highly beneficial. Artistic ensembles must leverage collective individual contributions to deliver a performance (product) that will attract and retain customers. Their performances must be delivered on time with close to zero defects. This must be accomplished in real time while the ensemble is subjected to continuous scrutiny.

- Jazz can serve as an inspiration and example for anyone seeking to improve skills of leadership, teamwork, innovation, and communication in today's knowledge-based economy. Jazz musicians constantly innovate and improvise in response to unexpected change.

- Companies such as IBM have demonstrated that the practices of jazz can be scaled up.

PART I

Working

In this section, we discuss five fundamental principles that are essential to any collaborative venture. By applying these principles, organizations can establish healthy, high-performance teams that respond to challenges with agility.

1. Use just enough rules
2. Employ top talent
3. Put the team first
4. Build trust and respect
5. Commit with passion

CHAPTER 1

Use Just Enough Rules

*"Bureaucracy is the death
of all sound work."*
—Albert Einstein

The Need for Rules

Rules are important, and the world is full of them. Rules provide a safeguard against chaos and anarchy. Imagine driving on the road with no traffic rules whatsoever. No one would know which part of the road to drive on, when to stop or yield, or what speed to travel. Because of the way in which most of us have been raised and educated, it's in our nature to not only follow rules, but also to need them. Put most people in a situation without rules, and they will be lost or confused. When people find themselves in an unfamiliar situation, such as in a new job, they naturally ask questions to learn the rules of the road.

In the societies in which we and the organizations we work for operate, rules take the form of laws. We generally don't have much control over these rules, and unless we want to risk fines or imprisonment, we must follow them without fail. Companies are bound by an extraordinary number of laws, including those enforced at municipal, state, and federal levels. They govern the payment of taxes, protect the environment, define contractual relationships between parties, and oversee the trading of goods and services. Even such a brutally violent and apparently lawless activity as war is legally regulated. States that are party to the various conventions, treaties, and protocols of war must ensure that their military forces comply with those laws. The Hague Conventions of 1899 and 1907 and the Geneva Protocol of 1925 govern the use of weapons in war, and the Geneva Convention of 1949 covers the standards for humanitarian concerns such as the treatment of noncombatants and prisoners of war.

In addition to rules defined by the societies in which they operate, most organizations and teams have their own rules. Some of these rules are directed at internal processes to help organizations comply with laws and regulations. Often an organization defines other rules simply because they are believed to be necessary for conducting business. Think about the many rules you must follow in your job. They are encoded into the procedures, processes, and methodologies employed by your team and your organization. If asked, you could probably recite the most important rules you must comply with in your work. If you play a sport such as basketball or a game such as chess, you must play according to a set of rules. If you don't follow those rules, you may be penalized, suspended, or even disbarred from playing. Even when people play sports or games for recreation, they shun participants who break the rules.

The United States Army Rangers is an elite light infantry special operations force. Since 1960, U.S. soldiers attending Ranger School in Fort Benning, Georgia, have been taught 19 Standing Orders. They appear in the regiment's Ranger Handbook and, at various times in the past, they have been printed on a small pocket card for Rangers to carry at all times. As one study of the Rangers pointed out (Bahmanyar and Welply 2003), if a Ranger fails to memorize the Standing Orders, "he will find himself doing a lot of push-ups."

The Standing Orders include such rules as these:

> Before reaching your destination, send one or two men forward to scout the area and avoid traps.

> If an enemy is following your rear, circle back and attack him along the same path.

> When following an enemy force, try not to use their path, but rather plan to cut them off and ambush them at a narrow place or when they least expect it.

Of course, Rangers are taught far more than the 19 rules of the Standing Orders in their intensive, three-month-long combat leadership course. They receive instruction in many disciplines, including field craft, demolitions, mountaineering, squad-level mission planning, and, of course, combat. The Ranger Handbook is almost 250 pages long, and only 1 page is dedicated to the Standing Orders. Rangers are proficient in many techniques and methods and can execute all of them instinctively as a result of intense training. Yet when they are in the midst of a military operation, deep in hostile territory where lives and critical mission objectives are at stake, the Standing

Orders provide a set of fundamental rules that they can instantly recall and apply to almost any situation.

Employing Just Enough Rules

Sometimes rules get in the way of execution. They add overhead, cause delays, and hinder productivity until we find ourselves wishing the rules just didn't exist. We've all had occasion to deal with too many rules or rules that were too restrictive or so complex that complying with them was difficult or next to impossible. We might have made some comment about bureaucracy or micromanagement or a lack of freedom. The fact is that, although we need rules, we also crave, expect, and value freedom. More specifically, as participants in creative endeavors, we need to have freedom of expression.

Virtual Teams

Virtual teams come together to achieve a specific goal and then disband after the goal has been achieved. **Concurrent engineering** introduced the concept of product-focused, multidisciplined, or cross-functional virtual teams to help guide the development of a product from conception to delivery, on through to sales and support. Previously, the product development process pushed the product in its various states through different departments—research, marketing, finance, design, engineering, testing, sales, and support. The weakness in this process was that problems one department discovered late in the cycle then required potentially costly changes and delays, as well as a restart in the cycle. When stakeholders from each discipline are involved at the outset, problems are identified earlier. The result is shortened development cycles and lower costs.

If a team has too many rules or rules that are too complex, it may take a substantial amount of time to learn them. Anyone joining the team may have to learn most or all of the rules before they can be fully productive or be allowed to contribute without continuous supervision or review. That's especially a problem if a team is growing rapidly or if the composition of the team is subject to constant change. It's also a big problem for virtual teams that are established on demand. They cannot afford lengthy startup times and need to be immediately productive.

The other problem with having too many rules or rules that are too complex is that remembering them can be difficult. This can be particularly problematic when time is limited, when things are moving quickly, or when problems crop up unexpectedly and people already have their hands full. When they are under pressure, people often forget which rules they are supposed to follow. They may even purposely avoid the rules when pushed to meet a deadline or perform a critical task.

If we are to maximize performance, it is essential to employ just enough rules to afford autonomy, while at the same time avoiding chaos. **Autonomy** is the independence and freedom that enables people to act individually. It is necessary to foster the individual expression essential to both improvisation and innovation. Autonomy also facilitates agility as it limits the constraints placed upon individuals. All too often, people are swamped and forced to deal with conflicting priorities. Minimizing the number of rules helps to clearly dictate priorities and focus people on what really matters to the team.

Employ just enough rules to afford autonomy, while at the same time avoiding chaos.

Even a few simple rules may stifle autonomy if the rules are too specific and constraining—in other words, if they lead to micromanagement. Effective rules are limited to those that are necessary, that can be practically applied, and, above all, that are clearly defined, with each rule's importance adequately communicated. People are more likely to follow rules when they fully understand their benefits. Even though those benefits might be obvious, concrete examples that document their successful implementation remind people of their usefulness and importance. Many organizations regularly make the effort to motivate employees by highlighting the successes of their teams. They often miss the opportunity to demonstrate how their processes contributed to those successes.

Rarely does a single set of rules apply equally to every situation and for every person. The exact set of rules or the importance of specific rules may vary over time. Figure 1.1 shows an example of a software development project plan. Toward the end of each milestone and then throughout the endgame, especially during the final weeks of the project, stability is vital, and only important bug fixes should be applied to the code. To minimize the risk of mistakes during these critical phases, strict rules are enforced that require multiple people to inspect and approve any fixes. At these times, applicable rules from the Jazz Process would include "Make contributions count," "Stay healthy," and "Take measured risks."

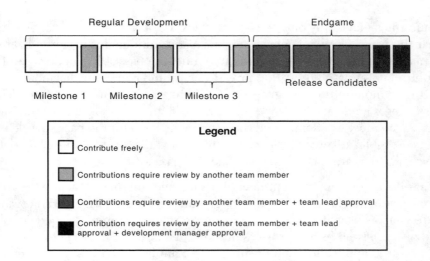

Figure 1.1   *Sensitivity to code changes during a software development project*

Figure 1.2 illustrates a jazz trio performing a piece of music. The performance begins with an initial statement of the form, with the lead instrument performing an interpretation of the precomposed melody. Each member of the trio then takes a solo. The order, length, and specific content of the solos are never known beforehand. Finally, the trio restates the melody and, in its final phrases, improvises an ending. Improvisation introduces uncertainty and the risk of instability at many points throughout the performance. At such times, Jazz Process rules such as "Lead on demand" and "Listen for change" become critically important to avoid disastrous train wrecks.

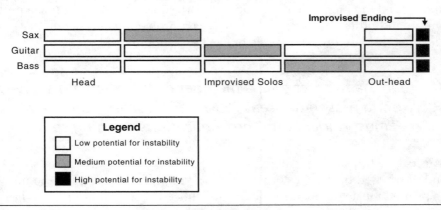

Figure 1.2   *Innovation and risk of instability during a jazz performance*

Some rules may apply only to specific roles. For example, in jazz, you often hear the bassist "walking a line." The bassist is fulfilling his or her obligation to play the harmonic roots. At the same time, the bassist fills in between the required notes with others that provide shape and a melodic, harmonic, and rhythmic momentum that gives the music forward propulsion. Improvising bass lines is an art itself. However, it's not just guesswork or an entirely subjective practice. A set of unique rules forms the basis for the bassist's role in a jazz ensemble. Likewise, a pianist, a drummer, and a saxophone player also have rules that are specific to their roles in a jazz ensemble.

In a software development project there are rules unique to each of the roles of project manager, software developer, and software tester. IBM's Jazz software enables users to define and customize rules pertaining to specific roles and different phases in a project's lifecycle. Thus, it provides necessary flexibility in the application and ensures that compliance with the rules makes sense for everybody at all times.

Breaking the Rules

Thus far, I've used the term *rule* for convention's sake and because I wanted to draw attention to the problems that arise when rules limit autonomy. In practice, we are talking about processes. A process can include principles, rules, practices, guidelines, conventions, rules of thumb, and so forth. Clearly, rules are far more binding than are guidelines. Rules in sports are, ideally, strictly enforced. If a team has a strict rule, a member of the team must have a very good reason to break it. More important, the member must understand the implications of doing so. Breaking a rule may not be a problem in and of itself; however, it usually is a problem when people have no idea that they are breaking a rule or can't explain the need to do so.

If a team has a strict rule, a member of the team must have a very good reason to break it. More important, the member must understand the implications of doing so.

Musical rhythms are organized into regularly recurring groups of stressed and unstressed beats. This organization is known as the meter of the music. In printed music the meter is delineated into bars, sometimes referred to as measures. A waltz, for example, has three beats per bar with a stress on the first beat: 1 2 3 | 1 2 3 .... A typical swing groove has four beats of music per bar with stresses on the first and third beats: **1** 2 **3** 4 | **1** 2 **3** 4 …. A bassist may alternate between playing *in two* by playing just two notes per bar on the first and third beats or by walking and playing four notes per bar. Playing in two imparts more of a relaxed feel, whereas playing *in four* gives the music more momentum and drive. For many kinds of songs, especially those based on specific musical forms or structures, it's common to play some sections in two and other sections in four when the melody is stated by the lead instrument. When solos are improvised, the bassist typically plays solely in four. Usually the members of a jazz rhythm section play the same groove together. So if the bassist switches from playing in two to playing in four, the drummer will play a different pattern to reinforce that groove. Sometimes, however, a drummer "breaks the rules" and elects not to follow the bassist. Or perhaps, by convention, playing in four would be expected and the drummer goes there, but the bassist purposely does not. Sometimes a bassist intentionally switches between playing in two and playing in four, while the drummer maintains a constant groove.

The "failure" of a drummer and bassist to agree on a specific groove may actually be an attempt to create tension in the music. Tension is important because it creates interest, which reaches a climax when the tension is resolved. In some classic recordings featuring bassist-drummer hookups, you can clearly hear the drummer wanting to play in four but the bassist refusing to go there. The tension is high, but when the bassist finally makes the transition, it is especially effective. Obviously, the need for a bassist and drummer to maintain the same groove is not a strict requirement—it's a convention, not a rule. If a rule is being consistently broken, perhaps it should be a guideline or convention instead of a rule. If the rule is being constantly broken and is not causing a problem, the rule may be unnecessary. On the other hand, some rules may be absolutely vital to the health or stability of a project or a team, and breaking them may be extremely damaging or costly.

Principles, rules, practices, and guidelines can—and often should—be defined and documented together. When it comes to rules, it is necessary to be very clear about the tolerance and the risks of noncompliance. Be realistic about what should be truly enforced and whether it can be enforced. It's an unfortunate reality that some rules seem to exist only to give those who define the rules plausible deniability. Such people sometimes define rules either knowing or not understanding that such rules cannot always be adhered to. Furthermore, they may set aggressive performance goals that can be met only by breaking these very rules. If something goes wrong, they can claim that people should have followed the rules.

Defining a Process

It should be possible to define a process that enables you to achieve any set of goals. But where do you start? "Use just enough rules" highlights the need to distill a process down to its essentials. The goal is to give a team the freedom it needs to be agile and innovative while ensuring that the critical success factors of the team's business are always addressed. What are your current challenges in meeting your goals? Is your team agile enough to respond to known and unforeseen competition and changes in your business environment? Is your team innovative and creative enough to deliver solutions that are more desirable than those of your competitors? Is your team performing optimally and making the most of its resources?

In recent years, the software development industry has witnessed widespread and growing adoption of a group of software development methods referred to as **agile methods**. The *Agile Manifesto* is a set of principles drafted in 2001 by 17 individuals who were interested in improving previous software development methods. Over the years, the agile software movement has been guided by the manifesto's four simple statements about the priority of values (Beck, Beedle, et al. 2001):

> *Individuals and interactions over processes and tools*
> *Working software over comprehensive documentation*
> *Customer collaboration over contract negotiation*
> *Responding to change over following a plan*

These values are pursued through the manifesto's 12 principles, which include such important rules as these:

> *Welcome changing requirements, even late in development. Agile processes harness change for the customer's competitive advantage.*
>
> *Build projects around motivated individuals. Give them the environment and support they need, and trust them to get the job done.*

The manifesto alone may not be enough to guide most software development teams. That's where specific methodologies come in. When you look at such methods, they are all remarkably lightweight. Their success is based not on a large set of specific rules to guide people in every situation (later I discuss why this is impossible), but on collaboration between like-minded, skilled, and experienced people.

The wonderful thing about great rules is that they are widely applicable.

One of the most popular agile software methods is Scrum. Many software developers either are unaware or have forgotten that absolutely nothing about Scrum is specific to software development. It was originally conceived as a method for general product development. The wonderful thing about great rules is that they are widely applicable. Many of the agile software methods are based on or inspired by twentieth-century manufacturing imperatives such as lean or just-in-time manufacturing, Total Quality Management, and Total Quality Control, all of which I reference later in this book.

As long as you are not violating intellectual property laws, there's nothing wrong with repurposing existing rules. *The Art of War*, a Chinese military treatise attributed to Sun Tzu, has been interpreted countless times and applied to contexts that the author would never have conceived. Consider, for example, Gerald Michaelson's book *Sun Tzu: The Art of War for Managers—50 Strategic Rules* (2001), which interprets *The Art of War*'s military advice for business managers.

The second rule of the U.S. Army Rangers Standing Orders is this:

> *Have your musket clean as a whistle, hatchet scoured, sixty rounds powder and ball, and be ready to march at a minute's warning.*

While the fifteenth rule is:

> *Don't sleep beyond dawn. Dawn's when the French and Indians attack.*

These rules were written 250 years ago. Obviously, times and technology have changed. Yet the Rangers still apply these rules, although they clearly don't interpret all of them literally. Many people, even those familiar with the Standing Orders, are surprised to learn the real story behind their origin. Popular belief has it that the 19 rules, often referred to as Rogers's Standing Orders, were written by Maj. Robert Rogers, who led a unit attached to the British Army during the French and Indian War (1754–1763). Rogers's Rangers was arguably the first special operations forces in history, tasked with reconnaissance and special operations against distant targets. Rogers did write 28 "Rules of Ranging," also known as "Plan of Discipline," in 1757. However, the truth is that the U.S. Army Rangers Standing Orders are fiction based on fact, as documented in a U.S. Army article (Cosner 2003):

> *Originally included in a 1936 Kenneth Roberts historical fiction novel, Northwest Passage, Rogers' Standing Orders were never actually penned or spoken by Rogers himself. Instead, Roberts based his hero's standing orders off of Rogers' real-life writings, published as 28 "Rules of Discipline" in Rogers' 1765 Journals, a fact most recently revealed in a re-released version of Rogers' autobiographical book.*

Despite this, the U.S. Army Rangers have made Roberts's version of Rogers's wisdom their own for half a century. The lesson here is that it doesn't matter how a set of rules evolves or is created. What's important is that they work and help a team to collectively function more productively and efficiently.

Documenting a Process

Users of a process must be able to readily and easily access documentation and guidance for that process. Jazz musicians clearly don't have time to stop and read documentation. They have mere microseconds in which to make decisions. Yet they must comply with critically important rules at all times. Jazz musicians internalize their performance process through years of training and experience, performing in all kinds of situations and playing all sorts of material. The same is true for many other performance artists and athletes.

Endings in Jazz

Endings are vital to any performance or project. A weak ending can mar an otherwise strong performance, whereas a strong ending can improve people's perception of a weak performance. Although perceptions may change when the performance as a whole is scrutinized, it is certainly rewarding to elicit a desirable response immediately after the performance, whether by a standing ovation at the close of a concert or a commitment from a customer to purchase a product in response to a sales pitch.

In improvised jazz, it's never clear to the musicians exactly how they will end a piece of music until they arrive at that point. The same musicians can play the same piece five times and end it differently each time. Although it may appear otherwise, many rules may be in play at that time.

Some songs may end by "tagging," or repeating the final phrase multiple times, or the song may end by moving into a vamp section in which the rhythm instruments repeat a riff or groove for an indeterminate time while a lead instrument improvises over the top. Sometimes the musicians perform a dramatic ending in which the music gradually slows and pauses while a lead instrument plays a short cadenza, a virtuosic display in "free" time, and then the band plays a final chord together. These are just a few of the many ways a piece might end, and myriad variations exist for each.

No matter how an ending evolves, good musicians always make it sound great. What's rather impressive is that, although extended endings such as vamps may be longer, all of this collaborative decision-making happens in real time in the space of perhaps 15 to 30 seconds.

Documenting a process can help flatten the learning curve when the process is updated, when new people join a team, or when a team is initially formed. In some cases, the problem space may be so broad that although it may be possible to define a process comprised of simple rules and practices, it may require a large number of those rules and practices. An activity may also transition through a large number of phases, and each phase may require different rules of engagement. Guidance may be provided in many forms, including upfront or ongoing education and on-the-job mentoring. Technology can often be used to great effect and is an obvious choice for workers who are already computer bound. Software developers, for example, spend the bulk of their time working on computers and using software development tools to capture requirements, design architectures, and write, debug, test, and deploy code.

IBM built process awareness into its Jazz platform by allowing users to define their own processes as collections of roles, practices, rules, and guidelines used to organize and control the flow of work. IBM also included sample templates that capture the practices of well-known processes. Jazz-based tools such as Rational Team Concert "understand" these processes and help users comply with them. When team members violate a rule, instead of just telling them that they have done something wrong, "advisors" suggest how to fix the problem. In its Team Foundation platform, Microsoft implemented process guidance that lets teams document the process for team members to follow, along with the different roles that may be assumed and the activities that must be completed. Tools built on Team Foundation enact these processes, which foster compliance whenever they are used. In this way, Jazz and Team Foundation let software developers "teach" tools about their organization's best practices. As their practices evolve, they can change the process definitions, and the tools then enforce the updated process.

For an example of how guidance can be structured, refer to the table of contents in this book. Note that the Jazz Process includes 14 principles. Notice that the names are short and easy to remember. Because even 14 principles are a bit much to keep in mind, they are divided into four groups, as you can see in the operating framework presented in the Introduction in Figure I.3. You'll notice that each group has progressively fewer principles: five for working, four for collaborating, three for executing, and two for innovating. Each quadrant in the Jazz Process is a prerequisite to those that follow in the sequence. Teams must be able to work together before they can truly collaborate and achieve synergy. Only then can they execute at the highest levels and create unique offerings through innovation. All this structure in the definition of the Jazz Process makes the broad concepts easier to remember and comprehend.

Evolving and Improving a Process

These examples are a reminder that sometimes teams must evolve their processes. Rules maintained simply for tradition's sake may deny a team the freedom to evolve and adapt. In the worst case, this can lead to critical failure. A response to change is often the catalyst for teams to evolve their processes. Such change might originate from within the team or organization. For example, when people leave or join a team, the size and capabilities of the team may change. Processes that work in one context may not scale to a larger context. Processes that depend on critical skills may need revision when those skills are no longer available. Organizational restructuring may increase or alter the goals and responsibilities of a team, and that may require it to change its methods.

Change can originate externally from a team's business or operating environment. The actions of competitors can be compelling catalysts of change. In sports, teams often alter their game to account for the strengths and weaknesses of an opposing team. If an opposing team has a particularly strong player, a team might institute specific rules or guidelines to deal with that player. As another example, a hockey team cannot approach every game with the same strategy. If its game plan is sound and the team consists of highly skilled and talented players, it might be able to win many games, but eventually another team will identify and target weaknesses in its game. Most winning sports teams are constantly changing their game plan, and they do it not just between games, but during games. During a baseball game, a manager might make a trip to the mound to instruct a pitcher on how to pitch to a particular batter. Before a game, a batter might scrutinize video of the opposing pitcher's delivery, and after each game, the manager, the coaches, and the team might do a post-game review in which they analyze every play of the game.

Winning teams seek to constantly improve their processes in pursuit of higher levels of performance. They do it not just because they are forced to respond to change, but simply because they want to do better. In reviewing their performance in retrospect, the members of a team need to ask themselves only such simple questions as "What worked well?" and "What problems did we encounter?" and "How can we do better or avoid those problems in the future?" Software development teams can perform such retrospectives at the conclusion of an iteration or after reaching a particular milestone. Jazz musicians are constantly trying to improve their level of performance and their process of playing and engaging with others. They ask themselves such questions as, "How can I play more in tune?" and "How can I 'lock in' better with everyone else?" and "How can I make my solo more engaging or meaningful?" This process of continuous improvement is so automatic that the musicians often don't realize they are doing it. The same is true of any performance athlete, such as the pitcher on the mound who is thinking about what he or she can do differently to get that next ball past the batter and into the catcher's mitt. In researching how the U.S. military developed its most elite fighting forces and what business could learn from the process, consultant Andrew Sobel observed the importance of "constant feedback," noting, "A key feature of SOF [Special Operations Forces] training is constant and relentless feedback about performance." (Sobel 2009)

Of course, changing one's way of working is not to be taken lightly and should be done only with thoughtful consideration. In some situations, however, you do not have the luxury of time in which to analyze the pros and cons of changing your process. During a performance, artists and athletes do not try to change their fundamental approaches to performance. They use the knowledge and the techniques already available to them and change the priority and extent to which they are employed. This is especially true when rules or aspects of a process offset or trade off with one another. Later we look at two rules, "Stay healthy" and "Take measured risks" that complement each other in this way. In the next chapter, we discuss the importance of "Employ top talent," a principle that has the potential to compromise the team cohesiveness facilitated by the principle "Put the team first."

When all team members dedicate themselves to giving their best and then constantly improving each performance, they become capable of delivering great results not only once, but again and again, even in the face of changing conditions. In sports, just as in the arts and in business, the truly successful teams are not the "one-hit wonders" that deliver a single great performance, but those that deliver repeatedly with consistent results.

Recapitulation

- Rules are essential to avoid chaos. However, too many rules can get in the way of execution, add unnecessary overhead, cause delays, and hinder productivity. It's important to employ just enough rules to afford autonomy while avoiding chaos.

- Some rules can be broken. If you break a rule, you must have a good reason, but more important, you must understand the implications of doing so.

- The goal in defining a process is to give a team the freedom it needs to be agile and innovative, while constantly addressing the critical success factors of the team's business.

- Users of a process must be able to readily and easily access documentation and guidance for that process.

- Process improvement is critical to long-term success. When all team members dedicate themselves to giving their best and then constantly improving each performance, they become capable of delivering great results not only once, but again and again, even in the face of changing conditions.

CHAPTER 2

Employ Top Talent

*"Art is the most intense mode of
individualism that the world has known."*
—Oscar Wilde

The Human Element

In their quest for greater productivity, many teams look to tools and technology when the greatest resource they have, or should have, is already within the team. The U.S. military is the best-equipped fighting force in the world, with hardware that soldiers in many other countries can only dream about. One would think that if any U.S. military units would have easy access to that hardware, it would be the elite Special Operations Forces (SOF). Yet although the SOF might find it easier to get access to advanced equipment and weaponry, its personnel realize that their most critical success factor is not technology, but people. This basic principle is encoded in four rules, known as the SOF Truths. Gen. David Baratto, who became the first chief of operations of the U.S. Special Operations Command (USSOCOM) in the late 1980s, defined the first of these truths as follows: "Humans are more important than hardware." Linda Robinson, author of *Masters of Chaos: The Secret History of the Special Forces* (Robinson 2004, 114), noted that the Special Operations Forces "view the individual soldier and his brain as the key factor in the fight." Gen. Wayne Downing wrote this in the foreword to *Special Operations Forces: Roles and Missions in the Aftermath of the Cold War* (Downing, et al. 1996, 3):

As USSOCOM moves into the 21st century, we have formulated a strategic plan. We must continue to evolve to meet the changing security environment. The most important factor in this evolution is people. Indeed, the most important component of success in all our missions is the people we commit to them. We are continually seeking new and innovative ways to select the right people, to train them thoroughly, and to develop them professionally throughout their career. We know that the best equipment in the world without the right person operating it will not accomplish the mission. On the other hand, the right person will find a way to succeed with almost any equipment available. All of our major programs for the future start with the premise that we must have the right people in the right place with the right training if we are to succeed.

Clearly, the Special Operations Forces believe that they must always employ top talent. They are renowned for staffing their teams with the best of the best personnel the military has to offer. Entry into these units is exceedingly difficult. The U.S. Army's Special Forces Assessment and Selection (SFAS) has a historic attrition rate of approximately 70 percent, with another 10–15 percent lost in the Special Forces Qualification Course. After they're accepted, SOF members receive continuous training of the highest order to ensure that the SOF remains among the most elite fighting forces in the world.

Although their missions might not be critical to the security of a nation, successful musical leaders live by the "Employ top talent" rule. They understand that a mediocre group comprised of regularly rehearsing average musicians will never be a match for a team of great musicians even if they are working together for the first time. Jazz leaders know this especially because improvisation, the ability to deal with the unknown and to adapt, plays such a large part in their music. General Downing wrote, "The challenge to Special Operations Forces is to prepare for an uncertain future while operating in an ever-changing present." Jazz leaders know that experienced and skilled jazz musicians can adapt to almost any situation and deliver a dynamic performance packed with spontaneity, creativity, and energy, even if they have never performed as a collective. Established but fundamentally weak groups performing packaged material might be able to dazzle with a handful of well-rehearsed tunes, but give them something new or unexpected, and their weaknesses will be revealed.

Individuality

How do you go about staffing a high-performance team? What sort of qualities and skills should you look for? In jazz, top marks are awarded for creativity and individuality. An important part of jazz is improvisation, the basis of which is the unique and personal expressions each musician offers. Duke Ellington was arguably the most successful jazz composer ever. His output of more than 4,000 works is notable not only for its quantity, but for its amazing breadth and depth. Much of what we hear in his recordings was written by Ellington and his composer colleague, Billy Strayhorn. They wrote notes that the musicians had to play and included opportunities for improvisation. The rhythm section often improvised all the detail in their parts. Even though Ellington's sidemen had to play the notes the composers wrote, their individuality came shining through in every piece. Ellington wrote for specific musicians just as William Shakespeare wrote for specific actors. Ellington's original parts bear the names of each musician, not just generic labels such as "Trumpet 1." He considered their unique strengths and abilities and wrote parts that featured their greatest talents, such as the plunger mute work of trumpeters "Bubber" Miley and "Cootie" Williams, and trombonist "Tricky Sam" Nanton, or the screaming high register of trumpeter "Cat" Anderson, or the seductive tone of lead alto-saxophonist Johnny Hodges. The individualism of these musicians, even when channeled through Ellington and Strayhorn's writing, contributed to the greatness and uniqueness of the compositions.

Any company seeking to develop unique products or services can also benefit from the talents of creative individuals. Unfortunately, businesses have tended to assume that they need only abstract thinkers and creative people in traditionally creative disciplines such as marketing. All disciplines can benefit from strong individuals with creative talents. In recent years, an increased focus on creativity has led companies to look to the arts for inspiration and education. In his book *A Whole New Mind* (Pink 2005), Daniel H. Pink makes a compelling case that creative-thinking right-brainers will rule the future. Seeking to reduce costs and leverage the global workplace, companies are moving more work to regions where intellectual labor is cheaper. The message is clear: If you want to be in demand, you need to be right brain-enabled. In his book *Linchpin: Are You Indispensable?*, prolific business author Seth Godin proclaims that one of the ways to establish yourself as an indispensable resource in an organization is to deliver unique creativity (Godin 2010).

Individuality is about more than self-expression and creativity. It's also about the confidence to play a unique part without any backup. In a jazz orchestra, individual parts have little redundancy. Every part is critical to the combined sound. Even when no improvisation is required, the musicians must be strong enough to play their unique parts without assistance. The same is true of any lean, cross-functional team on which everyone plays a specific role. The team is truly only as strong as its weakest link. Imagine a product development team in which the representative from engineering significantly overestimates the ability of the team to get the job done. The project could end up a disaster and waste everyone's time.

Individuality in Music

In classical music, the symphony orchestra is the equivalent of a small organization. It consists of smaller departments known as sections. The largest section is the string section, which is further subdivided into the first and second violins, violas, celli, and basses. A symphony orchestra may have as many as 100 musicians.

The jazz equivalent to the symphony orchestra is the jazz orchestra, sometimes known as a "big band," which has, at most, 20 musicians. The jazz orchestra also consists of sections such as the trumpets, trombones, saxophones, and rhythm sections.

Jazz harmony is much more complex than the classical harmony of Mozart's time. As a result, less duplication or doubling of parts occurs, making each part more unique. In a symphony orchestra, on the other hand, a lot of doubling occurs. Sixteen first violins may all be playing the same part, with 14 second violins all playing another part, and so on.

A person's ability to make high-quality contributions is an asset in and of itself. Some individuals are just very good at what they do, regardless of whether their skills or contributions are unique. Perhaps you've been to a concert that featured a soloist playing a concerto that demanded great technical facility on a particular instrument. The soloist not only managed to play all the notes perfectly, but he or she imbued the performance with a unique interpretation and musical expression that was truly engaging. In music, this level of virtuosity is prized. In any field of endeavor, an analogous level of proficiency makes someone a standout, superstar, or guru. The person may be able to forecast markets, close on sales, write code, succinctly communicate complex concepts to customers, or design an elegant architecture like no one else. Sometimes these superskilled practitioners can do what others do in far less time or with less effort. These virtuosi can achieve feats unmatched by most, if not all, of their peers. A hundred mediocre people may never be able to match the achievements of one genius, no matter how much time they have.

A hundred mediocre people may never be able to match the achievements of one genius, no matter how much time they have.

In his book *The Tipping Point: How Little Things Make a Big Difference*, Malcolm Gladwell identified the central role specific people can play in the growth and spread of **social epidemics**, a term that describes the viral spread of ideas, messages, and products. He stated, "The success of any kind of social epidemic is heavily dependent on the involvement of people with a particular and rare set of social skills" (Gladwell 2000, 33). Gladwell also invoked the **Pareto principle** (also known as the 80-20 rule and the Law of the Vital Few) to quantitatively suggest the extent to which these key individuals might be responsible for an epidemic's success.

The Manhattan Project, the 1940s effort to develop the atomic bomb, is surely one of the most famous efforts of creative collaboration. Business professor Warren Bennis and journalist Patricia Ward Beiderman included the project as one of six "Great Groups" in their book *Organizing Genius: The Secrets of Creative Collaboration* (Bennis and Ward 1998). In response to Nazi Germany's effort to develop an atomic weapon, the United States, the United Kingdom, and Canada engaged in a joint effort to design a weapon that would decisively end World War II. This was a race against time with not only the Germans, but also the Japanese, who were working toward the same goal. The Manhattan Project employed more than 130,000 people, but a small group of individuals, the project's scientific and engineering geniuses, were most vital to the project. Without them, the Manhattan Project would very likely have never succeeded, and the outcome of history might have been quite different.

One of the most influential groups in the history of jazz was Miles Davis's second quintet that performed from 1963 to 1968. Davis has been quoted as saying (in typical fashion) of his 1960s quintet, "I knew right away that this was going to be a motherf***er of a group." (Coolman 1997, 58). Perhaps not the words we would all choose, but arguably undeniable. Many have acknowledged the band as the greatest small jazz combo ever. The influence of the members' individual playing styles, ensemble work, and compositions is indisputable. Listening to the live recordings of this group is like going on a roller-coaster ride. The group drew its energy from its soon-to-be-superstar drummer, Tony Williams. Hailed as a child prodigy, he stamped his influence on every performance. Davis was quoted as saying, "Man, to play with Tony Williams you had to be real alert and pay attention to everything he did, or he'd lose you in a second." (Coolman 1997, 35).

Ron Carter, on bass, was the anchor of the quintet. Dubbed "Checkpoint Charlie" by Williams, he kept things together when William's polyrhythmic drumming threatened to blow the group apart. Together the pair played havoc with tempo and form, modulated meter in all manner of ways, and stopped and started on a whim. Herbie Hancock, on piano, was equally adventurous with harmony. He brought with him an impressionistic sound and lyricism that recalled Bill Evans's style from Davis's 1958–1961 sextet. George Coleman filled the tenor saxophone chair in 1963 and stayed until spring 1964. His replacement was Wayne Shorter, whom Davis had previously failed to recruit when Shorter had been committed to drummer Art Blakey. Both Coleman and Shorter were technicians of the highest caliber. As he had done with John Coltrane in previous groups, Davis used Coleman and Shorter as foils for his own less technical and more lyrical and introverted style of playing. In this respect, Shorter was better suited for the group and for Davis. He was a more aggressive and adventurous player than Coleman, who was apparently never completely at ease in the band and, as the oldest sideman with an established style, was less open to the exploration the others wanted to pursue.

Davis was already an acknowledged master, although he was still only 37 when the new quintet came together in 1963. His sidemen were all substantially younger by 10 to 20 years. Their energy, exuberance, and explorations pushed Davis and made him work in ways he hadn't since joining Charlie Parker's quintet in 1945. Hancock said, "The level of musicianship was so high that you either had to rise to the occasion or you better get another job" (Coolman 1997, 42). Davis was a great trumpet player. More important, he was a superb leader who understood the importance of employing top talent. He knew how to identify the best musicians and match them with other equally talented but often very different individuals.

The Importance of Awareness

The ability of Miles Davis's second quintet to collectively create such amazing music on the fly reminds us that being highly skilled is about more than individual contributions. As we see later in Chapter 14, "Take Measured Risks," inventors rarely make great discoveries in isolation. Similarly, jazz musicians create unique music not alone, but by collectively innovating. One of the most important skills of highly effective people is their ability to allocate a sizable portion of their personal bandwidth to collaboration. Think about the work-related tasks you can complete most proficiently. Chances are, you can do some of them on autopilot, allowing you to simultaneously perform another task or even two. Or perhaps you can easily complete these tasks in less time than it would take someone without your level of proficiency.

We each have limited cycles, but the more proficient we are at the routine tasks, the more aware we can be of our surroundings. Imagine a drummer who has to think constantly about where to place his or her limbs, how to hold the sticks, which drums to hit, and how to coordinate both arms and legs. A person doing all that will find it extremely difficult, if not impossible, to maintain awareness of what is going on with the other musicians, the audience, and the combined sound. Now imagine a drummer for whom playing is a routine exercise. He or she can perform all the necessary fundamentals and still have sufficient personal bandwidth to monitor everything else that is happening, communicate with the other musicians, respond to changes, and engage in interplay.

One of the most important skills of highly effective people is their ability to allocate a sizable portion of their personal bandwidth to collaboration.

Being personally competent requires a high level of *personal awareness*. Musicians, for example, are constantly aware of the sounds they are producing and what they have to do to produce those sounds, play in tune and in time, and express the nuances of the music. Armed with this ability, one musician may be able to deliver a great solo performance. However, most music is performed not by one person alone, but by ensembles. Performing in a group requires strong individual awareness, as well as heightened **social** or **situational awareness** of what others are doing and how one must interact with them. Both individual and situational awareness should be valued as highly as any skills proficiency or problem-solving ability. Phil Jackson, one of the greatest coaches in the history of the National Basketball Association (NBA), wrote this in his book *Sacred Hoops: Spiritual Lessons of a Hardwood Warrior* (P. Jackson 1995, 50–51):

Basketball happens at such a fast pace that your mind has a tendency to race at the same speed as your pounding heart. As the pressure builds, it's easy to start thinking too much. But if you're always trying to figure the game out, you won't be able to respond creatively to what's going on. Yogi Berra once said about baseball: "How can you think and hit at the same time?" The same is true with basketball, except everything's happening much faster. The key is seeing and doing. If you're focusing on anything other than reading the court and doing what needs to be done, the moment will pass you by.

Jackson also wrote:

Basketball is a complex dance that requires shifting from one object to another at lightning speed. To excel, you need to act with a clear mind and be totally focused on what everyone is doing. Some athletes describe this quality as a "cocoon of concentration." But that implies shutting out the world when what you really need to do is become more acutely aware of what's happening right this very moment.

Figure 2.1 illustrates two individuals, one who is highly proficient and the other less so. The highly proficient individual can do the same work as the other, with less concentration. Consequently, that person can spend more time monitoring his or her context, including interactions with other team members.

If you drive a car or ride a bike, or even if you've just walked the streets as a pedestrian, you've had the chance to observe and interact with literally hundreds of thousands of motorists. You've probably seen people demonstrating a lack of personal awareness as they drive. These are the people who cruise down the road with their indicators blinking, although they have no intent to turn. They drive around at night without their headlights on or are unaware that they are blinding other motorists with their high beams engaged. They're driving at highway speed in fourth gear in a five-speed car or driving in that same gear while they slowly make their way up a really steep hill, taxing their engine to the point of near-stalling. You've probably also seen drivers demonstrating a lack of social awareness. They change lanes without even realizing that someone is in their blind spot, or they reach a four-way intersection and nearly cause an accident by proceeding without waiting their turn. You've no doubt been in social situations where you've observed people unaware that their zippers are undone or their sweaters are inside out. Perhaps you've heard someone make an insensitive comment in a social or business situation, unaware that they've deeply offended the person standing right next to them. Countless examples from our everyday lives illustrate how essential individual and social awareness is to the way in which we operate.

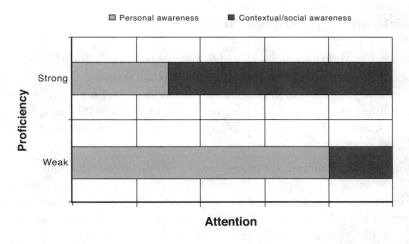

Figure 2.1   *How effective individuals rely on awareness*

You might expect *Executive Genius,* by John Selby and Ahmos Netanel (Selby and Netanel 2008), to be a book about problem solving or strategizing. However, the book's main focus is awareness. Subtitled *How to Build a High Awareness Company,* Selby and Netanel's book is based on the premise that the higher a leader's core awareness level, the greater that leader's chance of success. They make a compelling case for both personal as well as corporate awareness. In his book *Practical Intelligence* (Albrecht 2007), Karl Albrect describes forms of awareness as forms of intelligence. He defines **emotional intelligence** as the awareness and management of one's inner experience and **social intelligence** as the ability to understand social contexts and deal with people. Stephen R. Covey, author of the bestselling book *The 7 Habits of Highly Effective People,* describes a somewhat different model in *The 8th Habit* (S. R. Covey 2004). Covey suggests that emotional intelligence is "one's self-knowledge, self-awareness, social sensitivity, empathy and ability to communicate successfully with others." Regardless of how you look at it, heightened awareness on multiple planes is a critical element for success in almost any situation. Phil Jackson wrote: "Being aware is more important than being smart." (P. Jackson 1995, 113). Before he became a coach, Jackson had been a player. He recalls learning from New York Knicks coach Red Holzman that "awareness is everything," (P. Jackson 1995, 35) while Knicks forward (and later senator) Bill Bradley helped him realize the "gift of awareness." (P. Jackson 1995, 37)

Enabling Organizational Agility

Agility is the ability to move quickly, an essential capability when one must respond to change. Organizational agility is difficult, especially for large organizations, but it begins with agile individuals and teams. Put together teams of talented people who can react promptly to change and improvise solutions, and you'll enable an agile organization that can respond readily to challenges.

Although organizational agility can be enabled through individual agility, one should resist the urge to "bulk up" in pursuit of greater strength. When building a team, aim for the quality of people, not quantity. In fact, this is the second of the SOF Truths: "Quality is better than Quantity." The third is "Special Operations Forces cannot be mass produced." Teams that are staffed with quality over quantity in mind end up being both good and lean. This reduces costs and increases agility.

> *When building a team, aim for the quality*
> *of people, not quantity.*

The idea of lean thinking is not new. It began in modern manufacturing with Henry Ford around 1910 and evolved in just-in-time manufacturing when the Toyota Motor Corporation based its production system on an American supermarket chain. Lean principles originally applied to the reduction of stored inventory and manufacturing and processing operations. However, the mindset can and should be applied to every facet of an organization's operation, including the elimination of bureaucracy and unnecessary people. Recently, economic uncertainty, global competition, volatile oil prices, and war have forced a renewed focus on lean thinking. In fact, all organizations and teams should be lean, regardless of the forces to which they are subject—not so lean that they must compromise their ability to function or produce, but enough that they are not carrying unnecessary overhead. Lean operations force teams to deal with human resource constraints and, consequently, to select only the best people.

Although lean is good, it does have its drawbacks. The Special Air Service (SAS) special forces of the British Army is the oldest of all modern special forces and has served as the model for many other special forces units around the world. In *The SAS: The Official History*, Philip Warner wrote (Warner, 1982, 5):

> *A basic point of SAS philosophy is that a small group is more likely to reach its objective than a large one. Small units do not require much in the way of supplies, they can move unobtrusively, and rarely cause the alarm which a larger formation would arouse.*

Think about Warner's reference to the enemy as a business competitor. If you're the SAS, you want to make your move without letting your enemy know what you are doing until you are ready to reveal it yourself. Warner continued:

> *There is, of course, no room for mistakes in a very small unit; there is no one to cover up and every man is vital.*

Therein lies the risk of running lean: Each member of a team becomes a more critical resource. Small teams are clearly more impacted than large teams by a reduction in staffing or capability. As I noted in the description of a military A-team in the Introduction, in some contemporary special forces, redundancy is built in to avoid crippling the unit if one or more personnel are lost. Keep this in mind.

Managing Human Resources

So far, we've focused on recruitment. What about achieving our objectives with existing human resources? Can you develop an existing team into a collective of highly skilled, creative individuals with the ability to respond to change and improvise solutions when they are needed? It's not impossible, but by analogy, you also can't get blood from a stone. If you have the time and opportunity to develop existing talent, which is not always the case, the efforts can be rewarding for both teams and individuals. One lesson about developing and promoting individuals can be learned from the world of open source software development. Open source projects operate as meritocracies, with appointments based solely on contributions. Committers, with the right to own parts of the project and make important decisions that could affect the project's future, are appointed after first proving themselves as contributors and then being voted in by all the existing committers. This model of human resources has proven to be hugely successful for open source projects, as well as for commercial software developments that have adopted similar practices. A similar emphasis on ability is evident in the Special Operation Forces. Consultant Andrew Sobel noted, "In SOF, being able to pull your weight and having a depth of combat experience are more important than rank…. Their respect for one another is rooted more in the recognition of capabilities than in titles." (Sobel 2009)

We've covered hiring and developing top talent, so we need to briefly discuss the uncomfortable subject of letting people go. It's a tough job that no one wants to do, but too many teams carry dead weight. It's important to help people succeed and put them in positions where they can achieve success, but sometimes people need to move on, for their own good and that of the team. To keep them in positions where they cannot fully contribute is unfair to both.

Recapitulation

- People are your most important asset. Experienced and skilled people can adapt to almost any situation and deliver a dynamic performance packed with spontaneity, creativity, and energy, even if they are working together for the first time.

- Any team seeking to develop unique products or services can benefit from the talents of creative individuals. Individuality is about more than self-expression and creativity. It's also about the confidence to play a unique part without any backup.

- Highly effective people are able to allocate a sizable portion of their personal bandwidth to collaboration because they are highly proficient in their fundamental skills.

- Organizational agility begins with agile individuals and teams. Put together teams of talented people who can react promptly to change and improvise solutions, and you'll enable an agile organization that can respond readily to challenges.

- People should be given more responsibility only after they have demonstrated an ability to contribute positively.

- It's important to help people succeed and put them in positions where they can achieve success, but sometimes people need to move on, for their own good and that of the team.

CHAPTER 3

Put the Team First

"The way a team plays as a whole determines its success.
You may have the greatest bunch of individual stars in the world,
but if they don't play together, the club won't be worth a dime."
—Babe Ruth

Putting the Team First

Working within a high-performance team requires a tradeoff between virtuosity and collaboration. In his paper *Creativity and Improvisation in Jazz and Organizations: Implications for Organizational Learning*, Frank Barrett (1998, 617) noted that in jazz:

> *It is not enough to be an individual virtuoso. [O]ne must also be able*
> *to surrender one's virtuosity and enable others to excel.*

We've discussed the need to staff a team with top talent. Unfortunately, many high-achieving individuals tend to focus predominately on achieving their own goals. This is often the reason for their great personal success. As NBA coach Phil Jackson wrote of basketball (P. Jackson, 1995, 80):

> *Our society places such a high premium on individual achievement,*
> *it's easy for players to get blinded by their own self-importance and*
> *lose a sense of interconnectedness, the essence of teamwork.*

Building a team composed of amazing virtuosi who can't subjugate or blend their egos is a recipe for disaster. For any team to succeed, it must achieve a balance between individual and group performance. Jackson (1995, 89) writes:

This is the struggle every leader faces: how to get members of the team who are driven by the quest for individual glory, to give themselves over wholeheartedly to the group effort. In other words, how to teach them selflessness.

While this is clearly important for teams where egos may be at-large, even a team with well-tempered personalities can benefit from a team-centric perspective. The goal is to function in synergy, not simply as a group of talented individuals. It begins with a commitment to "Put the team first."

Jackson (1995, 4) recalls that when he became head coach of the Chicago Bulls, "[m]ore than anything, [he] wanted to build a team that would blend individual talent with a heightened group consciousness." Explaining the success of the Bulls, Jackson wrote:

No team understood better than the championship Chicago Bulls that selflessness is the soul of teamwork. The conventional wisdom is that the team was primarily a one-man show—Michael Jordan and the Jordanaires. But the real reason the Bulls won three straight NBA championships from 1991 to ['}93 was that we plugged into the power of oneness *instead of the power of one man, and transcended the divisive forces of the ego that have crippled far more gifted teams.*

Consultant Andrew Sobel (2009) noted that in the Special Operations Forces, "selfish behavior will get you kicked out, whereas in private-sector organizations, it may very well be tolerated as long as the individual is perceived as making money for the company. Punishing the wrong behavior is just as important as rewarding the right behavior—studies have shown that when executives publicly reprimand freeloaders, greater organizational collaboration will result. Business leaders must get much tougher about doing this."

The notion of team first is clearly important in a jazz ensemble. You simply cannot make music, let alone create amazing, unique music on the fly, if you're dealing with a clash of titans or a failure to connect. Astute jazz listeners can often recognize these troublesome group dynamics. They will remark, "The drummer and the bassist were fighting one another all night long" or "There was no exchange between any of the players."

People with the team-first mindset understand that their individual contribution is vital to the team's success. They also know that without the rest of the team, they alone could not achieve the same success. This mutual dependence must be accompanied by mutual accountability. In jazz, the musicians are accountable not only to the leader of the group, but to every person in the group and to the ensemble as a whole. Trust, which we discuss in detail in the next chapter, is another vital ingredient. As Jackson (1955, 21) wrote, "Good teams become great ones when the members trust each other enough to surrender the 'me' for the 'we.'"

In jazz, the musicians are accountable not only to the leader of the group, but to every person in the group and to the ensemble as a whole.

In the last chapter, we discussed how a small jazz group might handle the ending to a piece of music. Endings are a good example of the need to maintain team cohesiveness. When the musicians reach that point in a piece they are playing, no one knows exactly what will happen. Likely someone will take the lead and others will follow. Someone else might then take up the lead and continue with or evolve an idea that the first person started. Regardless, what's most important is that the musicians work together toward a final resolution. Their individuality is required to help make the ending unique and memorable, but it should never be at the cost of the team's combined effort. In jazz, all of this happens in real time with only limited means of communication, either through the music or visually. Total commitment to the collective result is critical.

When a team includes many strong individuals, each with distinctly specialized skills and experience, cross-fertilization among individuals can unify the team. Sobel (2009) noted of special forces operators, "They usually have a core specialty—such as weapons, communications, or medicine—but everyone on a six- or 12-man team knows something about everyone else's expertise, and it's the job of each specialist to conduct ongoing training for his teammates. Collaboration is enhanced by this shared vocabulary and body of SOF operating practices." This approach can both generate respect between team members and build redundancy that increases the robustness of a team.

Absorbing Mistakes as a Team

The ability of every individual in the team to put the team first is often tested in a time of crisis. Some years ago, I was conducting an orchestra in a performance of a wonderful suite of music. The suite was designed to be performed as a single continuous piece, with each movement flowing immediately into the next. It was very difficult music, and we didn't have a lot of preparation time. At the dress rehearsal, which was rather rushed due to a scheduling limitation, we discussed and briefly played through the transitions between the movements. The entire performance of the suite was great except for a near train wreck during one of the transitions. One part of the ensemble went one way with me, and the rest of the ensemble did not. I recall thinking for a very brief moment that I might have to stop the performance and restart from the beginning of the movement. However, within about three seconds, the ensemble had come to agreement and we continued on. It's not clear how many people in the audience were aware of the hiccup, but I was certainly glad that we were able to absorb it as a team and maintain the integrity of the performance.

On another occasion, I was performing with the same group, but I was playing bass, and we had no conductor. At the sound check, we decided on a last-minute change to the ending of a piece featuring solo trumpet. The ending involved an extended trumpet cadenza, after which the ensemble entered on the second beat of a bar. We decided to alter it so that a drum fill would set up the tempo for the ensemble, with the drums ending on the first beat and the ensemble entering on the second beat. Unfortunately, one of the trombonists was not present for the sound check. As the leader of the group, I should have informed him, but things were rather frantic and it slipped my mind. Consequently, during the performance, he entered before the drummer had begun to set things up for the ensemble entry. Others might have followed and amplified the mistake, but fortunately, the rest of the ensemble absorbed the mistake and stayed with the plan, and we finished strong.

The ability to absorb mistakes is one of the most important capabilities of an effective team. "Team first" is a team-centric mindset that gives more consideration to team results than to individual ones. The team succeeds and takes the credit together, and the team fails and takes the blame together. As Jon R. Katzenbach and Douglas K. Smith (1993) wrote in their bestselling book *The Wisdom of Teams*, "No group ever becomes a team until it can hold itself accountable as a team." When a team can collectively deal with mistakes and failures, it can absorb them more readily and lessen their impact.

The ability to absorb mistakes is one of the most important capabilities of an effective team.

Ideally, a team doesn't need to deal with mistakes to prove its collective mindset. Another way to demonstrate team cohesiveness is through a willingness to tackle a challenge or traverse a risky path. A unified team negotiates that path with commitment.

Avoiding Groupthink

Teams that single-mindedly pursue team-first thinking face a potentially dangerous downside. **Groupthink**, a term coined by psychologist Irving Janis in 1972, refers to a collective mindset that is manifested when a team's quest for cohesiveness leads it to all but abandon individual creativity and critical thinking. As a result, team members may fail to innovate. Worse still, they may make huge mistakes together. The individuals who question their team's direction fail to speak up for fear that their comments will not be well-received. Well-known examples of groupthink include the failure of the U.S. military and government to anticipate the Japanese attack on Pearl Harbor in 1941, the decision of John F. Kennedy and his advisors to authorize the Bay of Pigs invasion of Cuba in 1962, the failure of NASA administrators to prevent the Challenger Space Shuttle disaster in 1986, the collapse of Enron in 2001, and the Bush administration's decision to invade Iraq in 2003.

Groupthink can occur when a team's quest for cohesiveness leads it to all but abandon individual creativity and critical thinking.

The tendency to resort to groupthink can be exacerbated by a team's tendency to self-select likeminded people and rid itself of people who don't think like the rest of the team. It's important to find a workable balance between strong individual talents and team-centric collaboration, and to ensure that people always feel empowered to speak out.

Team-first thinking should also focus on the overall strength, integrity, and, where applicable, longevity of a team. A strong team should regularly deal with such issues as these:

- Recruiting new team members
- Developing existing team members
- Understanding the team's strengths
- Identifying and addressing the team's weaknesses
- Identifying opportunities to collaborate with other teams
- Helping the team do a better job with existing cross-team collaborations

Team Awareness

You've undoubtedly seen high-performance teams and marveled at the brilliance of the teamwork. It might have been a team of professional chefs preparing a sumptuous banquet for 500 people, a company of acrobats performing a dazzling routine, or a baseball team turning a perfectly executed triple play. The ability of a team to execute at the highest level is predicated on a heightened awareness among team members. When everyone in the team knows what everyone else is doing, they can coordinate efforts and avoid unnecessary duplication of work. This is an example of the social awareness we discussed in Chapter 2. In describing "The Myth of the Superhero" in basketball, Phil Jackson wrote (1995, 17):

> *Basketball is a sport that involves the subtle interweaving of players at full speed to the point where they are thinking and moving as one. To do that successfully, they need to trust each other on a deep level and know instinctively how their teammates will respond in pressure situations. A great player can only do so much on his own—no matter how breathtaking his one-on-one moves. If he is out of sync psychologically with everyone else, the team will never achieve the harmony needed to win a championship.*

In a jazz ensemble, each musician must be constantly aware of what the other musicians are doing. As the great jazz pianist Oscar Peterson said, "It's the group sound that's important, even when you're playing a solo. You not only have to know your own instrument, you must know the others and how to back them up at all times. That's jazz." The ability to do this requires strong team awareness. To maintain a solid groove and then keep in time and in tune with one another, each musician must constantly monitor the combined output of the ensemble and make adjustments to individual output. To take the music to a level at which each musician can individually or collectively innovate, they all need to be even more intimately engaged. Heightened team awareness can make someone highly effective in a collaborative environment.

"It's the group sound that's important, even when you're playing a solo. You not only have to know your own instrument, you must know the others and how to back them up at all times. That's jazz." —Oscar Peterson

---

It's no surprise that IBM built the notion of team awareness into Rational Team Concert. Team awareness is especially important when you consider that many software development teams are distributed across multiple geographic locations. Technology can give these teams the same advantages that physically colocated teams take for granted. Software development teams can tell Team Concert about their project teams, including their roles, relationships, capabilities, and artifacts they work on. This information can help team members stay informed of events that may be of interest to them. Team members can browse or directly access specific information or subscribe to newsfeeds that automatically notify them of events of interest. IBM integrated instant messaging (chat) and virtual presence into Team Concert. As a result, any mention of a team member in project artifacts is accompanied with the person's chat status. Chat sessions can be initiated without having to go to a separate tool and find the person there. Views such as Team Artifacts, Team Central, and Team Organization all reinforce the idea that the team is working together, even if the members are functioning in isolation or are scattered across the globe and working at completely different times of the day.

Heightened team awareness can make someone highly effective in a collaborative environment.

Acknowledging Everyone's Efforts

Focusing on the team helps people recognize the value of everyone's contributions. Few people who attend a symphony orchestra concert can later recall the names of the artists, apart from those of the conductor and soloists. Sports fans all remember who made the winning shot of a championship basketball or hockey game, but rarely do they recall the players who made the passes to set up the score. In politics, people remember influential leaders for their actions and words, but not the advisors and speechwriters who empower those leaders. Unfortunately, people tend to remember the accomplishments of only a team's most noticeable individuals, even if those individuals did not make the most significant or valuable contributions. That is why it's important for leaders and the stars who receive all the accolades to acknowledge the contributions of their colleagues. Acknowledging the "everyday heroes" builds trust and empowers every member of the team to achieve higher levels of performance.

When I'm on stage as the leader of a musical ensemble, I always make it a point to acknowledge each and every member by introducing them to the audience. I always introduce myself last. I do this regardless of whether the ensemble has 5 or 50 musicians. Even if I'm conducting the orchestra, I never take a separate bow, make a separate entry onto the stage, or do anything that in any way acknowledges me with greater significance than any of my colleagues. To me, each person in the ensemble deserves to be equally acknowledged and credited. Despite my consistent efforts, many people, including the press, still treat me special. It is easier for them to identify with a single individual than with many individuals. That's why it's all the more important for me to make extra efforts to acknowledge and credit everyone whenever I can.

Not surprisingly, the "Put the team first" and "Employ top talent" principles are related. They have a symbiotic relationship in that they keep one another in check. They are two of the most fundamental principles of the Jazz Process and proof that people play the biggest part in both the successes and failures of teams. The trick for leaders is to follow both of these principles, harnessing individual talents and combining the collective output in synergistic attainment of common goals.

Avoiding Team Elitism

We've discussed the need for individuals to work within a team, but this philosophy extends outside the team as well. Organizations consist of large teams that are made up of smaller teams and so forth. In military organizations, there are armies, corps, divisions, brigades, regiments, battalions, platoons, squads, and so on. When high-performance teams exist within larger teams or organizations that may not be so productive, there is a danger that tension can develop between the two. Writing about the SAS, Philip Warner (1982) noted:

> "Special" forces are often the subject of envy, dislike and misunderstanding, because they are usually selected for secret missions, trained on a wider variety of weapons than other soldiers may use, and are issued with equipment which is often more lavish than that provided to their parent units. Often they wear a distinctive marking, a badge or specially coloured beret, and this, whether they like it or not, gives them a certain glamour. Further, they have a more exciting and varied life than the comrades they have left behind them. Some

*will envy them, some will curse them and others will say with consid-
erable conviction: "Better you than me, chum."*

For this reason, the SAS has worked hard to avoid these kinds of problems.
Warner wrote:

> *Nobody in the SAS looks down on any other unit of the army as being
> less important; no regiment in the entire army is so well aware of the
> essential attributes of what are often dismissed contemptuously as
> "administrative" troops.*

> *The SAS man, the fighting soldier par excellence, suffers from no
> delusions about his own importance. He knows his role is vital but he
> knows that a cipher clerk, or a cartographer, or even the skill of the
> opposing general's cook, may in fact be more important to the success
> of the campaign than quite a number of daring soldiers.*

Putting the team first means not just your immediate team, but the larger
team as well. Every person has something to contribute.

Recapitulation

- Working within a high-performance team requires a tradeoff between virtuosity and collaboration.

- Team players understand that their individual contributions are vital to the team's success. They also know that they alone could not achieve the same level of success without the rest of the team.

- Members of a team are accountable not only to the leader of the group, but to every person in the group and to the team as a whole.

- Cross-fertilization within a team can generate respect between team members and build redundancy that increases the robustness of a team.

- The ability to absorb mistakes is one of the most important capabilities of an effective team. A strong team succeeds and takes the credit together, and the team also fails and takes the blame together.

- Groupthink can occur when a team's quest for cohesiveness causes members to all but abandon individual creativity and critical thinking.

- The ability of a team to execute at the highest levels is predicated on a heightened awareness among team members. When everyone in the team knows what everyone else is doing, they can coordinate efforts and avoid unnecessary duplication of work.

- Leaders and the stars who receive all the accolades should acknowledge the contributions of their colleagues. Acknowledging the "everyday heroes" builds trust and empowers every member of the team to achieve higher levels of performance.

- Avoid team elitism that may result when high-performance teams exist within larger teams or organizations that aren't so productive. Putting the team first means not just your immediate team, but the larger team as well.

- Acknowledge everyone's contributions and not just those of the most visible individuals.

- Avoid divisiveness between high-performance teams and other less-capable parts of an organization.

CHAPTER 4

Build Trust and Respect

"In any organization, trust must be developed among every member of the team if success is going to be achieved."
—Mike Krzyzewski

Trust and Respect

If you trust someone, you are confident that you can depend on that person to fulfill an obligation. If you respect someone, you likely admire that person and hold his or her work in high regard. Another form of respect, which we consider separately, is the willingness to consider what others have to contribute. We can associate trust and respect with people or with teams or organizations. Sometimes we base one on the other. For example, we may trust and respect someone because that person works for a company we hold in high regard, or we may trust a team because it includes individuals with a history of positive results.

The people and entities in which we place our trust and respect depend on personal and subjective judgments. Our trust is complex, defies precise measurement, and can seldom be turned on or off at will. Nor can it be demanded or coerced. Conversely, you can't make anyone trust or respect you. Trust and respect can only be given freely, and often that can happen only when people feel they have a reason to trust or respect someone. As is often stated, trust and respect must be earned. If a team is to work effectively, every member of the team must trust and respect each of the other members. A potentially complex network of mutual trust and respect exists in every strong team. Creating this network may take time and can also be difficult. As much as mutual trust and respect are desirable, reciprocation is never guaranteed.

Although it is true that trust and respect must be earned, it is also true that these qualities are sometimes implicit and easily developed. Consider trust as an example. Trust in other people is one of our most primitive and essential notions. From the moment we are born, we must depend on others for our sustenance and well-being. Consequently, we instinctively develop bonds of trust with those who care for us. Roderick M. Kramer, a professor of organizational behavior at the Stanford Graduate School of Business, has conducted extensive research on the social psychology of trust and distrust and how it relates to teams. He observed, "We're born to be engaged and to engage others, which is what trust is largely about." He noted that we have a tendency to approach many situations without suspicion (Kramer, 2009, 70–71):

> Unless we've been unfortunate enough to be victims of a major violation of trust, most of us have had years of experiences that affirm the basic trustworthiness of people and institutions around us by the time we become adults. Things seldom go catastrophically wrong when we trust, so it's not entirely irrational that we have a bias towards trust.

Kramer's observations certainly have merit. When we cover the perception of authenticity in our discussion of "Act transparently," we will see that many variables can lead us to develop a perception of authenticity. What makes our context unique is that we are typically dealing with high-performance teams comprised of talented individuals working in challenging situations. The bar is set high, and not just anybody can deliver. If you inserted an unknown basketball player into an NBA basketball team, an unknown violinist into a world-class string quartet, or an unknown soldier into a U.S. Navy SEAL Team, how apt do you think the other members of these ensembles would be to immediately extend trust to the newcomer, especially in a critical situation? In all likelihood, the other members would be highly suspicious and nervous. In these and similar situations in which the level of performance is high, establishing trust requires work and proof of delivery.

Trust and respect can only be given freely, and often that can happen only when people feel they have a reason to trust or respect someone.

Benefits of Trust and Respect

What are the essential benefits of trust and respect? Trust and respect can engender loyalty, motivation, satisfaction, and honesty. They are binding agents that keep a team together and help it maintain strong and healthy relationships even in the face of change and adversity. In recalling some of the storms weathered by the Chicago Bulls, Phil Jackson wrote, "Once the game starts, the players know how to tune out those distractions because of the trust they have for each other. The untold story of the Bulls, says [point guard] B.J. Armstrong, is 'the respect each individual has for everybody else'" (P. Jackson, 1995, 159). The mutual dependence that binds a team together requires that each member trust the other members to do their parts. Without that trust, people may spend precious time and energy wondering whether other people will fulfill their obligations to the team. Placing trust in people gives them the freedom to work. That freedom is especially important if their approach to a task differs from that of others. It's important to remember that sometimes more than one path may lead to success.

Another important reason to create an environment of trust and respect is the comfort, happiness, and satisfaction of team members. Nobody wants to work in a dysfunctional team. People are more likely and more willing to do a better job when they are happy in their work environment. In music—and especially in jazz, where self-expression is such a vital part of the art form—the artists' inner feelings come through in their performances. This holds true in most other forms of self-expression: developing software, writing a speech, delivering a sermon, or putting together a project plan.

When people make great efforts, deliver under challenging or difficult conditions, or excel at their tasks, they generate respect for their efforts and abilities. When people are respected, they feel pride in themselves, their efforts, and their results. Too much pride can be a bad thing, leading to overconfidence and, consequently, mistakes. In the right amounts, however, pride generates genuine care about what one produces. When people don't have pride in themselves and their work, they often don't care enough to correct mistakes or take the extra steps that produce a standout offering. Going that extra mile may well be exactly what is required to edge out the competition.

The attainment of complete and unwavering trust and respect among every person in a team is a lofty goal. Think about what your answer would be and what your colleagues at work would say if you asked them whether they unequivocally trusted everyone else in their team and had complete respect for them. Many people would rightly ask for clarification on the scope or the context of the question. Consider these examples of trust and respect:

- Tom trusts Mike to fix a complex bug in the server code, but there's no way he'd trust him to even touch the user interface layer.

- Bob doesn't really trust Jin Li to interview the candidates for the financial controller position by herself, but he has great respect for the way she handled the termination of the previous financial controller.

- Lily is constantly amazed by the results John delivers as a project manager, but she doesn't have much respect for the way he goes about meeting his objectives.

- Sharon really respects Lee for giving her the time and the opportunity to grow into a new role, even though she had trouble in the beginning.

- Sanjeev trusts his brother-in-law to repay a loan but is pretty sure that he can't trust him to keep a secret.

These examples demonstrate that not only are there different levels of trust and respect, but the two do not always go together. You can trust someone even though you may not respect him or her. It's also possible to respect someone even though you may not trust that person's abilities.

Developing Trust and Respect

In *The 8th Habit*, Stephen R. Covey introduced The Speed of Trust, a concept he attributed to his son, Stephen M.R. Covey. Several years later, the younger Covey wrote at length about the idea in his own book, *The Speed of Trust,* arguing that the presence of trust affects the speed and cost of operations. When trust is present, things move faster, and costs are lower. For example, Covey wrote that when Warren Buffett's company, Berkshire Hathaway, acquired McLane Distribution, a $23 billion company previously owned by Wal-Mart, they did "no due diligence" because, as Buffett pointed out, they trusted Wal-Mart (S. M. Covey, 2006, 14–15). In activities in which time can be sacrificed, the absence of trust may cause delays that frequently result in increased costs. The 9/11 terrorist attacks reduced the effective speed of air travel and increased the cost to travelers and governments. The Sarbanes-Oxley Act, passed in response to corporate failures such as Enron and WorldCom, has significantly increased the time and cost of complying with financial regulations. In activities in which time must remain fixed, scope or quality may suffer. A software project may be delivered on time but may lack important features or contain more bugs. The speed of delivery is not negotiable for a jazz performance because jazz must be delivered in real time. Trust and respect help musicians perform with confidence, enabling them to take creative risks that help create unique performances. Without trust, the musicians may never dare to explore new pathways; one musician may pass up the opportunity to develop an idea offered by another.

Because good jazz musicians want to deliver strong, unique performances, they must quickly establish trust, especially if they are performing together for the first time. Doing so enables them to safely and comfortably explore myriad musical possibilities. They begin this process by showing basic respect, accepting that each person has something to contribute, and respecting each contribution. Listening with open ears, accepting with open minds, and appreciating with open hearts, the musicians foster a camaraderie that encourages each individual to give his or her best. This is the other form of respect that I mentioned briefly at the beginning of this chapter—the willingness to consider what others have to contribute.

One of the wonderful points about jazz is that self-expression is never suppressed. When a team is trying to create something novel or unique, as jazz musicians often are, creative, individual statements are most needed. You will often see jazz musicians praising or encouraging one another even in the middle of a performance. Exclamations along the lines of "Yeah!" or "Say it, man!" are not uncommon. Depending on the situation, these exclamations either are made discreetly from one musician to another or are delivered with gusto and incorporated into the performance. Either way, they are evidence of the positive attitude that jazz musicians bring to their product. As the musicians perform, they make contributions that establish their credentials as jazz musicians, their intent for the direction of the music, their ability to fulfill the essential parts of their role, and their willingness to help the team manage change and create a unique offering.

Listening with open ears, accepting with open minds, and appreciating with open hearts, the musicians foster a camaraderie that encourages each individual to give his or her best.

Whatever your job may be, your team has some basic expectations of you. In most jazz ensembles, a bassist is expected to outline the harmony and provide a pulse for the time. The pulse is especially important if the group has no drummer. To deliver on these requirements, the bassist must negotiate the chord changes and maintain a strong and steady pulse. By immediately and consistently fulfilling these requirements, the bassist establishes trust and respect for his or her abilities. The other musicians know that the bassist will always be there to provide a harmonic and temporal foundation. This, in turn, gives them freedom to innovate in their respective domains. Ingrid

Monson, a noted musicologist, wrote about the jazz performance process in her book *Saying Something: Jazz Improvisation and Interaction*. In the book, she quoted drummer Ralph Peterson on the subject of musical trust (Monson, 1996, 174–175):

> *Another thing about bass players that's very important is their ability to concentrate when I or another member of the ensemble moves away from the basic pulse beat—and start playing against the time, if you will. It's not always the best idea...when somebody else starts playing against the time—to hear that and go with them, because somebody has to stay grounded .... When a bass player has the ability to concentrate and...the wisdom to know when to...play against the time and leave me as the centerpoint, that's very important and it's not anything that I would want to have to teach anyone....It's some- thing that has to be there...the ability to absorb large amounts of rhythmic variants without being thrown.*

Peterson's words ring true for me as a bassist. When the rhythms within the ensemble become complex, it can be hard to remain grounded even though I know this is precisely what the group needs at that time. To fail may cause the performance to go off the rails and ultimately crash and burn.

Reliance upon others is necessary, too, for the bassist. It's a common misconception that the responsibility for keeping time falls solely to the drummer or to the bassist in a drummerless group. In fact, it is the responsibility of all the musicians to help maintain a steady pulse to the music. Knowing that the other instruments can also keep good time allows the bassist freedom. In certain sections of the music, most notably during an improvised solo, he or she can let the pulse become a secondary concern. Pianist Bill Evans is one of the most famous figures in jazz. A great solo artist and leader in his own right, he is also well-known for playing all the tracks but one on the classic Miles Davis album *Kind of Blue*. In the early 1960s, Evans put together a trio with bassist Scott LaFaro and drummer Paul Motian. This group became one of the most famous and innovative trios in the history of jazz. Although they played traditional jazz standards, they performed them with a previously unheard level of collective improvisation and collaboration. LaFaro, who tragically lived only to age 25, shunned the traditional role of the bassist. Instead of clearly delineating the harmony and time, he continuously played fragments of melody or counter-melody, effectively soloing continuously, as did the other members of the group. This feat was possible only because LaFaro had complete trust in the other trio members to fulfill their respective roles. Listen to any of the trio's four albums—*Portrait in Jazz*,

Explorations, Sunday at the Village Vanguard, and *Waltz for Debby*—and you will be in for a real treat.

By acting with complete openness and transparency, jazz musicians speed up the process of establishing trust.

Covey points out (S.M. Covey, 2006) that one way to build trust quickly is to have transparency. By acting with complete openness and transparency, jazz musicians speed up the process of establishing trust. They do this by clearly communicating their intents and actions. Trust and respect can be built only with genuine, uncompromised communication. In small-group jazz settings, it is hard to do anything else, given all communications occur in real time and within the proximity of the ensemble. In business teams, where communications may be delayed and relayed via telephone and e-mail, facts can be distorted, mistakes can be covered up, weak contributors can be overlooked, and poor results can be conveniently ignored. Large, distributed teams are most in need of quality communications. People are less likely to trust someone if they don't know who he or she is or if they have no idea of how that person is contributing to the team's efforts. They are also less likely to trust the team's collective abilities if they don't know how the team is doing.

Acknowledging Efforts and Results

Spreading the word about the efforts and results of individuals helps to build trust and respect for those people. Similarly, communicating the progress of the team can help build trust and respect for the team. We live in an era when speed and timeliness are paramount and organizations are subjected to constantly changing conditions. Organizations need to develop practices that help teams rapidly establish trust and respect just as jazz musicians do.

In Rational Team Concert, IBM built an engine to automatically collect metrics for a wide range of activities. These metrics provide the data sources for real-time reports, dashboards, and alerts that enable each member of a software development team to estimate, measure, and compare efforts and results for individuals and for the team. Statistics such as bugs reported and fixed and build health are readily accessible. This capability is simply an automated form of teamwide communication that demonstrates efforts and results. It gives a team or a project's stakeholders an accurate real-time picture of how individuals are contributing and how they and the team are faring relative to goals or objectives. When things are not going well, the feedback can help people get back on track. When things are going well, the positive results can encourage, inspire, build confidence, and generate trust and respect for individuals and the team. Because the metrics are collected in real time, they are always available and always up-to-date, and each interested party can customize the exact queries and presentation.

Every team and project can benefit from collecting similar metrics and providing people with the means to access them as they see fit. Of course, metrics are only numbers. They alone may not be sufficient to provide people with the feedback they need to build trust and respect. This is why it's useful to have both quantitative measurements and personal messages. It's particularly important that communications be genuine. Companywide broadcasts acclaiming the work of teams and key individuals are all too often ignored and given the immediate "send to trash" treatment because employees don't trust the sources or feel inundated with what they consider superficial communiqués.

Most people know when they aren't getting straight talk, and deceitful or filtered communication can only lead to a loss of trust and respect. Covey lists "Talk straight" as the first of 13 behaviors to help build trust in relationships (S.M. Covey, 2006). As an example, he cites the letter that Warren Buffett writes each year for Berkshire Hathaway's annual report. In these letters, Buffett highlights the year's successes and failures with a direct matter-of-factness. In reference to his actions in 2008, he wrote (Buffett, 2008, 5):

> *During 2008 I did some dumb things in investments. I made at least one major mistake of commission and several lesser ones that also hurt. I will tell you more about these later. Furthermore, I made some errors of omission, sucking my thumb when new facts came in that should have caused me to re-examine my thinking and promptly take action.*

He took great care to admit sole responsibility for these mistakes (Buffett, 2008, 16):

> *I told you in an earlier part of this report that last year I made a major mistake of commission (and maybe more; this one sticks out). Without urging from Charlie or anyone else, I bought a large amount of Cono-coPhillips stock when oil and gas prices were near their peak. I in no way anticipated the dramatic fall in energy prices that occurred in the last half of the year. I still believe the odds are good that oil sells*

far higher in the future than the current $40–$50 price. But so far I have been dead wrong. Even if prices should rise, moreover, the terrible timing of my purchase has cost Berkshire several billion dollars.

I made some other already-recognizable errors as well. They were smaller, but unfortunately not that small. During 2008, I spent $244 million for shares of two Irish banks that appeared cheap to me. At yearend we wrote these holdings down to market: $27 million, for an 89% loss. Since then, the two stocks have declined even further. The tennis crowd would call my mistakes "unforced errors."

In contrast, the management letters in most other annual reports attempt to make the company look as good as possible. They rarely list the mistakes of management and usually put some kind of spin on any problems they cannot avoid mentioning. Buffett has become as famous for his straight talk as he has for his financial success. His unvarnished truths have made him a trusted source for financial investors. Each year, thousands of such investors make the pilgrimage to Omaha, Nebraska, for Berkshire Hathaway's annual shareholder meeting, which has come to be known as "Woodstock for Capitalists." In 2008, the meeting drew 31,000 people for a weekend in which the highlight was a six-hour question-and-answer session with the man himself. Clearly, many people trust Buffett's advice.

When Trust and Respect Are Lost

It can take time to establish trust and respect. Yet they can be lost in a flash, and restoring them can be difficult. When looking for ways to regain trust and respect, we can look to the principles of the Jazz Process for inspiration. I don't mean to suggest that this book will provide the answers to all such situations, but it's not hard to find examples where a lack of attention to these principles has caused people to lose faith.

For instance, consider the principle of "Act transparently." During the time I have been writing this book, most of the world has been dealing with an economic crisis. The Group of Twenty Finance Ministers and Central Bank Governors, more commonly known as the G-20, called the crisis "the greatest challenge to the world economy in modern times" and recognized the need to "restore confidence" and "rebuild trust" (G-20, 2009). Many reasons have been given for the root cause of the global financial meltdown, but one that is increasingly repeated is the lack of transparency that has allowed poor management, corporate excess, political corruption, and fraud to remain hidden from consumers and investors. When it comes to criminal activity related to the crisis, we know of those whose dishonest actions were discovered, but what about those who managed to get away with their crimes? A nationwide U.S. poll conducted in October 2008 found that 81.7 percent of Americans felt that political corruption played a major role in the financial crisis (Judicial Watch, 2008). Kroll, a leading risk consultancy company, has identified a multitude of "frauds which contributed to today's financial crisis" (Slavek and Donato, 2009). In February 2009, the United States Federal Bureau of Investigation announced, "The FBI has more than 530 open corporate fraud investigations, including 38 corporate fraud and financial institution matters directly related to the current financial crisis" (Pistole, 2009).

Transparency International, a nongovernmental organization dedicated to fighting corruption, claimed that the "financial crisis [is] a betrayal of public trust" and called on leaders of the G-20 to "ensure that transparency, integrity and public accountability become the foundation of the vital reforms needed to rebuild the world's financial system" (Transparency International, 2008). The Global Reporting Initiative (GRI) produces a widely adopted standard for consistent reporting of economic, environmental, and social performance by organizations, including businesses and public agencies. In March 2009, the board of the GRI issued The Amsterdam Declaration on Transparency and Reporting, concluding, "The root causes of the current economic crisis would have been moderated by a global transparency and accountability system" (Board of Directors of the Global Reporting Initiative, 2009). The Task Force on Financial Integrity and Economic Development, a consortium of government and nongovernmental organizations focused on achieving greater transparency in the global financial system, claimed that the "heart of the current worldwide economic crisis is a lack of transparency in the global financial system" (Task Force on Financial Integrity and Economic Development, 2009).

People lose trust and respect for others for a variety of reasons. Table 4.1 considers some of these and how they map to principles of the Jazz Process.

Table 4.1 Using Jazz Process Principles to Prevent or Restore Loss of Trust or Respect

Reason for Loss of Trust or Respect	Preventative or Restorative Measure
Failures or poor performance due to excessive bureaucracy	Use just enough rules
Lack of faith in people's abilities	Employ top talent
Lack of teamwork or excessive egos	Put the team first
Lack of enthusiasm, motivation, or follow-through	Commit with passion
Sense of being ignored or failing to respond	Listen for change
Lack of initiative	Lead on demand
Suspicions of poor management, fraud, or corruption	Act transparently
Conflicting efforts	Make contributions count
Poor efficiency, waste	Reduce friction
Inability to deliver on time or lack of communication	Maintain momentum
Constant breakdowns, defects, errors, low productivity	Stay healthy
Lack of innovation or creativity	Exchange ideas
Lack of excitement or inability to compete	Take measured risks

In addition to the failed application of these and other best principles, specific mistakes or oversights may lead to a loss of trust or respect. To avoid such a loss or to restore trust and respect, you must always accept accountability for any mistakes and make it a priority to correct them wherever possible. Failing to do so may allow the mistake to snowball into an even bigger problem. Recovering may involve taking active steps to correct the mistake, or you may have to continue on without correction, but with candid recognition that the mistake was made. Occasionally, situations will arise in which mistakes are unavoidable. At such times, it is important to clearly communicate the circumstances to all parties to avoid a loss of trust and respect. I discuss this further in Chapter 9, "Make Contributions Count."

The worst kind of mistake is one that goes completely unnoticed because the person who made it has no clue he or she did something wrong.

Accepting responsibility for a problem is not simply a matter of issuing an apology. You must acknowledge your understanding of the problem and your role in it. The worst kind of mistake is one that goes completely unnoticed because the person who made it has no clue he or she did something wrong. Not surprisingly, a logical conclusion is that the person will likely make the mistake again in the future. This is even more of a problem if someone ignores a mistake by pretending it never happened. Ignorance is excusable, at least the first time, whereas deceit only leads to a further loss of trust and respect.

Recapitulation

- Trust and respect can engender loyalty, motivation, satisfaction, and honesty. They are binding agents that keep a team together and help it maintain strong and healthy relationships even in the face of change and adversity.

- The presence of trust affects the speed and cost of operations. When trust is present in activities in which time must remain fixed, things move faster, and costs are lower. In real-time activities, trust helps people perform with confidence, enabling them to take creative risks that help create unique performances.

- Jazz musicians establish trust rapidly by showing basic respect, accepting that each person has something to contribute and respecting each contribution.

- One way to build trust quickly is to have transparency. Jazz musicians speed up the process of establishing trust by communicating their intents and actions openly, clearly, and in a timely manner.

- Spreading the word about the efforts and results of individuals helps build trust and respect for those people. Similarly, communicating the progress of the team can help build trust and respect for the team.

- To avoid a loss of trust and respect or to restore trust and respect, always accept accountability for any mistakes and make it a priority to correct them wherever possible.

CHAPTER 5

Commit with Passion

*"Wheresoever you go,
go with all your heart."*
—Confucius

Commitment

Rules provide the framework for talented people to work collectively in a team. Trust and respect bind the team together and keep it in good health. Commitment contributes to the stability of the team and helps its members execute even when they must overcome challenges.

When people commit themselves to a team, they pledge their time, attention, and energy to help the team achieve its goals. That pledge must include a statement of priority and importance if the commitment is to have any real meaning. Agreeing to help, but then bailing out or delivering late when other things get in the way, is nothing less than a complete letdown for a team.

Ideally, teams would have their members pledge total commitment. However, gaining such a level of commitment may not always be realistic. Companies all too often wonder why their employees are not more committed to their work, when, in fact, they should be asking themselves what they can do to achieve a higher level of commitment from their employees. To paraphrase John F. Kennedy's famous inauguration speech, "Ask not what your team can do for you; ask what you can do for your team." Often the organization, not the individuals, must make the extra effort. For example, if a team is saddled with unrealistic goals that members believe are impossible to meet, their commitment likely will be equally unrealistic or superficial. If a team has set extremely demanding, albeit attainable, goals, its members may be willing to commit to them, provided that they are sufficiently motivated.

Many things can motivate a person to make a substantial commitment to a team, and what motivates one person may not motivate another. Money can be an effective motivator. Organizations that pay their employees, especially those that pay generously, can and should expect a basic level of commitment in return. However, not all organizations are equipped to offer financial motivation. For example, some organizations operate with limited budgets or as not-for-profit or charitable organizations; they rely primarily on the efforts of volunteers to achieve their goals.

Companies all too often wonder why their employees are not more committed to their work, when, in fact, they should be asking themselves what they can do to achieve a higher level of commitment from their employees.

All too often, companies resort to superficial means to motivate employees. "Rah-rah" or "pep up the troops" activities such as lavish corporate gatherings, team-building exercises, or inspirational speeches from senior management may temporarily increase morale or inject energy into a stagnant work environment. But if a team has underlying problems, such activities may only frustrate people. These efforts may have an uplifting effect on low-performing individuals and teams. However, self-motivated high performers, who always give 110 percent to anything they do, often regard them as a waste of their time. If you follow the "Employ top talent" principle, you will find that high-level performers have a strong sense of pride in their work. They routinely go the extra mile simply for their own personal satisfaction. They often relish a challenge, and when one is presented, they rise to the occasion. If they are team players who believe in the principle "Put the team first," they already have the willingness to go to the ends of the Earth for the benefit of a team.

When you're dealing with top talent, the question is not one of how to motivate people, but of how to avoid undermining their motivation. One needs only look at the Jazz Process for clues. For example, let's go back to "Use just enough rules." If there's one way to kill people's motivation, it's to burden them with bureaucracy. Instituting too many rules or strict rules that don't make sense can lead to frustration and wasted time and effort. If people feel that the team does not "Employ top talent," especially if they consider themselves to be top talent, they may think that either the team is not up to the tasks at hand or that the weight of the team's efforts unfairly rests on the shoulders of a few capable hard workers. If employees believe that others are not likely to "Put the team first," they will question why they should do so. If they feel that the team does not "Build trust and respect," not only will they be prone to put forth little effort, but they may well depart the team in the near future. Nobody likes to work for an underperforming team. People will quickly lose motivation if they have to work on a failing project. The importance of the principles "Stay healthy," "Maintain momentum," and "Reduce friction" will become apparent later. For now, it's enough to recognize that it's not just the team that people expect to function well; it's also the specific project to which they are assigned. This is particularly true for teams that don't have a track record of successful operation.

When you're dealing with top talent, the question is not one of how to motivate people, but of how to avoid undermining their motivation.

A weak commitment to a team or the team's work may result in a weak delivery. Although this can detract from a performance and potentially disappoint audiences, the greatest danger is that it may introduce instability into a production. This maxim may seem obvious in the context of an artistic performance, but it holds true in other situations as well. As a fan of *Star Trek*, I often like to paraphrase lines from its fictional universe—my favorite is, "We're losing structural integrity." I'll even say this if I'm eating a burger or a sandwich and the thing starts to fall apart on me. It also often comes to mind when I hear ensembles in which the musicians seem unable to deliver their contributions with total commitment. Especially in the world of jazz, which is full of unknowns and constant change, a failure to commit may result in a loss of structural integrity—and, in the worst case, it can lead to the loss of one's "ship."

Less Work Requires More Commitment

Even if you're not intimately familiar with the work of William Shakespeare, you can imagine the first meeting of the two star-crossed lovers from the Bard's famous romance *Romeo and Juliet*. Shakespeare crafted their conversation into a beautiful 14-line sonnet in Act One, Scene V. It begins with Romeo taking the initiative. He employs all his skill to convince Juliet to let him kiss her. Young and innocent, she does as Romeo asks, not even moving when he asks her, "Then move not while my prayer's effect I take." After a first kiss, Juliet gains confidence and becomes almost playful. She entices Romeo with "Then have my lips the sin that they have took" so that he might kiss her again to take back the "sin" he placed upon her lips with the first kiss. When he does just that, she follows up with the arguably cheeky comment, "You kiss by th' book."

Even if you don't know the music by name, you would probably recognize Edvard Grieg's famous orchestral piece "In the Hall of the Mountain King." Grieg composed the music in 1876 as part of his *Peer Gynt* suite at the request of Norwegian dramatist Henrik Ibsen, who needed incidental music for his play, *Peer Gynt*. The famous music begins with a light-footed theme that is played slowly and quietly to illustrate the scene in which Peer Gynt sneaks into the Mountain King's castle. The original music or the themes have been used countless times in films, television, and video games, usually to portray an impending ominous event.

In both of these scenes, one theatrical and the other musical, the respective characters, Juliet and Peer Gynt, must appear to be hesitant or tentative. The delivery must be delicately handled. This is especially important because of what follows. Within minutes, "In the Hall of the Mountain King" develops into a vigorous chase scene in which Peer must escape from the King and his trolls after having insulted the King's daughter. In *Romeo and Juliet,* Juliet's state of mind changes within the microcosm of the sonnet. Shakespeare uses the sonnet to foretell the transformation Juliet will undergo in the play. She begins as a young and innocent girl but develops such great passion for Romeo that, in the play's final scene, she ends her life rather than live without him. In both Shakespeare's play and Grieg's music, these respective stories and characters begin in a cautious state and then evolve into a more dramatic one. It's natural that artists will want to convey these stories in their performances. The simple way to do that is to demonstrate the contrast between the two states.

Even when delicacy and sensitivity are called for, artists must deliver their performances with unfailing conviction so that the scene and the story are clearly conveyed to every member of the audience. When such precision is required, performing with conviction is all the more important and requires great skill if one is to avoid a weak delivery. Performing with conviction is actually much easier when the script calls for obvious gusto. Think about the dramatic fight scene in Act Three, Scene I of *Romeo and Juliet,* or the vigorous "Trepak" (Russian Dance) from Tchaikovky's *Nutcracker* ballet music that calls upon the full force of the orchestra.

Imagine that you're at a sports game and all around you people are shouting out the name of their team, jeering at the players on the opposing side, yelling encouragement when their team is about to score, and hurling epithets at the officials when a decision favors the opposition. It's easy to get caught up in these festivities, and before long, you find yourself joining in. You then notice someone moving through the crowd toward you. He has a microphone in his hand, and he's being followed by another person toting a broadcast camera on his shoulder. A hush falls over the crowd as they notice your image up on the big screen. Just as you're thinking that the image is probably also being broadcast to millions of homes across the country, the person with the microphone shoves it in front of your face and asks if he can conduct a short interview with you to get your thoughts on the game and your team. Is it easier to partake in the interview, or is it easier to cheer along with the rest of the crowd? What happens if you agree to the interview but you're speechless or can only manage to blurt out incoherent and uninspired responses?

It's not so difficult to join in and contribute when there is a high level of activity among the members of a team. If you happen to make a mistake, it may well be absorbed by the team. However, when most activity has ceased and everything hinges on the success of a single, critical task, contributing becomes more difficult, and mistakes can be a lot more costly. Think about a software release in which a critical bug is discovered in the last couple days before the software is due to ship. The bug must be fixed in such a way that no new bugs are introduced and no previous bug fixes are undone. As we discover later, it is critical that we always "Make contributions count." Regardless of the circumstances, you must perform with as much confidence and conviction as possible.

Regardless of the circumstances, you must perform with as much confidence and conviction as possible.

If I'm working with musicians on a difficult or unusual section of music, I often find myself remarking to the group, "It sounds like we are unsure," and the cause is often exactly that: The musicians are in doubt. They play tentatively, and it comes through in the performance. A couple years ago, I was fortunate enough to lead the Impressions in Jazz Orchestra in a 50th anniversary performance of Duke Ellington and Billy Strayhorn's marvelous Shakespearean suite, also known as *Such Sweet Thunder.* Composed in 1957, this work is a brilliant example of jazz orchestra composition in which Ellington and his musical partner composed 12 musical vignettes depicting characters, scenes, and events from Shakespeare's plays. One of the stand-outs in the suite is an unusual little masterpiece entitled "Up and Down, Up and Down (I Will Lead Them Up and Down)," reflecting the comedic chaos of *A Midsummer Night's Dream.* In a seven-voice fugue,[1] Puck, represented by the solo trumpet, gets into mischief, causing great confusion among the lovers Demetrius and Helena, Lysander and Hermia, and Oberon and Titania, who are depicted by the clarinets, alto and tenor saxophones, violin, and valve trombone. From the very beginning, the dissonant contrapuntal chaos tells the story of the romantic mix-ups. It's a difficult and unusual piece that features both frequent dissonance and off-beats[2] in the bass part. We had rehearsed the piece only once or twice before the performance, and never with all seven of the lead voices present. Shortly before the performance, I gathered all the essential people together for a run-through. The initial attempts were less than stellar. The musicians were hesitant because it didn't feel right and sounded odd. In fact, it's supposed to sound odd, and once I explained that and encouraged the musicians to just set aside their concerns and play their parts with conviction, it all came together. Once we had played it with a good measure of confidence, it inspired us to try again. We did so with even more confidence, resulting in an amazing performance.

Be Willing to Make Mistakes

Jazz musicians often take risks when they are improvising a solo. Occasionally, something doesn't come off exactly the way they intended. Perhaps a note was slightly out of tune or a sequence of notes didn't speak clearly, or

---

1 A fugue is a type of contrapuntal composition that developed during the seventeenth and eighteenth centuries and reached maturity in the works of Johann Sebastian Bach. Perhaps the most popularized example is Bach's "Toccata and Fugue in D Minor." As with any piece built on counterpoint, a fugue features multiple voices that appear to perform independently while they also interact. The overall effect of combining the voices is harmonious. One voice may state a theme that another voice then imitates and develops, and so forth.

2 When we discussed our first rule, "Use just enough rules," I explained how bassists often switch between playing in two, with the notes falling on the first and third beats ("ONE ___ THREE ___"), and playing in four, with the notes occurring on every beat ("ONE TWO THREE FOUR"). Throughout much of "Up and Down, Up and Down," the bass plays only on every even or off-beat ("___ TWO ___ FOUR"), and the resulting effect can be very disconcerting to the rest of the ensemble. These off-beats are usually the weakest beats, and emphasizing them inverts the basic rhythmic pulse of the music. Ellington likely used the device to illustrate the oddity of what was happening in the play. The other instrumentalists have to concentrate intently to avoid getting thrown off by the bass part.

perhaps they lost their place in the musical form after attempting something that was rhythmically complex. Some people may say that such events are mistakes because they're not what the musician intended. Miles Davis is supposed to have said, "There are no mistakes in jazz—only opportunities." The idea is that, in jazz, something is a mistake only if you make it sound like a mistake. If you make it sound like you intended it, it's just part of the solo. Not *what* you play, but how you play makes the difference. If you play every note with confidence and conviction, any mistakes you make don't seem so significant. Of course, that's only a perception; the actual magnitude of any mistake is not actually reduced. However, that clarification highlights the key point: In a live performance, what's done is done, and there's little point in focusing on mistakes until the performance is over. Furthermore, if you play tentatively, you are much more likely to stop or lose your place when you make a mistake, causing you to fail to "Maintain momentum."

"There are no mistakes in jazz—only opportunities."
—Miles Davis

The idea that you can just ignore mistakes doesn't necessarily hold true in all situations. It depends on the exact nature of what you are producing and on the mistake itself. If you're working on a software release and discover a bug, the severity of the problem may be low enough that you can ignore it and fix it in the next release. On the other hand, it may be so critical that it must be fixed immediately, even if the entire schedule is delayed as a result. It's interesting to note that when jazz musicians are in a recording studio where they have the luxury of recording another take when a mistake is made, they often pass on the opportunity. In jazz, creativity and self-expression are core components of the product. Often the "mistakes" lead to some of the most interesting moments. As drummer Ralph Peterson said to Ingrid Monson (Monson, 1996, 176):

> It's not what you play when you're playing, but what you play after you f**k up that really counts, you know. It's not that you f**k up, but how you clean it up that matters, because a lot of times those are the most musical moments, because the desire to compensate for the ... mistake ... often leads to a special moment in music where everybody begins to come to the support.

Miles Davis's *Kind of Blue*, recorded by his sextet in 1959, is one of the most famous jazz recordings and a seminal masterpiece in jazz history. For many people, it served as an introduction and, in some cases, even a conversion to jazz. For many years, it was the best-selling jazz album of all time, and some would argue that it still rightly holds the title. Ever since its release, *Kind of Blue* has been studied, imitated, and seen as inspiration for generations of musicians. What most people don't realize is the degree to which spontaneity played a role in the creation of *Kind of Blue* and the number of "mistakes" present in the recording. In the album's liner notes, pianist Bill Evans wrote:

> *Miles conceived these settings only hours before the recording dates and arrived with sketches which indicated to the group what was to be played. Therefore, you will hear something close to pure spontaneity in these performances. The group had never played these pieces prior to the recordings, and I think without exception the first complete performance of each was a "take."*[3]

One of the most incredible pieces on this album is "Flamenco Sketches," a hauntingly beautiful piece with interesting musical properties. Musician Bill Kirchner fittingly wrote (Kirchner 2001, 15): "That 'Flamenco Sketches' was used to conclude the album seems inevitable; nothing could follow its brooding ending." In an interview described by both Kahn (A. Kahn 2000, 134) and Kirchner (Kirchner 2001, 12), Evans stated that he and Davis had written the piece in Davis's apartment on the morning of March 2, 1959, just hours before the first recording session. A wonderful photograph in Kahn's book (A. Kahn 2000, 132), taken during the second recording session on April 22, 1959, shows a scrap of music manuscript paper on the music stand of alto saxophonist Julian "Cannonball" Adderley. The five scales accompanied by the words "Play the sound of these scales" was all the musicians received,[4] along with the clarification by Davis and/or Evans that they could

---

3 There is actually some disagreement about this. In writing about the recording sessions, Ashley Kahn (A. Kahn 2000, 96) points out some of the issues, including the fact that Evans had not played regularly with Davis's group for more than three months, that drummer Jimmy Cobb claimed they had played one of the tunes ("So What") once or twice on gigs, and that even Davis himself admitted that another number ("All Blues") had started out as a live tune and then evolved over six months. Despite this, there is no doubt that the recording represents a high degree of spontaneity. This is evidenced by the comments from the musicians on the studio tapes (A. Kahn 2000), some of the obvious mistakes in the playing, and the undisputed background of the other pieces on the album.

4 It's especially notable that the "Spanish" sound, and hence the basis for the title of the piece, comes from the use of the fourth mode in the tune. Known to some musicians as "Spanish Phrygian" or the "Flamenco Scale," it is referred to as the "Hijaz" in Middle Eastern music and was brought to Spain by the Moors. At the recording session, producer Irving Townsend wrote "Spanish" as the tune's temporary title.

play each scale for as long as they wished, as long as they played them in sequence. Since the rest of the band would not know exactly when to follow the soloist to the next scale, the coordination would have to be done on the fly. Besides having no specific form for the piece, it had no supplied melody. Most pieces have a melody stated at the beginning and the end of the piece with solos in the middle, yet every note of "Flamenco Sketches" was improvised, from beginning to end.

Evans's statement about the number of takes was true for every piece except "Flamenco Sketches." The band gave it two complete takes. Fortunately, the first take has been made available on the CD reissue of the album, where it is usually labeled as "alternate take." One of the most wonderful parts of "Flamenco Sketches" is that the spontaneity and lack of specific form provide an opportunity to hear how the musicians had to respond to one another, to ensure that they maintained the structural integrity of the performance. Listen especially to Paul Chambers on bass and Evans on piano, following—or, in some cases, guiding—the soloists. The first take is at a slower tempo. You can sense the hesitation. The second take is both faster and more confident. Any "mistakes" are simply incorporated into the performance. The musicians use the unexpected as jumping-off points to further evolve the music. This kind of collective, spontaneous, creative development is possible only with total commitment throughout the ensemble. All the players are dedicated to moving forward and maintaining momentum, while always maintaining structural integrity.

Those Who Support the Team

In jazz, bassists have a special role to play in this respect. Because they are playing the roots of the harmony and maintaining a constant groove, such as a walking bass line, they have the potential to make strong harmonic and temporal statements. Consequently, they are relied upon to help keep things together in more ways than one. When Larry Blumenfeld asked Kareem Abdul-Jabbar who he would be in a jazz-playing basketball team, he replied (Blumenfeld 2008): "I'd be the bassist who soloed a lot." If scoring points is akin to soloing, then Abdul-Jabbar soloed more than anyone else in the history of basketball. At 38,387 points, he remains the top NBA scorer of all time, and with a lead of almost 7,000 points over second-place Wilt Chamberlain, it's a record that may never be broken. Yet Abdul-Jabbar was more than just a high scorer. When he left the game of basketball in 1989 at the age of 42, he held the records not just for scoring, but for blocking more shots and winning more Most Valuable Player awards than anyone else. In his first season with the Milwaukee Bucks, he led the team to a 28-game turnaround. In his first season with the Los Angeles Lakers, he led them to a 10-game turnaround. Abdul-Jabbar's greatest asset to a team was not simply his ability to score, but his ability to help make a failing team successful.

Milt Hinton, one of the world's greatest bassists, once described the bass by saying, "Bass is the base—the bottom—the support. We hold the thing up—like Atlas of the music world." (Levin 2000, 139). Bassist and guitarist Jerome Harris said, "Everyone in the band is affected if the bass player isn't on the case" (Monson 1996, 50–51). Many people, especially those who are not familiar with jazz, don't really think much about the role of the bass. Not surprisingly, they tend to focus on the lead instruments. This is understandable because that's where a lot of the exciting things are happening. The minute the bass stops playing, however, they instantly realize that something is wrong. In many teams, some people help keep things together in a similar way. They may not be the leaders of the group or the most noticeable contributors, but they understand the importance of maintaining stability, and their understanding and their actions are absolutely vital to the team's success.

Performing with Passion

In jazz or any artistic performance, the artists and audiences expect more than strong commitment. They expect the performers to have passion for what they are doing. People can see, feel, and hear the passion of a performer, and when passion is lacking, it is obvious. Passion is the enthusiasm that drives us to do something even when obstacles must be overcome. When people are passionate about something, they believe in what they are doing and feel compelled to do it well. Passion isn't something you can easily fake. It is generated by a sense of authenticity and a belief that something is worth doing. If you don't believe in what you are doing, it's pretty hard to be even mildly passionate about it.

Passion is infectious.

The world is full of people who are passionate about things they do, whether it's performing jazz, developing software, selling products, teaching children, designing floral arrangements, or something else. Many people may not exhibit obvious passion most of the time, and it's a mistake to discount such people for an apparent lack of enthusiasm. When he wasn't playing jazz, John Coltrane exhibited a soft-spoken and humble demeanor. In his book *John Coltrane: His Life and Music,* Lewis Porter wrote about Coltrane's personality in a chapter entitled "The Man: 'A Quiet, Shy Guy.'" He quoted people who knew Coltrane (Porter 2000, 250–251):

> *"He was very quiet, very humble." (Ira Gitler)*
>
> *"John was a quiet, shy guy ..." (David Young)*
>
> *"He never talked a whole lot unless you engaged him in conversation ..." (James Forman)*
>
> *"I found him very quiet ..." (Kitty Grime)*

Playing jazz ignited a passion in Coltrane that would bring out a completely different side of his personality. In his autobiography penned with Quincy Troupe, Miles Davis wrote about Coltrane (Davis and Troupe 1990, 223):

> *It was like he was possessed when he put that horn in his mouth. He was so passionate—fierce—and yet so quiet and gentle when he wasn't playing. A sweet guy.*

Not everyone's passion is their work, and a great many people have absolutely no passion for the job that helps them put food on their tables. Martin Luther King, Jr., the Baptist minister, American civil rights leader, and Nobel Peace Prize winner, was a truly passionate man if there ever was one. He spent a great deal of his life inspiring people to take pride in themselves and their work and to always give their utmost. On a number of occasions in the years before he was assassinated, he gave speeches in which he used what I call the "street-sweeper" words. The exact words varied on occasion. I'll quote the ones he used when he spoke to a group of students at Barratt Junior High School in Philadelphia on October 26, 1967. The speech is often referred to as the "What Is Your Life's Blueprint?" speech because he began by saying, "I want to ask you a question, and that is: 'What is your life's blueprint?'" Moments later, he said these words:

> *And when you discover what you will be in your life, set out to do it as if God Almighty called you at this particular moment in history to do it. Don't just set out to do a good job. Set out to do such a good job that the living, the dead, or the unborn couldn't do it any better.*

If it falls your lot to be a street sweeper, sweep streets like Michelangelo painted pictures, sweep streets like Beethoven composed music, sweep streets like Leontyne Price sings before the Metropolitan Opera. Sweep streets like Shakespeare wrote poetry. Sweep streets so well that all the hosts of heaven and earth will have to pause and say: "Here lived a great street sweeper who swept his job well."

The most wonderful thing about passion, besides the fact that it drives people to do their best work, is that passion is infectious. When audiences see jazz musicians enjoying themselves, they, in turn, enjoy the performance more. Similarly, musicians are spurred on by the passion of their fellow performers. We are all performers in some way. Of course, we're always performing within our teams; it's typically how our contributions and efforts are valued and how we are rewarded in return. However, the performing I'm referring to is the contact we have with people outside our teams and organizations. A team must perform each time it delivers its product or service or engages with customers or stakeholders.

Performing in Social Media

Over the last couple decades, people, teams, and organizations have found themselves performing with great frequency and in ways they've never previously imagined. The introduction of social media and social networking, powered by the Internet, has us engaging with interested parties and revealing more about ourselves and our work progress and plans than ever before. For many organizations, blogging is now a routine activity. Junior employees and executives alike are bypassing the active filters of marketing and legal departments and are regularly writing in their own words within the framework of loose corporate blogging guidelines. In doing so, they give their customers—and, unfortunately, their competitors—insight into their thoughts, opinions, plans, and progress. Much danger accompanies this. People may accidentally leak confidential information, disparage a competitor's product, or state opinions that are not representative of their companies. The upside is that people's passion for their work and their companies' offerings can come through in their statements. Because those statements are personal and not formulated, people may be more likely to believe they are genuine. Demonstrating your passion can inspire others, including your customers and partners.

Demonstrating your passion can inspire others.

People "perform" daily on social networking websites such as Facebook and MySpace. They take great pride in telling their friends and family what they are doing at all hours of the day. They communicate their passion for their jobs and their favorite hobbies, bands, movies, books, and just about anything that excites them. These Internet-enabled media are not simply unidirectional. Consumers are no longer satisfied with the passive consumption of information in the traditional forms of radio, TV, print, or even simple web pages. They now demand the ability to respond, question, contribute, and share in kind. In some cases, they may respond negatively and even induce "flame wars" that can quickly become an Internet sensation. However, on the positive side, they have the opportunity to share in the passion of "performers" and, in doing so, become engaged in what those performers have to offer. In some situations that can lead to intentional or unplanned *viral marketing,* which is when awareness of a product or service increases through the use of self-replicating viral processes not unlike biological and computer viruses. Powered by the Internet, such awareness can spread very rapidly.

Teams don't necessarily need to worry about getting people to be passionate. If you "Employ top talent," those people are already passionate about what they do. This is likely the reason they are so good at it in the first place. The most important point is not to kill people's passion by failing them. One sure way to do that is to ignore best principles such as "Use just enough rules," burdening people with so much bureaucracy that they spend all their time on everything but the one thing they are passionate about. Passion is extremely powerful, and many people will stick with something they are passionate about even when problems frustrate them. There are limits, however. It makes much more sense to let people direct the full energy of their passion into helping their teams achieve their goals.

Recapitulation

- Commitment helps a team maintain stability even when it must overcome challenges.

- Any commitment to a team by its members must include a statement of priority and importance if the commitment is to have any real meaning.

- When you're dealing with top talent, the question is not how to motivate them, but how to avoid undermining their motivation.

- When the level of general activity within a team is low, contributions become more important, and mistakes become more costly.

- Jazz musicians know that not *what* you play, but *how* you play it makes the difference. If you play every note with confidence and conviction, any mistakes you make don't seem so significant.

- In a live performance or any real-time activity, what's done is done; there's little point in focusing on mistakes until the performance is over.

- Passion isn't something you can easily fake. It is generated by a sense of authenticity and a belief that something is worth doing.

- Passion is infectious. Demonstrating your passion can inspire others, including your customers and partners.

Collaborating

In this section, we begin by establishing a framework for effective, continuous execution. In that context, we discuss four principles that can help teams collaborate effectively within their teams and with consumers, customers, partners, and suppliers.

Essentials of Execution
6. Listen for change
7. Lead on demand
8. Act transparently
9. Make contributions count

Essentials of Execution

Figure 1 illustrates how the principles of the Jazz Process form a continuum, moving from strategy to execution, to differentiation. In the first section of this book, we focused on five fundamental principles that set the strategy for success. In this section and the next, we deal with principles that specifically focus on execution. Before delving into those discussions, we must build the essential framework that will put each of these execution principles in context. It's a detour, but one that is filled with fascinating stories from history.

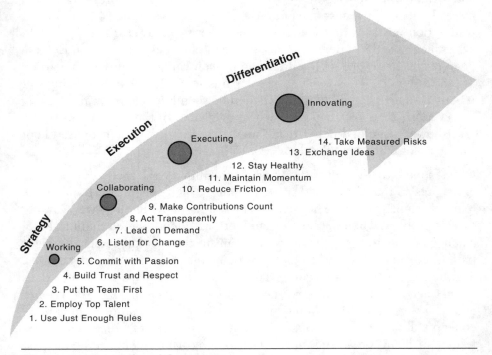

Figure 1 *Principles of the Jazz Process*

Feedback and the Birth of Cybernetics

Our detour begins in World War II, when two of the greatest threats faced by the Allies were the submarine U-boats of the German *Kriegsmarine,* hunting Allied vessels in the North Atlantic, and the bombers of the *Luftwaffe,* conducting intense bombing raids on Great Britain.

In response to the naval threat, the Allies sought to determine the locations and movements of the U-boats. This ultimately became a cryptographic problem because the Germans were coding their radio communications with mechanical encryption devices known as Enigma machines. Although the Germans thought the Enigma codes were unbreakable, cryptanalysts at Britain's Bletchley Park were able to decode various Enigma ciphers throughout the war. Their success may not have been possible without the work of the Polish *Bióro Szyfrów* (Cipher Bureau), which had made great advances toward breaking the Enigma codes with the aid of French-supplied intelligence (Wesolkowki 2001, 6). In 1939, the Poles supplied France and Britain with the results of their work. Britain's code-breaking efforts were also aided by access to captured Enigma hardware and codebooks, not to mention mistakes that German cipher clerks made (D. Kahn 1998, 69). The Allies gave the codename Ultra to the intelligence gained from Enigma decrypts because the fact that they had broken Enigma codes was regarded as "ultra-secret." They went to great pains to protect Ultra, sending out reconnaissance planes where they would be seen by the enemy and leaking false reports that spies had obtained intelligence. In the end, however, the Nazis' own misguided belief that Enigma could not be compromised kept the secret of Ultra safe (Ratcliff 2006, 158).

One response to the Luftwaffe threat was to improve the accuracy of antiaircraft guns so that they could track and target high-speed dive bombers. A team of scientists at the Massachusetts Institute of Technology was working on this problem when mathematician Norbert Wiener joined them in 1943. Their goal was to develop a servomechanism that could predict the flight path of a plane by taking into account elements of its previous trajectories. The behavior of such a servomechanism would mirror what a hunter does when tracking a moving quarry. In developing the servomechanism, Wiener and his assistant, electrical engineer Julian Bigelow, began to form general concepts about feedback, observing that both intelligent mechanical systems and living organisms make decisions by using feedback about past actions. The servomechanisms used the "experience" of past trajectories to make targeting decisions.

In their research, Wiener and Bigelow developed ideas about the health of systems. They noticed a strange problem in the servomechanisms in which certain conditions, such as lack of friction or excessive input, could allow a servomechanism to fall into a mode of potentially uncontrollable oscillatory "hunting." This led them to seek the help of Mexican neurobiologist Arturo Rosenblueth, from whom they learned of **purpose tremor**, an involuntary trembling or quivering that can be caused by pathological conditions such as Parkinson's disease.

In 1943, Wiener, Bigelow, and Rosenblueth published their seminal article "Behavior, Purpose, and Teleology," in which they compared servo devices with the behavior of living organisms. In 1948, Wiener published *Cybernetics,* a name he had coined from the Greek word *kubernts,* meaning "steersman" or "ship pilot." The book was subtitled *Or Control and Communication in the Animal and the Machine.* As the study of "control and communication" in both technological and biological systems, cybernetics is routinely referenced through common scientific metaphors. Cognitive scientists refer to the human mind as "software of the brain" (Block 1995), behavioral psychologists write about "reprogramming old habits," and molecular biologists talk about "coding" the DNA molecule (Rheingold 2000, 99). Cybernetics has become a broad field of study with principles that have been applied to a diverse array of problems, from the beginning of life to the end of the universe. Its principles are especially appropriate to the ways in which individuals, teams, and organizations work.

Feedback Loops

In cybernetics, a feedback loop is a process in which some proportion of the output signal of a system is fed or looped back to the input and is then used to control the dynamic behavior of the system. Two types of feedback loops exist: positive and negative. These terms refer not to the desirability of the outcome, but instead to the nature of the change in response to feedback.

A positive feedback loop is also known as a self-reinforcing or synergistic loop. It tends to accelerate a system away from equilibrium. An example is a crowd of spectators observing an unusual event such as the site of a traffic accident. When the crowd attracts people, it grows; in doing so, it attracts more attention, resulting in even faster growth. The reverse is also true and is still a positive feedback loop. As people begin to leave the crowd, it becomes less of an attraction and people leave faster. The case of the growing or shrinking crowd is known specifically as an **information cascade**, referring to the way people make decisions based on observing the actions of others. Growth or sudden decline in the stock market is also a positive feedback loop. As an asset increases in value, more people want it. The higher demand drives up the value. In a crash, when the value of an asset falls, more people offload it, which causes others to panic and sell, causing the price to fall even further. Systems with unchecked positive feedback loops may lead to catastrophic situations as they repeatedly amplify their output. A nuclear chain reaction or explosion is a perfect example. Emotions such as anger can also behave as positive feedback loops, escalating into violence and rage. On the other hand, many positive feedback loops have beneficial results. Henry Ford exploited **economies of scale** by parlaying his initial success in building one-off vehicles into mass production. More productive methods of manufacturing enabled Ford to produce cars that he could sell at lower cost, thus increasing sales and enabling Ford to spend more on research; that then fueled more innovation and even more productive methods of manufacturing.

One of the most important elements of the theory developed by Wiener, Bigelow, and Rosenblueth is negative feedback loops. In such cycles, when an action causes an effect, the response is to reduce or discontinue the action, to offset the effect. For this reason, such a loop is also known as a self-correcting, regulatory, or balancing loop. It tends to bring a system into equilibrium. A thermostat corrects rising heat by switching off the heat when it reaches a certain temperature. In the same way, people around a campfire stoke the fire when they get too cold. Cruise control corrects a car that is traveling too fast by reducing the throttle and possibly applying the brakes. In a quality control system, when an action results in a defect, the response is to change the action, to avoid further defects. Many political and social systems rely on negative feedback loops to ensure equilibrium. In international politics, a **balance of power** allows nations to keep each other in check so that no one nation can become so powerful that it can act solely according to its own interests. Similarly, in the United States Constitution, a **separation of powers** keeps the executive, legislative, and judicial branches of government distinct, to avoid abuses of power. Each branch has powers that it can use to check and balance the powers of the other two branches so that no one branch can wield all the governmental authority.

Hunting Cause 1: Trying Too Hard

One of the most fundamental skills for all musicians is to be able to sing or play their instruments in tune. This process, known as **intonation**, is especially crucial if the musician is playing in an ensemble where any tuning errors will be magnified in the presence of other voices or instruments. The method of determining the pitch varies with each instrument. On a piano, the pitch of each note is fixed. A note is sounded with the frequency predetermined by the tuning of the strings, and the pianist has no opportunity to easily alter that frequency. For wind and stringed instruments, pitch is semi-fixed. Wind instruments such as the saxophone and trumpet have keys or valves. Guitars have frets. These provide players with a way of quickly producing a note that is guaranteed to be more or less in tune, assuming that the fundamental tuning of the instrument has been set correctly. The fundamental tuning on wind instruments is altered by changing the length of an instrument's sounding pipe. This can be accomplished by pulling out or pushing in a tuning pipe or the mouthpiece on the neck of an instrument. On a guitar, the fundamental tuning is altered by changing the tension of the strings. Tension is decreased by unwinding the strings, and tension is increased by winding them tighter. Once this fundamental tuning is set and a specific note is determined through the use of specific combinations of keys, values, or frets, the note is still only somewhat in tune. For various reasons, often due to deficiencies in the basic design of an instrument, some notes may be less in tune than others For example, when you play a note that involves pressing down the third valve on a trumpet, the notes are usually sharp. The player must use a small third-valve slide to compensate. Other factors, such as temperature and humidity, can also affect an instrument's pitch. Intonation is most difficult on variable-pitch instruments such as double bass, violin, or trombone because there are no keys, frets, or other obvious mechanisms or points of reference for each note. The positions are there, but they must be approximated each time a note is played. Thus, the possibility for tuning error is greater.

Each time a note is played on an instrument where the pitch can be varied by even a small degree, the musician must correct the pitch within milliseconds of the initial sound so that the final result sounds in tune. If the note is too flat, the note must be sharpened; if the note is too sharp, it must be flattened. You can probably already tell that the process of intonation is a negative feedback loop. It is absolutely critical that the musician zero in on the correct pitch as quickly as possible. Ideally, this requires only a single adjustment, a movement of a finger or a tightening of the lips. If the musician overcorrects, the result could be ruinous. Hunting, in this case, would be heard as the pitch of the note meandering back and forth.

Now imagine that a software developer is tasked with fixing a bug. The bug manifests itself only intermittently, but when it does, it causes the program to crash spectacularly. The developer engineers what she believes is the right fix for the bug, but in doing so, she actually creates another, more serious bug. She then attempts to fix that bug but only creates another bug.

These are all examples of negative feedback loops that hunt for the right solution but never get there or have trouble getting there as a result of overcorrection. Just as positive feedback loops can sometimes get sick and degenerate into catastrophic situations, negative feedback loops can develop health issues. Wiener and Bigelow learned from Rosenblueth that purpose tremors could be caused by medical conditions, but they also found that such oscillatory hunting can develop for other reasons. When we are nervous or fearful or overconcentrate on a goal, it can cause us to fail. You are already familiar with this concept if you've ever had difficulty threading a needle or pouring liquid into a small-necked bottle. Your hands are steady, but they begin to shake just as you approach the target. Athletes may perform a move perfectly in practice but "choke" when faced with the same challenge at a critical moment in a game. These kinds of failures are caused by an overabundance of correction, or negative feedback. In many cases, this happens subconsciously. The solution is to back off, relax, and avoid trying too hard. We look at this again when we discuss the principle "Reduce friction."

Hunting Cause 2: Reacting Too Slowly

Hunting can also be caused by simply taking too long to react to feedback. By the time the system (or person) adjusts to the feedback with the next action, the correction is no longer sufficient or valid. Picture a car negotiating a curve. The driver is driving at the limit and enters the curve slightly and then proceeds to accelerate through the curve. Suddenly the car loses traction at the rear wheels. The car is now in a state of oversteer. This occurs when the rear wheels do not follow behind the front wheels, but instead slide out toward the outside of a curve, turning the car farther into the turn. If left unchecked, oversteer can develop into a spin. It can be corrected by applying opposite lock, which involves steering in the opposite direction. If the car is turning toward the left, the driver corrects by steering to the right. If a driver waits too long to react when a car is in oversteer, the rear of the car may already have slid too far by the time any corrective action takes place. When the driver finally begins to apply corrective steering, he or she must apply it judiciously to correct the now substantial oversteer. If the vehicle regains traction, the correction may be too great. The end result is overcorrection, which then requires a further correction. As this cycle continues, the driver loses more control of the vehicle.

In this example, we imagined that oversteer was caused by excessive acceleration. Oversteer can also be caused by sudden deceleration while the car is negotiating a curve. If the car is cornering under power and the driver abruptly lifts his or her foot off the throttle, the vehicle will pitch forward, thus becoming lighter at the back end and possibly losing traction at the rear wheels. This is called trailing throttle oversteer (TTO) or sometimes lift-off oversteer. A correction for TTO is to transfer weight back to the rear by accelerating. This may seem counterintuitive when your brain is telling you to slow the car down so you can regain control. If you reduce power further by applying the brakes, the back of the car will become even lighter and the situation will get worse. In effect, you'll end up in a positive feedback loop that could crash—literally!

Reacting too slowly can cause a negative feedback loop to fall into a mode of hunting or to turn into a destructive positive feedback loop. A stock control system reacts to demands for availability. If a store does not have enough stock of a particular item that customers are requesting, the correction is to request more of the item from the central warehouse. If the demand for an item is low, with the excess taking up valuable space, the correction is to clear it from the store. This is achieved by sending some of it back to the central warehouse or by discounting the item, in the hope that it will be sold. If there are requests for an out-of-stock item but it takes the store too long to restock, customers may decide to purchase the item elsewhere. In addition to losing revenue, the store will then end up with excess stock.

Breaking Out of Positive Feedback Loops

Audiences express their appreciation and approval for jazz performances with applause and other less obvious gestures, such as nodding their heads and tapping their feet. The musicians interpret all of this as positive feedback. Creativity and innovation are key performance goals for jazz musicians. The musicians respond to the positive feedback from the audience with further creativity and innovation. This can lead to wonderful results. However, if the process continued in this way, with the musicians innovating further and further and continuing to evolve the music way beyond its original starting point, the performance could eventually become unstable and lead to a "train wreck." The danger with positive feedback is that it amplifies the possibilities for divergence, evolution, and change. If this process continues unchecked, it can eventually become a problem.

What can you do about this? Quite simply, you must the break the loop. Who hasn't experienced the terrible screech when a microphone is held too close to a speaker cabinet in a public address system? This is the result of a positive feedback loop in which the sound from the speaker cabinet is picked up by the microphone, which is then sent back to the amplifier and broadcast even more loudly through the speaker cabinet, and so forth. The howling noise can be stopped only by moving the microphone away from the speaker cabinet so that it breaks the feedback loop.

John Boyd and the OODA Loop

Col. John Boyd was a maverick U.S. Air Force fighter pilot. He was one of the first instructors at the Fighter Weapons School at Nellis Air Force Base in Nevada, where he wrote the curriculum on dogfight tactics. There he earned the nickname "Forty Second Boyd" for a standing bet involving a challenge in aerial combat. Boyd bet $40 that, beginning with the challenger on his tail, he could maneuver within 40 seconds to a point at which the positions were reversed. Many took up the challenge, but Boyd never once lost the bet. Franklin C. Spinney, a former analyst for the Pentagon, counted Boyd as a friend and a mentor for more than 20 years. He recalled, "One of Boyd's lifelong friends, Ron Catton, a retired fighter pilot, and one of the few ever to graduate from the Fighter Weapons School with a perfect score, told me that Boyd usually needed only 20 seconds to win, but liked a little insurance in case something went wrong" (Spinney 1997).

By the late 1950s, Boyd was widely regarded as the finest fighter pilot in the U.S. Air Force, but his abilities went way beyond superiority in the skies. According to Spinney, "Boyd had a very spooky way of thinking. To make matters worse, he had an IQ of only 90, which he claimed was an advantage because it forced him to be more efficient" (Spinney 1997).

Boyd put his practice into theory in the early 1960s when he devised the Energy-Maneuverability (E-M) theory of aerial combat. He used it to save the U.S. Air Force's F-15 Eagle project from disaster. Boyd transformed the F-15, originally designed as an 80,000-pound behemoth with sluggish performance, into a highly agile 40,000-pound fighter. He was a proponent of air agility and believed that fighter aircraft should be highly maneuverable, unlike the F-4 Phantom II, F-111, and other cumbersome U.S. jet fighters of the 1960s. The F-111 was an 85,000-pound sloth designed to be everything for every potential buyer. It was supposed to land on carriers, fly long distances, and engage in dogfights, yet it was unable to do any of these well. I believe this is what usability researcher Bill Buxton would refer to as a weak general system rather than a strong specific one (Buxton 2001). Boyd's concerns rang true during the Vietnam War, when U.S. pilots found themselves outclassed by Soviet and North Vietnamese pilots in MiG-17 and MiG-21s.[1] Subsequently, the U.S. Air Force established the Light Weight Fighter Project, which resulted in the development of the F-16 Fighting Falcon and F/A-18 Hornet. Boyd is often called the father of these highly successful fighter aircraft.

Although his contributions to aircraft design were more than enough to establish him as a legend in military circles, Boyd's work on a feedback loop earned him a place in history. Sometimes known as the **Boyd Cycle**, the **OODA Loop** is a decision cycle named for four processes:

- **Observe**—Acquire data by means of senses
- **Orient**—Analyze and synthesize data to form a perspective of the situation
- **Decide**—Determine a course of action based on the perspective of the situation
- **Act**—Implement the decision

During the Korean War, Boyd wondered how the pilots of the American Saber F-86 were able to rack up a ten-to-one kill score against their North Korean counterparts in their Soviet-made MiG -15s. The MiG-15 had a higher flight

---

1. Only 5 American pilots become aces during the Vietnam War, but 16 North Vietnamese and 1 Soviet pilot earned the same honor. When ranked by victories, the American aces all rank at the bottom, with five or six victories, whereas the top North Vietnamese ace, Nguyen Van Coc, had nine victories. There is an argument that the statistics fell in favor of the North Vietnamese because they had the home-turf advantage, with superior radar and command center support, and the overwhelming number of U.S. aircraft gave them more target opportunities. Yet there is no doubt that the MiG-17 and MiG-21 jets were more agile than the F-4 Phantom II in direct one-on-one confrontations, and the F-105 Thunderchief was a "sitting duck" for the MiGs. The U.S. forces introduced the Dissimilar Air Combat Training (DACT) and TOPGUN programs as a direct result of the aerial combat losses in Vietnam.

ceiling and a higher sustained turn rate, which meant it could hold a tight turn for a longer period than the Saber. The Saber, Boyd observed, had a higher instantaneous turn rate, enabling it to transition more quickly from one maneuver to another. In other words, whereas the MiG-15 could *outperform* the Saber, the Saber could *respond more quickly.* In addition, the Saber had a bubble canopy, which afforded its occupants an unobstructed 360-degree field of view, allowing American pilots to observe more quickly than the MiG-15 pilots. Boyd became convinced that success in dogfights lay in the ability to make superior decisions and execute them more quickly than one's opponent. This formed the basis for his OODA theory. Boyd understood the need for agility in terms of not just aircraft maneuverability, but also people's ability to respond to constantly changing, life-threatening situations. His colleague Harry Hillaker, chief designer of the F-16, wrote about the OODA theory in a posthumous homage to Boyd (Hillaker 1997):

> *Time is the dominant parameter: the pilot who goes through the OODA cycle in the shortest time prevails because his opponent is caught responding to situations that have already changed.*

When pilots can achieve ultimate success in an OODA loop, their opponents end up in a hunting mode as a result of being too slow to react to feedback. We know that hunting in a negative feedback loop can lead to disaster. In the case of an aerial dogfight, losers usually pay the ultimate cost: their lives. In aerial combat, agility translates to superiority. Hillaker wrote:

> *The key is to obscure your intentions and make them unpredictable to your opponent while you simultaneously clarify his intentions. That is, operate at a faster tempo to generate rapidly changing conditions that inhibit your opponent from adapting or reacting to those changes and that suppress or destroy his awareness. Thus, a "hodge-podge" of confusion and disorder occur to cause him to over- or under-react to conditions or activities that appear to be uncertain, ambiguous, or incomprehensible.*

> *Put more succinctly, deny your opponent the use of his maneuvering advantages against you while you convert your strengths into an advantage over him and cause him to make a wrong move, one that can be easily defeated.*

Boyd's work on the OODA Loop has prompted some to proclaim him the greatest military strategist since Sun Tzu. Studies of his work reveal the depth of his research. His original sources (Osinga 2005) included Gödel's Incompleteness Theorem, Heisenberg's Uncertainty Principle, the Second

Law of Thermodynamics, and Darwin's Theory of Evolution. Just as with *The Art of War*, the OODA Loop has been applied to many other domains, including business, politics, sociology, and sports. Hillaker wrote:

> *After his retirement from the Air Force, Boyd elevated his theories to a higher plane to encompass the total battle and not just the air battle. He refined and expanded his combat theories of fast reaction and mobility and incorporated them into a four-hour "Patterns of Conflict" briefing that he presented to the Army and Marines to illustrate how his concepts could be adapted to the land battle. … Many of the tactics used in Desert Storm were patterned after Boyd's theories.*

Management guru Tom Peters frequently quotes Boyd's OODA theory. In his book *Re-Imagine! Business Excellence in a Disruptive Age* (Peters 2003, 210), Peters wrote:

> *John Boyd, an Air Force Colonel, said that whoever has the fastest "OODA" Loop wins. OODA Loop: Observe–Orient–Decide–Act cycle. Confuse and confound the "enemy" by your speed per se. While the Champions of Inertia are busy scheduling the next "planning review," you swiftly get the job done … and go public with it.*

In later years, Boyd himself studied the applicability of his theory to business, specifically the just-in-time Toyota Production System (C. Richards 2008, 8). Software development consultant Steve Adolph wrote about Boyd's theory as it applies to software development in his paper "What Lessons Can the Agile Community Learn from A Maverick Fighter Pilot?" (Adolph 2006). Whether by design or by accident, many other cycles of decision and action bear similarity to the OODA Loop. Plan–Do–Check–Act (PDCA), also known as the Deming Cycle, Shewhart Cycle, or Deming Wheel, is one such example.

The Lessons of Blitzkrieg

Boyd also studied the tactics of the *Blitzkrieg*. Many myths and controversies surround the Blitzkrieg concept and its use by German forces during World War II. Many have propagated and continue to propagate the false notion that *Blitzkrieg* was primarily a strategy of repeated "shock and awe" tactics that relied on overwhelming force directed through military hardware such as the armored divisions of the German *Panzerwaffe*. Military historian Julian Jackson observes that newsreels portrayed the German army as a mechanized juggernaut, when, in fact, the German army had 3,350 tanks and 650,000 horses when it attacked the Russians in 1941 (J. Jackson 2004, 218). The real advantage of *Blitzkrieg,* which is German for "lightning war," was speed and mobility.

At the end of World War I, the Treaty of Versailles imposed strict restrictions on German military forces, limiting them in both size and scope. The task of reorganizing the German military within these restrictions fell to Hans von Seeckt. A general who had served in numerous high-level positions in the German army during World War I, Seeckt realized that agility was the key to success. Robert Citino, an American history professor, wrote about Seeckt's thought process in *The Path to Blitzkrieg* (Citino 1999, 9):

> *During [WW I], all European armies had increased in size and decreased in effectiveness: their huge mobs of half-trained solders had been incapable of forcing a decision. [Seeckt] felt their immobility was the root cause.*

Citino quotes Seeckt, "The mass cannot maneuver, therefore it cannot win." Under Seeckt's leadership, the German Army developed a new military doctrine called *Bewegungskrieg,* or "maneuver warfare." To enable this new method, the army also developed a new leadership system called *Auftragstaktik,* or "mission tactics." In previous approaches, every decision German forces made involved taking time to gather information (observe), analyze the information (orient), make a decision (decide) and then communicate the orders throughout the military hierarchy, where soldiers were commanded to carry out the orders (act). Seeckt's quest to improve mobility led to tactics that "necessitated the nearly complete decentralization of command, the surrender of much of an officer's authority to the squads, fire teams, and individual soldiers making the assault" (Citino 1999, 9). By giving unit commanders more autonomy, German forces were able to improve agility. Instead of waiting for explicit orders, they were made aware of the strategic intents of their superiors and expected to use their own creativity and initiative, and make their own decisions to help implement the strategy. In this way, German forces were able to make decisions and act more quickly than their opponents. The actions of individual units were less predictable, and the units were able to adapt more quickly in response to the specific threats or conditions they encountered. By continuously maintaining a more rapid tempo, German units were able to paralyze enemy forces, locking them into a mode of constantly reacting and often hunting in a negative feedback loop. We discuss the concept of decentralized leadership in more detail later.

Boyd himself was fond of proclaiming, "People, ideas, hardware—in that order" (Coram 2002, 354). It's not surprising that he embraced the notion of reducing the time of decision cycles through a cultural change instead of a technological one. Influenced by his study of the *Blitzkrieg* and other research during the 1970s, Boyd developed a framework that he called "Organizational Climate for Operational Success (C. Richards 2004, 51). Others sometimes referred to this as Principles of the *Blitzkrieg*, although Boyd himself disliked the term because of its Nazi connotations. He did use the German words for the four cultural and organizational principles that he identified:

- **Unity/Trust** *(Einheit)*—The mutual trust that binds an organization together.
- **Skill/Expertise** *(Fingerspitzengefühl)*—The ability to know just what to do. This comes from years of training and experience.
- **Intent** *(Auftragstaktik)*—The intent communicated by senior leaders. In many ways, this is a contract whereby the leaders communicate what is required and people agree to accomplish it and are then held accountable to their commitment. It's important that the leaders not prescribe how the work shall be done.
- **Vision** *(Schwerpunkt)*—Focus and direction given to the efforts of all within the organization. In theory, this helps people make decisions when they are unsure or confronted with ambiguity. ("Will this help us achieve our vision?")

It's easy to see how these map to principles of the Jazz Process:

- **Unity/Trust** *(Einheit)*—Build trust and respect
- **Skill/expertise** *(Fingerspitzengefühl)*—Employ top talent
- **Intent** *(Auftragstaktik)*—Lead on demand and use just enough rules
- **Vision** *(Schwerpunkt)*—Put the team first and commit with passion

OODA and the Jazz Process

Figure 2 illustrates a model of execution based on OODA theory. The illustration shows how the principles of the Jazz Process can help improve execution. The principles of working and executing have a constant effect on the entire process, and the principles of collaborating and innovating act on specific elements of execution. "Build trust and respect" has a specific bearing at two points in the execution loop: 1) Act to generate trust and respect from others, and 2) extend trust and respect to others when considering a situation. Similarly, "Exchange ideas" has a specific bearing at two points: 1) Offer ideas to others when acting, and 2) consider the ideas of others when gathering data about a situation.

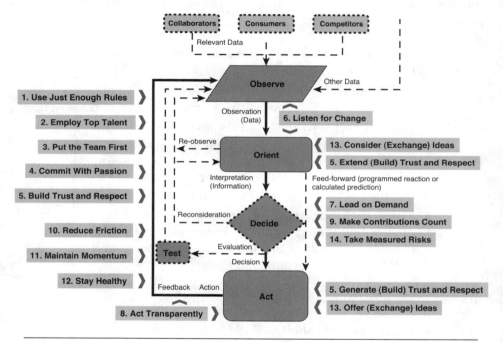

Figure 2 *Jazz Process Cycle of Execution*

In looking at this figure, you can see a number of dashed lines connecting various OODA steps. This is because, in reality, the path of execution does not always neatly follow the steps of Observe–Orient–Decide–Act. The various dashed lines represent the exceptions:

- **Reobserving**—Sometimes we have to look twice. We may see something and suspect that our observation is flawed. We have to do a "double take" and reacquire the data. Another reason to reobserve is to ensure that we are equipped with the most up-to-date data. One of the dangers of simply thinking of execution as a linear sequence of steps moving from Observe to Orient, to Decide, to Act is that it implies that you are only observing part of the time. That can be a problem: You might miss something important when you look away. Although observing clearly is one step in the process, one must never forget the importance of continuous observation. If you take longer than expected to orient to what you observe, you may have to go back and reacquire the data. Reobservation can also occur in the decision-making phase, especially if the decision is complex and things don't seem to add up.

- **Reorienting**—Sometimes you have to reconsider what you have observed. You might be sure that the data is correct but still have trouble making heads or tails of it.

- **Feed-forward**—In a feedback system, some proportion of the output signal is fed back into the input and used to control future behavior. In contrast, a feed-forward system is one in which decisions and their resulting actions are based on predicting possible future outcomes. For example, in a feedback system, a thermostat turns on the heat when the temperature in a house drops below a certain level. A feed-forward system might detect that a door has been left open and that the temperature outside the house is cold. It can use this data to predict that the temperature in the house will eventually drop and can turn on the heat to prevent that situation. A feed-forward approach to control is often used when a system is slow to respond to changes. In social systems, people are often able to feed-forward based on experience. Feed-forward has special significance for educators, mentors, and leaders. Although it's often necessary for them to provide negative (corrective) feedback to others when things go wrong, it's much more important that they provide feed-forward and help people avoid costly mistakes before they happen. Feed-forward allows highly trained and talented individuals to reduce the time spent making decisions and instantly react with an optimal response. This capability is developed from continuous learning and extensive experience. It is based on remembering unique decisions and actions, and then either recalling the respective past outcomes or rapidly deducing the possible outcomes for the present. In routine or simple situations, feed-forward allows people and teams to operate on autopilot, issuing preprogrammed responses. Of course, it's critically important that such responses be correct, especially when they are based on assumptions of déjà vu. How many times have software developers corrected a bug using a fix they had used previously because they thought it was a bug they had seen before, when, in reality, it was a subtle variation that required a different fix? It is also possible to feed-forward when you know for certain that the situation will allow you to do the right thing with virtually any reasonable action. Finally, it is possible to skip the decision phase entirely without feeding forward. In other words, you can take a wild guess and hope for the best, although such an approach is not usually recommended!

- **Evaluation**—In some cases, the only way to make a decision is to first evaluate one or more possibilities by testing them. Within a team, the "evaluate and test" microloop depicts an important activity that occurs for individuals in certain contexts. For example, in software development, individual developers usually try out their changes locally before unleashing them on the rest of the team. Collaborative programming systems such as Rational Team Concert support such activities. Personal workspaces and personal builds let people work and test changes locally. When they are satisfied with the results, they can deliver their contributions to shared integration streams, where they are combined with contributions from the rest of the team. Many activities require constant microevaluation before committing to a substantial decision and action. When people are confronted with unfamiliar problems, they often perform small, sometimes undetectable local testing to ascertain the limits and responsiveness of their situations. Jazz musicians do this all the time by trying out musical ideas. Sometimes these evolve into great things. Other times, they go by largely without fanfare.

Another problem with thinking of the loop in an exclusively linear fashion is that if your goal is to get through the cycle as quickly as possible, you may be inclined to make rash decisions. We know that two problems can lead to hunting in a negative feedback loop: trying too hard and reacting too slowly (reacting too quickly is just another form of trying too hard). Making bad decisions quickly leads to the need for a corrective action. You can then end up hunting in a negative feedback loop. Taking longer to make the right decisions can actually speed up the overall tempo.

As you read through this book, I believe you'll find that much of what we discuss is best considered in the context of the execution cycle. The concepts are widely applicable, and I'll bet you can apply them to your own execution and that of the teams you work in.

Execution is a topic that deserved its own chapter in this book because the ability to effectively execute is an all-too-rare skill. Many people can talk, plan, strategize, and theorize, but not enough people know how to get things done and deliver quality, innovative solutions on time. This is the reason so many plans are never seen through to fruition and why so many companies fail to successfully navigate change. Additionally, a thorough understanding of execution allows leaders to create strategies that are more likely to succeed.

Recapitulation

- All intelligent systems maintain feedback loops that allow them to make decisions by using feedback about past actions.

- A positive feedback loop is also known as a self-reinforcing or synergistic loop. It tends to accelerate a system away from equilibrium. Positive feedback loops can be good or bad.

- The danger with positive feedback is that it amplifies the possibilities for divergence, evolution, and change. This can become a problem, so it's important to know how to break out of a positive feedback loop.

- A negative feedback loop is also known as a self-correcting, regulatory, or balancing loop. It tends to bring a system into equilibrium.

- Reacting too slowly or overcorrecting can cause a negative feedback loop to fall into a mode of hunting, which can also turn into a bad positive feedback loop. The solution is to back off, relax, and avoid trying too hard.

- Fighter pilot and military strategist John Boyd developed a decision cycle known as the OODA Loop. It consists of four stages: Observe–Orient–Decide–Act. The Jazz Process principles act on this loop.

- Boyd studied the tactics of the *Blitzkrieg* and learned that the key to agility is to decentralize leadership and give people the authority to make decisions that affect them.

- The ability to effectively execute is an all-too-rare skill. Many people can talk, plan, strategize, and theorize, but not enough people know how to get things done and deliver quality, innovative solutions on time.

- A thorough understanding of execution allows leaders to create strategies that are more likely to succeed.

CHAPTER 6

Listen for Change

"A good hockey player plays where the puck is;
a great hockey player plays where the puck is going to be."
—Wayne Gretzky

Observing

What does it mean to listen? In his paper "Creativity and Improvisation in Jazz and Organizations: Implications for Organizational Learning," Frank Barrett wrote about why jazz musicians need to be good listeners. I have quoted from Barrett's paper here and added a few annotations (Barrett 1998, 617):

> In order to "comp" or accompany soloists effectively, jazz musicians need to be very good listeners. They need to interpret others' playing [Orient], anticipate likely future directions [Maintain momentum], make instantaneous decisions in regard to harmonic and rhythmic progressions [Decide]. But they also may see beyond the player's current vision, perhaps provoking the soloist in different direction [sic] [Exchange ideas], with accents and chord extensions. None of this responsiveness can happen unless players are receptive [Trust and respect] and taking in one another's gestures [Exchange ideas]. If everyone tries to be a star and does not engage in supporting the evolution of the soloist's ideas [Put the team first], the result is bad jazz. When they listen well to others' soloing, they help the soloist reach new heights. Usually we think that great performances create attentive listeners. This notion suggests a reversal: attentive listening enables exceptional performance.

Barrett begins and ends with specific references to listening, but the details in between demonstrate how "listening" can be more than simply hearing music. Not surprisingly, jazz musicians place great importance on the skill of listening. If one jazz musician remarks that another jazz musician has "big ears," it's a compliment that means the person is constantly aware and ready to respond to change and open to exchanging ideas.

The OODA Loop, discussed in Part II's opening section "Essentials of Execution," begins with the act of observing. The Jazz Process Cycle of Execution begins with listening. In a general sense, observing and listening are the same. The different verbs reflect different contexts: The original perspective of OODA was the cockpit of an aircraft, whereas the Jazz Process has its origins in jazz performance. Regardless of the setting, the aim of observing in any cycle of execution is to acquire the relevant data that will enable the best decisions to be made and acted upon. As with the first step in any process, listening is critically important because any failure potentially compromises everything that will follow.

Uncompromised observation begins with an unimpeded field of view. Remember what John Boyd realized about the bubble canopy on the Saber in "Essentials of Execution?" Physical or systemic limitations may limit your ability to acquire data, but it's amazing how many people impose such constraints on themselves. In a visual context, this is known as **tunnel vision**. Figure 6.1 illustrates a driver negotiating a curve. Instead of looking through the windshield and tunneling her vision, she looks to her left, which is the direction she is heading. More important, upon encountering a problem in the form of an obstacle on the road, she focuses not on the problem, but on the possible solutions to the problem. In defensive driving, a solution is often referred to as an **escape route**. In *The 7 Habits of Highly Effective People*, Steven R. Covey says, "Begin with the End in Mind." Hockey legend Wayne Gretzky is often quoted as putting it this way: "A good hockey player plays where the puck is; a great hockey player plays where the puck is going to be."

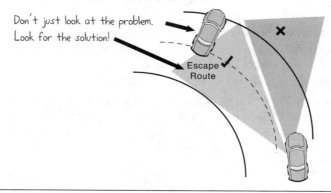

Figure 6.1   *Tunnel vision*

The opposite of tunnel vision is **peripheral vision**. Have you ever watched a juggler at work? When a juggler has many objects in play, it is impossible to look individually at each and every one. Instead, the juggler focuses on one point in midair. Objects that fall outside of that immediate space are observed in peripheral vision. Our field of vision is quite wide, but although we may see things, we may not actually observe them unless we make a conscious effort. Seeing is not the same as observing, just as hearing is not the same as listening. Your eyes or ears may receive data, but unless you actually pay attention, you may well miss what's important.

Figure 6.2 illustrates a situation I routinely face when I embark on the drive from my house to downtown. When I approach the on-ramp to the highway, I'm always concerned that there might be construction or some other problem that has caused traffic to back up. The path I pursue depends on the exact problem. If the problem is localized, I do a U-turn farther down the road and enter the highway from the other side. If the back-up of traffic is severe, I have to drive farther ahead and take a completely different route. Whenever I encounter this situation I must quickly observe the flow of traffic at multiple points. This helps me answer the following questions:

- Is there a problem?
- If so, what is the source of the problem?
- What is the severity of the problem?

Points of observation are indicated by the numbers on the figure. My process of observation and orientation might be as follows:

1. I need to observe the situation ahead because I don't want to run into the cars in front of me. The source of the problem might simply be a blockage on or near the ramp. On the other hand, if the traffic is backed up on the on-ramp, the problem may be quite severe.
2. Observing the traffic on the highway to my left helps clarify the situation. If the traffic is backed up there, it confirms that the blockage may not be confined to the on-ramp.
3. If the traffic is backed up to my right, the severity of the problem may be even greater than initially observed.
4. If I turn my head and look farther down the highway, I may be able to see the source of the problem.

5. If I turn my head to the right and look farther back up the highway, I may be able to obtain even more data to help determine the severity of the problem. If the traffic is backed really far up the highway, I know it's a very bad situation.

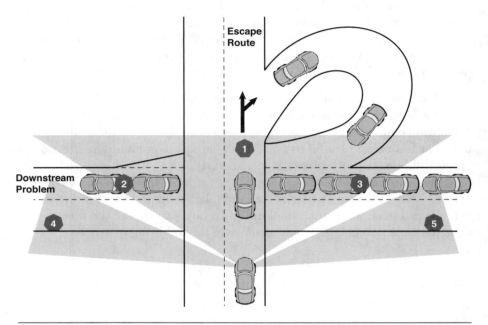

Figure 6.2 *Peripheral vision*

Individuals and teams that want to improve their execution must begin by expanding their field of view, opening themselves to all the relevant data that may affect their performances. When I think about the importance of observing, I am often reminded of the "all-seeing eye." If you have access to a U.S. $1 bill, you'll find the Great Seal of the United States on the reverse side. The seal includes the Eye of Providence positioned at the zenith of a pyramid. The Eye of Horus appears frequently in ancient Egyptian symbolism. An eye in a triangle was an explicit image of the Christian Trinity in Medieval and Renaissance iconography. Perhaps the most commonly seen manifestation of this symbolism in recent years appears in the 2001–2003 *Lord of the Rings* movie trilogy. Sauron is described in the Tolkien books as having an all-seeing eye, but in the movies, he appears as a large flaming eye. In all these cases, the "all-seeing eye" represents the ability to see all and miss nothing, a useful ability for a highly effective individual, especially one of deific magnitude! The notion of watching over and protecting is often associated with this symbolism and is also very applicable. In our case, the quality and integrity of the performance needs to be protected.

What We Observe

Figure 2, Jazz Process Cycle of Execution, in the "Essentials of Execution" section, illustrated five sources of data:

1. Feedback as a result of our actions
2. Relevant data from collaborators we work with
3. Relevant data from consumers we work for
4. Relevant data from competitors we work against
5. All other data relating to a specific situation

Figure 6.3 shows this in greater detail, including the personal awareness and situational awareness we discussed in Chapter 2, "Employ Top Talent," and the team awareness discussed in Chapter 3, "Put the Team First."

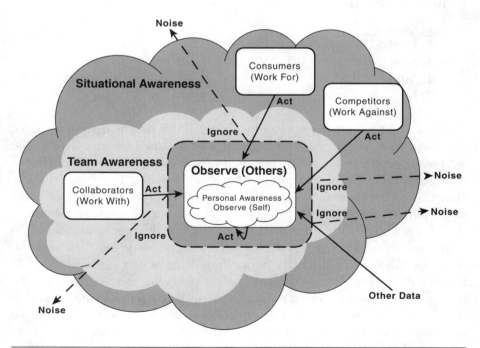

Figure 6.3 *Observing and orienting*

Paying attention to the feedback from your own actions is clearly critical. How else can you ensure that what you are doing is correct and optimal? When people with a high level of personal awareness perform an action independent of the actions of others, they often have a good idea of the outcome. Things become much more complex when the simultaneous actions of collaborators are factored into the mix. This is true whether they are performing music in an ensemble, playing basketball with four other people on a court, or contributing code during a development cycle while 50 other software developers do the same. Driving would surely be much easier if yours were the only vehicle on the roads. Interacting with all these other people requires that we look, listen, or otherwise acquire the data that represents their past, present, and future actions, whether they be collaborators, consumers, or competitors. This is the social awareness that we discussed in Chapter 2. Observing and understanding what others are doing is not only essential to execution—it's also essential in following the rule "Put the team first." This is what Stephen R. Covey declared the ultimate degree of listening in a continuum that he defined in *The 8th Habit* (S. R. Covey 2004, 192):

Listening Continuum

1. Ignoring
2. Pretend listening (patronizing)
3. Selective listening
4. Attentive listening
5. Empathic listening

The downside to opening up and receiving all this data is the potential for data saturation. We may have to deal with a lot of data if we are collaborating with many people. Even if each person is not very active, the total amount of data generated by a large team can be overwhelming. The president of a company with a thousand employees simply can't keep track of what every single person is doing. That's why he or she collaborates primarily with vice presidents who provide summary information that the president can use. In turn, each of those vice presidents receives summary information from directors, who obtain summary information from senior managers, and so forth. With so many steps between the people collecting the data and the person at the top of the organization hierarchy, a danger of losing important details exists. There is also a danger of costly delays because it takes time for information to bubble up to the top of the command hierarchy. In recent years, technology has enabled people to build tools that alleviate some of these dangers. Such tools allow executives, senior managers, and other stakeholders to gain direct access to information based on live data.

However, without the ability to filter the data and summarize the information, you can easily be bombarded with too many details.

Rational Team Concert promotes team awareness by notifying users when other team members perform actions that might be of interest to others. This is especially useful when some of those team members are in other locations. The Team Central view displays a constant stream of event notifications. Users can configure this so that they have control over the types of events they will see in this view. Figure 6.4 displays the configuration options.

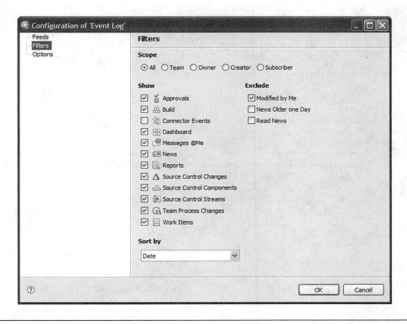

Figure 6.4 *Configuring the filter for the Event Log in Rational Team Concert*

Work items in Rational Team Concert track specific work efforts, such as fixing a bug or developing a new feature. In addition to pertinent details about the work effort, such as its severity, priority, ownership, and so forth, each work item tracks a discussion between any parties that want to contribute a comment. In this way, software developers can collaborate and interact with people who file work items, whether they are other developers, customers, testers, or other stakeholders or interested parties. Users are subscribed to a work item automatically when they contribute to that work item's discussion. They can also subscribe to a specific work item to track its progress, and they can subscribe other users to a work item if they want that person to be kept informed of the work item's progress. It's also possible to explicitly mention someone in a work item discussion without subscribing that person. This is simply accomplished by referencing the user ID with the "@" prefix:

@psmith do you think we can delay fixing this until the next release?

This can be useful if you want to ask someone a question or keep them informed without requiring that they track the ongoing progress of the work item. Users can be notified if they are mentioned in a work item or subscribed to a work item, or if a change is made, such as adding a comment or marking a work item resolved. With large teams and projects, users may be subscribed or mentioned in hundreds or even thousands of active work items, so there is great potential for them to be bombarded by too much data. This is addressed by allowing users to specify the types of notifications they want to be informed of (see Figure 6.5).

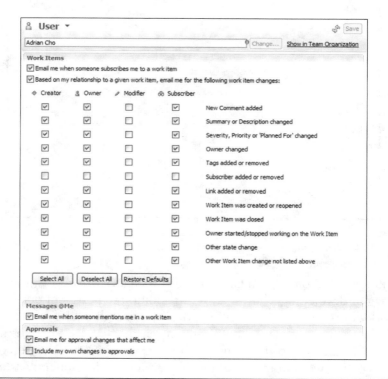

Figure 6.5   *Configuring e-mail notifications in Rational Team Concert*

Just as large teams can easily generate a large volume of data, so can a single, very active person. In 1958, jazz critic Ira Gitler used the term "sheets of sound" in the liner notes for John Coltrane's album *Soultrane*. Gitler was referring to Coltrane's style of playing extremely dense passages containing many notes at high speed. Coltrane often used this approach to outline specific harmony, suggesting up to three stacked chords at a time. He also realized the need for the device to have aesthetic as well as functional value, telling Gitler, "Now it is not a thing of beauty, and the only way it would be justified is if it becomes that. If I can't work it through, I will drop it" (Gitler 1958). When you first listen to Coltrane playing in this manner on albums such as *Kind of Blue* (1959) and *Giant Steps* (1960), your ears are assaulted with the sheer number of notes. Contrast this style with the sparse and lyrical playing of Miles Davis, who never used more notes than was necessary to get his point across. In the artistic milieu of jazz, neither style is better than the other. As we noted in our discussion of Davis's second quintet (see Chapter 2), Davis often employed players with note-intensive styles, to distinguish his own playing. The contrast between the styles creates interest and tension in the music. However, it takes the listener more time to decode the musical message embedded in a storm of notes.

Considering all the data from collaborators, consumers, and competitors can increase the potential for data saturation, but simply ignoring data from these sources is not an option. Can you imagine a jazz musician not listening to what the other members of the band were doing? This is as preposterous as a company ignoring customer feedback or an army ignoring the troop movements of enemy forces.

Identifying and Ignoring Noise

For purposes of this discussion, we label any data in which we are not interested as "noise." As you can see in Figure 6.3, we receive both relevant data and noise from any given source. When I'm playing jazz, my ears hear sound from many different sources. If I'm playing in a concert hall, the amount of ambient noise in the room may be low, with the audience listening in silence. If I'm playing in a club, there may be a lot of noise, with many conversations taking place simultaneously, none of which is relevant to my job as a musician. To borrow an electrical engineering term, when the amount of noise is proportionally high, the signal-to-noise ratio (often abbreviated as SNR or S/N) is low. This makes it harder to identify and acquire the data that we're really interested in. It's important to filter out the noise and increase the

SNR. This is a vital part of listening, and the concept is not exclusive to an aural context. Unwanted noise can be present in any medium. You have to deal with noise in your inbox when you receive junk e-mail or spam. With social networking, we are now connected more than ever. People receive updates from new services, friends, companies, and groups on services such as Facebook and Twitter. Although these services are great for staying in touch and keeping current with both private and public events, they often have a low SNR. Users of these services are often left trying to filter out the noise.

Separating the signal from the noise is often a challenge, but it's probably the most important part of observing.

In business and politics, the tactic of spreading disinformation is known as FUD, an acronym for fear, uncertainty, and doubt. FUD is an attempt to influence people's perception of something or someone by spreading negative information. This causes people to question the target of the FUD, usually a product or service, but sometimes an individual or organization. In politics, candidates usually broadcast a signal that communicates their stance on issues, cultivates a positive image, and implies that people would benefit if they were elected. The opposition may conduct a smear campaign based on false information. Bombarding people with the noise of FUD obscures the real issues and decreases the candidate's SNR. A candidate may also waste time combating the FUD. In the 2004 United States presidential campaign, supporters of George W. Bush were accused of using FUD against Democratic nominee John Kerry when *Swift* boat veterans and former Vietnam prisoners of war called into question Kerry's military service record, including his numerous military honors. Since that time, the term *swiftboating* has become synonymous with FUD-based political tactics.

In competitive sports, athletes must deal with constant noise. This includes not only audible noise in the form of cheering and jeering, but visual noise such as waving balloons, "thunder sticks" and those big foam hands, sometimes aimed at throwing the players off their game. This is particularly noticeable when basketball players are attempting free throws or soccer players are attempting penalty kicks.

Soldiers must deal with all kinds of noise in battle. Again, this is not simply audible noise such as the sound of gunfire or artillery, but it includes intelligence data that deals with the actions of both friendly and enemy units, the locations and status of strategic objectives, and so forth. What often appears to be interesting data may actually be noise in the form of a distraction created by the enemy. Entire battle plans have been drawn up and executed on the basis of military intelligence that turned out to be false information planted or purposely leaked by the enemy. Commanders have used whole armies as distractions on the field of battle, drawing opposing enemy forces away from important locations or deceiving them into exposing their flank or dividing their ranks. Squads and even individual soldiers regularly use similar diversionary tactics on a smaller scale.

Separating the signal from the noise is often a challenge, but it's probably the most important part of observing. The problem is that what's noise in one situation may be relevant data in another. Have you ever asked that your name be removed from an e-mail thread? Perhaps it was noise to you to begin with because someone mistakenly included you on the send list, or perhaps it was relevant to you in the beginning, but as the conversation took a different turn, it then became noise. These subtle cases can consume valuable time. So can the obvious cases because they may still divert your attention away from the data in which you are really interested.

Data Versus Information

You may have noticed that until this point, I have used the terms *data* and *information*. I've not used them interchangeably. In fact, I've been very particular about which term I used. **Data** is just raw, unstructured facts. It is meaningless until it has been processed, interpreted, and analyzed, at which point it becomes information.

When we were developing the second release of Rational Team Concert at IBM, I wanted to communicate specific information to the development team and to stakeholders. One of the cool points about the project is that we develop Rational Team Concert using itself. This metacircular existence means that we get to test our code all the time. One of the features of the product is the capability to construct dashboards to present customized information views based on live data. They are especially useful for summarizing information, highlighting and comparing specific facts, and aggregating data from multiple sources. Dashboards are displayed on web pages so they can be shared with any user with a web browser.

Figure 6.6 shows a dashboard with four viewlets. Each viewlet uses a bar chart to display the number of defects fixed in the endgame, which is the final phase of a development cycle. One of the prerequisites for entering the endgame is that all new feature work be complete. In the endgame, the focus is on achieving and maintaining stability. The project moves through a series of iterations, with a release candidate build produced at the end of each iteration.

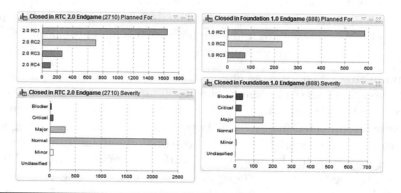

Figure 6.6   *Dashboard viewlets showing endgame shutdown*

Two teams are involved in the development of Rational Team Concert. One team works on Rational Team Concert (RTC) itself, and the other works on Jazz Foundation (a collaboration platform often referred to as simply Foundation), which underpins a number of different products. During the endgame for RTC 2.0 which was built on Foundation 1.0, 2710 defects were fixed in RTC, and 888 were fixed in Foundation. The effort to fix each of these 3,598 defects was tracked in a work item. Collectively, these work items contain a huge amount of data that can be mined to produce specific information. The dashboard viewlets enabled us to quickly communicate the manner in which the teams shut down their projects. As they moved through the iterations toward the end of the development cycle, stricter approvals were instituted, which reduced the tolerance for changes and increased stability of the code base. The result was a steady decrease in the number of defects fixed over time. This is shown clearly in the viewlets on the top row. The viewlets on the bottom row show different information from the same set of fixed defects: The components in Jazz Foundation fixed a higher proportion of serious "blocker" and "critical" severity defects than the components in Rational Team Concert.

As we progressed through the endgame and defects were being fixed, the dashboards changed in real time. Instead of having to constantly produce reports for the team and other interested stakeholders, I could simply point them to the web page with the dashboard viewlets, where they could check at any time and get the most up-to-date information. We used many dashboards in this way to quickly communicate specific information based on live data.

Military commanders, business executives, and heads of government all receive frequent briefs from analysts and advisers. In each case, they seek useful information, not just raw data, to help them make the best possible decisions they can. Regardless of what you may be doing, you will have similar needs. This is where the *orient* phase in the execution loop comes into play.

Measuring Success

One of the most useful pieces of information required in any situation is a score, a measure of how well a person or a team is doing. Dr. Saul Miller is a performance specialist who has worked with many sports teams in the National Basketball Association, National Football League, and National Hockey League, as well as Olympic athletes and PGA Tour golfers. In the chapter entitled "Feedback" in his book, *Why Teams Win: Keys to Success in Business, Sport and Beyond,* Miller writes matter-of-factly: "If you play to win, then you gotta keep score." He also adds (Miller 2009, 77):

> *To be successful a team needs to know how they are doing. They need high-quality feedback.* They need to know the score. *The ability to assess and adjust performance is critical to continuous improvement. Assessment must be based on clear and accurate information. Team members may think, "We're a great team." "We're winners." And, "We're doing fine." However, if the results of their actions don't translate into meaningful numbers on some scoreboard, then they may be deluding themselves.*

Miller highlights why this is important for businesses (Miller 2009, 88):

> *One of the parallels between business and sport is an awareness of and respect for the bottom line. Winning teams know what they have to do to win. They also know that the status quo is never good enough. What won last season rarely repeats. There is a continual push to be better. The scoreboard is an indicator of how they are doing.*

In business, metrics such as key performance indicators (KPIs) are used to keep score. When used effectively and appropriately, they are an essential part of observation in an execution cycle. Unfortunately, metrics can be overused and abused. Management by numbers exclusively can lead to misguided efforts and eventual failure. Quality guru W. Edwards Deming cautioned in his book *Out of the Crisis* that focusing solely on financial figures was one of the seven deadly diseases of management (Deming 2000, 121). He wrote, "[H]e that would run his company on visible figures alone will in time have neither company nor figures," adding, "[T]he most important figures that one needs for management are unknown or unknowable (Lloyd S. Nelson 20), but successful management must nevertheless take account of them." Deming attributed this last gem to his friend Lloyd S. Nelson, who was the director of statistical methods at Nashua at the time.

"Not everything that counts can be counted, and not everything that can be counted counts."
—Albert Einstein

Deming is often incorrectly quoted as saying, "You can't manage what you can't measure." Agile software experts Kent Beck and Martin Fowler were certainly not the first to cite this misquote, but to their credit they noted in *Planning Extreme Programming* (Beck and Fowler 2000, 107): "We're sure this isn't true, because lots of software gets shipped without any metrics being gathered." There is no evidence that Deming ever said such a thing, and his words in *Out of the Crisis* contradict the claim. Management guru Tom Peters is apparently in agreement, having said, "You can measure everything except what's important" (Kelleher 2009). John Bogle, the legendary investor and founder and retired CEO of The Vanguard Group, devoted a full chapter to this, entitled "Too Much Counting, Not Enough Trust," in his book *Enough: True Measures of Money, Business, and Life.* Bogle had harsh criticism for numerically centric thinking (Bogle 2008, 99–100):

> *Today, in our society, in economics, and in finance, we place far too much trust in numbers. Numbers are not reality. At best, they are a pale reflection of reality. At worst, they're a gross distortion of the truths we seek to measure. But the damage doesn't stop there. Not only do we rely too heavily on historic economic and market data; our optimistic bias also leads us to misinterpret the data and give them credence that they rarely merit. By worshipping at the altar of numbers and by discounting the immeasurable, we have in effect created a numeric economy that can easily undermine the real one.*

No more damning a case against the mindless pursuit of numbers can be made than in the story of Roger Smith, chairman and CEO of General Motors from 1981 to 1990. The timing is notable because *Out of the Crisis* was published in 1982 (it was then titled *Quality, Productivity and Competitive Position* and was renamed in 1986). By then, Deming had been teaching his concepts of quality for more than 40 years, most notably in Japan, where he was instrumental in helping establish Japanese manufacturing prowess after World War II. Smith has the unfortunate honor of being named one of the "Worst American CEOs of All Time" (Portfolio.com 2009), and his tenure at GM is regarded by many as a failure (Greenwald, McWhirter, and Szczesny 1992). In their book *Conquering Complexity in Your Business: How Wal-Mart, Toyota, and Other Top Companies Are Breaking Through the Ceiling on Profits and Growth,* Michael L. George and Stephen A. Wilson singled out Smith's misguided focus on net income, providing a textbook example of what Deming cautioned against (George and Wilson 2004, 35):

> In 1964, General Motors management inherited the edifice that Alfred Sloan had built. They presided over the fortunes of the largest, most successful company in history, operating in the economy's largest industry. They guided GM into the most catastrophic loss of market share in business history. What metric did management use to guide GM into the chasm?
>
> *"I look at the bottom line. It tells me what to do."*[1]
> —Roger B. Smith
>
> As your awareness of complexity increases, you begin to appreciate that a focus on earnings alone can lead management to make decisions that can destroy corporate value. GM's approach to conquering complexity in the 1980s was to build lookalike cars to reduce cost in a market that valued differentiation. The primary result was the acceleration of loss of market share.

During the 1980s, GM's market share fell from 46 percent to 35 percent under Smith's leadership (Greenwald, McWhirter, and Szczesny 1992). The company eventually filed for government-assisted Chapter 11 bankruptcy in June 2009, making it the fourth-largest bankruptcy in U.S. history, ranked by assets.

---

1 "The bottom line" is an expression synonymous with a company's net earnings, net income, or earnings per share. The expression comes from the fact that the net income almost always appears as the last line on a company's income statement.

Just as Boyd believed in people and ideas over hardware, Deming, despite being a statistician, believed that the path to success lay with people and management, not with measurements. In *Out of the Crisis*, he defined 14 points for transforming management (Deming, 2000 23–24), including this advice: "Eliminate management by numbers, numerical goals. Substitute leadership." In 1981, the same year Smith began his tenure as chairman and CEO at GM, Ford became one of the first big American corporations to seek Deming's help. As Andrea Gabor tells it in *The Capitalist Philosophers: The Geniuses of Modern Business—Their Lives, Times, and Ideas*, "At the time, Ford had begun to hemorrhage red ink, thanks to foreign competition and decades of slavish devotion to short-term financial figures" (Gabor 2002, 193). Although they were expecting advice about quality, after examining their culture and methods of management, Deming told them that management actions were responsible for 85 percent of all problems in developing better cars (Holusha 1993). By 1986, Ford had become the most profitable American car manufacturer, and for the first time since the 1920s, its earnings exceeded those of GM. At the time of writing, Ford is the only American car manufacturer that has not received bailout loans from the U.S. government as a result of the worldwide economic crisis that began in 2008.

You have to be realistic about the accuracy of metrics and the potential for measurements to be deliberately skewed. Many organizations attempt to control quality by setting targets and rules regarding defects. They mandate the number and classes of defects that can be tolerated. In some cases, products with minor defects or flaws are sold at a discount. The problem is that measuring and judging defects may be subjective. In software, it may be unclear whether a particular behavior is performing as designed or is not conforming to specification. The severity or impact of a defect may not be clear. A defect may have critical impact, but a temporary solution to work around the problem can reduce its impact.

For any score to be an effective gauge of success, the method of determining the score must be consistent over time and must be comparable to one or more points of reference. Everyone must agree that the method of scoring is a fair and useful measure of the team's success, and any caveats or limitations to the scoring should be well documented. In most complex situations, rarely can a small set of all-encompassing measurements be relied upon as sole measures of an individual or team's success. Even in a game such as basketball, in which the number of points is the primary measure of the score, a complete picture requires that you also know the quarter being played, the amount of game time remaining, the amount of time left on the shot clock, the number of individual and team fouls, who's on the court, and so forth.

The four dashboard viewlets in Figure 6.6 present useful information, but there are many things that they do not tell us. Although we can see the number of defects fixed, we have no idea how many are still open. While the team is fixing defects that have been filed, others are being constantly reported. Therefore, it would be useful to see the number of defects being submitted (opened) versus defects fixed (closed) over time. Incidentally, this is one of the many historical reports available in RTC, and it can be viewed in a dashboard viewlet alongside "current snapshot" viewlets, such as those in Figure 6.6.

Whatever method is used to score success, people must clearly understand the relationship between their efforts and the scoring. Measuring something that people feel they have no control over can only lead to frustration for everyone. Scores are useful for highlighting specific aspects of performance, but they should never be the sole input to decision making. The key to success is in managing not the score itself, but the underlying processes that produce the score.

Change Is Unavoidable

Whether you're observing numbers or measuring less quantitative data, the critical thing to look for and identify is change. What is change, how does it come about, and why is it important? Change is ever present in our world. If you place an object in deep space and give it a push in a certain direction, it will theoretically continue along that path until it encounters an obstacle. It's all theoretical because, even in space, the gravitational pull of celestial bodies such as planets, stars, and whole galaxies affects the position of other objects. After all, gravity from the sun keeps planets in orbit, and gravity from the Earth keeps the moon and other satellites in orbit. On March 3, 1972, NASA launched Pioneer 10, the first craft designed to leave our solar system. The power source on Pioneer 10 eventually degraded to the point that it was too weak to be detected from Earth. It was being monitored until April 27, 2002, however, despite being nearly 12 billion kilometers from Earth. When it was launched, a three-stage Atlas-Centaur rocket propelled Pioneer 10 to a speed of 51,810 kmph. As it passed Jupiter in December 1973, the huge gravity pull of the giant planet accelerated Pioneer 10 to a speed of 132,000 kmph. Since that time, its speed has slowed. It was always understood that this would happen due to the gravitational pull of our sun and planets in our solar system. However, Pioneer 10 has slowed even more rapidly than expected, a phenomenon that has become known as the **Pioneer anomaly** or **Pioneer effect**. Scientists are not sure exactly why this is happening. Suggested possibilities include pressure imposed by sunlight and solar wind, and gravitational effects from unseen masses such as cosmological dark matter and large asteroids in the outer solar system (Steel 2002).

Virtually any entity is subject to external forces, even in such a stark and remote environment as the vacuum of deep space. Business teams must deal with customers, competitors, economic conditions, and regulatory organizations. A sports team, even one that is strictly amateur and doesn't operate as a business, must contend with opposing teams, ruling officials, fans, and sports regulatory bodies. For any team, forces are acting to reduce momentum and alter direction.

Unforeseen obstacles may obstruct an object's path. Although the probability is extremely low, there is no guarantee that Pioneer 10 will not collide with an object in deep space. A ship traveling in the ocean must be vigilant to avoid collisions with other sea-faring craft, as well as to steer clear of bad weather. In many cases, the nature and behavior of these various obstacles can be hard to predict because they are constantly changing and sometimes not well understood. The good thing is that a team is like a ship; it has the ability to apply energy to maintain momentum, and it has the ability to make course corrections to successfully navigate the challenges and hurdles it encounters.

Even if a team is following a path that appears to lead to certain success, it must be prepared for unforeseen challenges. After game three of the 2008 NBA finals, the Boston Celtics were leading the Los Angeles Lakers two games to one. Determined to turn things around and stay in contention for the title, the Lakers came out with a vengeance in game four, finishing the first quarter with an impressive 35–14 lead, the largest first-quarter lead in NBA history. At one point, they were 24 points ahead. Things were looking great for the Lakers. They knew they had to win the game to prevent the Celtics from getting too far ahead in the finals, and it appeared they were on the right path to success. Then in the third quarter, the Lakers' fortunes took a turn for the worst. Somehow the Celtics scored 21 points in the same time the Lakers managed to score only 3. At the end of the third quarter, the score was 73–71, with the Lakers ahead by only 2 points. When they came back in the final quarter, the Celtics took the lead when reserve Eddie House scored with an 18-foot jump shot. From there, it was all Celtics, and they went on to win the game 97–91, and later the championship, by four games to two in the best-of-seven series. The coach of the Lakers at the time of this brutal defeat was none other than the great Phil Jackson, who had previously coached the Chicago Bulls to six titles and the Lakers to three. In 2009, he coached the Lakers to his tenth title, making him the record holder for the most titles won by any coach in NBA history. It's easy to see how the Lakers might have thought they were on a sure path to success, especially with a coach of Jackson's experience at their side. Yet that classic game demonstrated that, in sports, just as in business or any other field of endeavor, anything can happen.

Business professor Charles Rarick has written extensively and lectured internationally on Asian management practices. In summarizing the words of Sun Tzu from the classic *The Art of War*:

> *When ten times the enemy strength, surround him; when five times, attack him; when double, engage him; when equally matched, be able to divide him; when inferior in numbers, be able to take the defensive; and when you are no match for the enemy, be able to avoid him.*

Rarick wrote (Rarick 1996), "In the business of war, there is no invariable strategic advantage which can be relied upon at all times." No team can afford to rest on its laurels, no matter how well it is doing. Especially in highly competitive or volatile arenas, even a highly successful team that is apparently in full control of a situation can suddenly find themselves facing significant challenges that may lead to catastrophic failure. A team facing such serious challenges must be able to identify the issues, choose an appropriate course of correction, and execute with agility if they are to survive and succeed. In business parlance, the constantly changing conditions to which teams must react are referred to simply as "change." Not surprisingly, you'll find that change management is one of the most urgent themes in business because change can lead to the downfall and even the demise of those who are unable to successfully navigate through it.

Consideration 1: Cognitive Biases

Observing and orienting in an execution loop is not really as straightforward as I may have made it sound. People fail to account for numerous factors, many of which exist only in their minds.

We already know that two people can be in the same situation and observe different things. Even if they observe the same things, they can interpret their observations differently. One reason for this is the behavioral traits that affect observation, orientation, and, ultimately, decision making. One of the most dangerous tendencies that we all have is the proclivity to see what we want to see. When we face a situation with preconceptions, we may tend toward information that confirms our preconceptions. The psychological term for this is **confirmation bias**. We may also avoid or discount information that contradicts our preconceptions, which is **disconfirmation bias**. In the context of an execution loop and the tasks of observing and orienting, these and other cognitive biases can manifest in a number of ways:

- We observe and then orient, and then, failing to find what we seek, loop back and reobserve, in the hope of finding evidence that supports our hypotheses. In the worst case, we may even invent things that are simply not present in our situation. Alternatively, we observe and orient, and then, finding something we would really rather not see, we pretend to ourselves that we never saw it in the first place. This is known as **selection bias**.

- We observe and then orient with a skew. In other words, we interpret information to suit our needs. This is known as **assimilation bias**.

- We observe and then orient and decide to skip a decision and act by feeding forward based on a recollection of a previous identical or similar situation. Unfortunately, the recall is flawed. We either invent the previous situation or skew its characteristics or outcome. **Selective memory** is a form of this kind of bias.

These kinds of cognitive biases can often result from **cognitive dissonance**, which is the uncomfortable tension that results from simultaneously considering two conflicting thoughts. Cognitive dissonance increases with the importance of a decision and the difficulty of undoing it. In an attempt to resolve the tension, our judgment can become skewed. It's interesting to note the recent work of Roger Martin, dean of the University of Toronto's Rotman School of Management. In his book *The Opposable Mind: How Successful Leaders Win Through Integrative Thinking*, Martin defines **integrative thinking** after interviewing more than 50 highly successful leaders (Martin 2009, 6):

> [The leaders Martin has studied] have the predisposition and the capacity to hold two diametrically opposing ideas in their heads. And then, without panicking or simply settling for one alternative or the other, they're able to produce a synthesis that is superior to either opposing idea.

Martin describes people who are not only comfortable with the simultaneous consideration of opposing ideas, but actually use it to their advantage.

Many other cognitive biases can affect our ability to execute. **Information bias** occurs when we spend unnecessary time in observation and orientation, even though acquiring and analyzing more information will have no effect on our decision. This can happen if we are fearful of making a decision or we're trying to avoid a specific outcome. The opposite of this is **premature termination of search for evidence**, which is the tendency to accept the first alternative that looks like it might work. **Not Invented Here**, or **NIH**, is the tendency to ignore an existing solution that is seen as inferior or unreliable simply because another party developed it.

Biases are not limited to individual behavior. **Group polarization** is the tendency for people to make decisions that are more extreme when they are in a group. One form of this is the so-called **risky shift** or **cautious shift**, which is the tendency to choose a course of action with either greater or lesser risk when making joint decisions or when making decisions alone after a group discussion. This can be a good thing in some situations, but it can also lead to the groupthink that we discussed in Chapter 3. In military circles, the term **incestuous amplification** describes the individual behavior that may contribute to group polarization. In such situations, each person's OODA loop becomes more dysfunctional as their orientation overrides their observation. This leads to decisions and actions that are further misinterpreted. Thus, an amplification of behavior becomes increasingly disconnected from reality. Think about this, and you'll realize that it's a positive feedback loop. We know where this can lead if the loop is not broken. Research has shown that group polarization is more likely to occur in online discussions when participants are in distributed locations and can't see one another or when they are anonymous and cannot identify one another (Sia, Tan, and Wei 2002). That's of concern, given the increased use of online collaboration.

As individual human beings, our thinking is invariably skewed by good and bad experiences, likes and dislikes, fears, aversions, preferences, beliefs, and so forth. There's no escaping this. What's important is that we each understand our own thought processes, including when, how, and to what extent our individual behavioral traits affect our observations, interpretations, and decision making. If we understand our biases, we are in a better position to appropriately compensate for them. Understanding the cognitive aspects of decision making allows us to adjust our actions to compensate for the biases of others. We've only scratched the surface of this complex but fascinating topic. If you're interested in exploring further, I recommend that you look at the book *Project Decisions: The Art and Science*, by Lev Virine and Michael Trumper (Management Concepts 2007).

> *If we understand our biases, we are in a better position to appropriately compensate for them.*

Consideration 2: Thinking Outside the Box

When people talk about *thinking outside the box*, they are referring to the process of approaching a problem with a different perspective. To even begin that process, you must understand that everyone's box is different and is bounded by their experiences, including their biases. Thinking outside the box requires both observing and orienting outside the box. Accomplishing the first task is not too difficult. We've already discussed the examples of tunnel and peripheral vision. The second task is much harder. For starters, most people are not really sure where the boundaries of their boxes lie.

Boyd wrote about the need to "shatter the rigid conceptual pattern, or patterns, firstly established in our mind" in his classic paper "Destruction and Creation" (Boyd 1976). All orientation begins with a model that is based on preconception. When things are observed, they are merged into that model, effectively destroying the old model and creating a new one. Boyd could have chosen to describe this process as one of evolution, in which a mental model is incrementally updated with observations. Instead, he chose to describe the process in a way that allows for more radical differences between expectations and reality. This is important because people can have difficulty orienting to data that is outside their box. In the worst cases, they fail to orient and their decision-making ability becomes severely compromised. This can happen if the data is extremely unusual and unexpected, and it can be made worse if a person's box of mental conception is small and rigid.

U.S. Army officer Maj. Brian L. Steed refers to situations of extreme change as aberrations. In his book *Piercing the Fog of War* (2009), he studied seven famous battles in which unrecognized extreme change had a profound effect on victory or defeat. Aberrational events are not simply confined to war. Epistomologist Nassim Nicholas Taleb refers to aberrational events as Black Swans and wrote at length about the concept in *The Black Swan: The Impact of the Highly Improbable*. The term *Black Swan* comes from the seventeenth-century European assumption that "all swans are white" simply because no one had ever seen a black swan. This assumption fell apart when black swans were found in Western Australia in the eighteenth century. Taleb classifies Black Swan events as having low predictability and high consequence. People attempt to rationalize such events retrospectively by finding ways to explain how they could have been or were predicted. This illusion of retrospective predictability is yet another bias at work: the **hind-sight bias**. We are often encouraged to expect the unexpected. This seems somewhat nonsensical. If you could expect the unexpected, then it wouldn't be unexpected. Expecting the unexpected is really about being agile enough to respond to unexpected problems when they occur. Additionally, as Taleb recommends, instead of attempting to predict the unpredictable, you should build robust organizations and systems that can weather negative Black Swan events while exploiting positive ones (Taleb 2007).

When the unpredictable happens, we need to be able to react. Extreme change that is revolutionary and not simply evolutionary can shock people and leave them in decision-making paralysis, regardless of the context or domain. This can happen if people are not open to the complete destruction of existing mental models. Their orientation to a situation can be stifled or skewed, and they risk missing the potential effects of change. In reference to Boyd's ideas in *Destruction and Creation,* Steed wisely noted (Steed 2009, xiii): "[W]hat I learned from studying [Boyd's] ideas was that most of us will never be able to completely destroy our conceptual boxes. At the very best, we can only expand them to include different ideas and ways of thinking." As noted in our discussion of biases, **introspection** can help you understand your own box. In competitive situations, it can also be useful in understanding an opponent's box and the options that opponent might consider. In this case, **empathic thinking** can be useful in helping you put yourself in your opponent's mind. Both introspection and empathy are dependent on the individual and situational awareness discussed previously.

The ability to think creatively is also critical to effective orientation, especially in the face of extreme change. The more creative you can be, the less likely you are to be impacted by substantial change. Chapter 13, "Exchange Ideas," covers this topic in more detail.

Consideration 3: Seeing Through the Fog

The **fog of war** is the concept of uncertainty in war. The great Prussian military strategist Carl von Clausewitz described it in his famous military treatise *Vom Kriege,* translated into English as *On War:* "[T]he general unreliability of all information presents a special problem in war: all action takes place, so to speak, in a kind of twilight, which, like fog or moonlight, often tends to make things seem grotesque and larger than they really are" (von Clausewitz, Heuser, and Howard 2007, 89).

Clausewitz's colorful language (English translations of the original German *Vom Kriege* always vary) accounts for the multitude of factors that can make it hard to observe accurately. This is not the more obvious noise that we discussed earlier, but the haziness or ambiguity that can result from such issues as these:

- Lost details due to inaccurate observation resulting from poor eyesight or any kind of deficiency in the acquisition of data, including faulty equipment or bugs in test suites or tools
- Poor communication that may result from a lack of communication skills or information relayed through too many people
- Any kind of confusion or miscalculation

In the worst cases, the fog of war can lead to catastrophe. In military operations, friendly fire casualties may occur when friendly troops are mistakenly identified as enemies or are in positions where they are not expected to be. During the Six-Day War in 1967, Israeli jet fighters and torpedo boats mistakenly identified the *USS Liberty*, a neutral U.S. Navy research ship, as an enemy vessel. The subsequent attacks wounded 171 and killed 34 of the ship's crew. In 2002, four Canadian soldiers were killed and eight others were injured when an American F-16 dropped a laser-guided bomb on them after the pilot came to believe that he and his flight leader were under attack from what he thought was an anti-aircraft battery. The fire was actually part of an anti-tank and machine-gun night firing exercise.

Later, we will study **friction**, another concept to which Clausewitz refers. Whereas friction can adversely affect actions, fog affects observation, orientation, and, ultimately, decision making. In competitive situations, you must find ways to deal with your own fog and friction, while creating it for competitors.

Whereas friction can adversely affect actions, fog affects observation, orientation, and, ultimately, decision making. In competitive situations, you must find ways to deal with your own fog and friction, while creating it for competitors.

Responding to Change

You must look for and identify change so that you can react with an effective decision and action. If you fail to do so, you may compromise the integrity or result of your performance. If you could measure the impact of change on your team's performance and your own ability to respond to that change, what would you learn?

Figure 6.7 is a graph of data representing one team's performance over time in a hypothetical situation. The team could be engaged in any operation you can think of where it is subject to the actions of competitors, opponents, enemies or consumers, partners or customers, and where the team is also seeking to innovate or create something unique. The graph illustrates the following:

- Over time, the team is subject to external change from competitors and consumers. This measurement appears as the column below the axis of the graph, as the segment closest to the axis.

- Similarly, the team is subject to change from within its own walls. This is also shown in the column below the axis, but in the segment farthest from the axis.

- The team must respond to these changes as they occur. This is shown in the column above the axis.

- A failure to respond when a response is required affects the health and quality of the performance. This health is shown as the line at the top of the graph. When the line is below the top of the graph, the quality of the performance is less than optimal.

- The total amount of change over time can be measured as volatility. This is shown as the dashed line above the axis.

- The ability of the team to respond to change is shown as the solid line above the axis. If the team could respond ideally to every change, the responsiveness would always equal the volatility.

- Assuming in this particular hypothetical case that all changes within the team are made for the purpose of innovation and that they do not include mistakes made by individuals within the team, then these changes over time can be measured as innovation. This is shown as the dotted line above the axis.

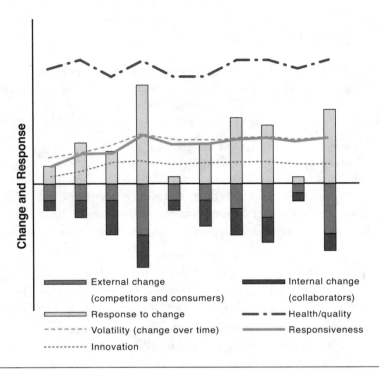

Figure 6.7 *A team's response to change over time*

One of the purposes of this graph is to demonstrate how the need to respond to change is a function of a number of variables. The first of these is **volatility**. In volatile situations, change may occur frequently. Basketball can be a highly volatile game because the action is constant. The ball changes hands often, and points are scored frequently. Consequently, in close games, the lead can move rapidly back and forth between teams. Contrast this with a game such as soccer, in which only one goal may be scored in an entire game. In basketball, if your team has a large lead, two points scored against you may not have much of an impact. But when the opposing team follows it up with a few three-pointers, your team may find itself in danger. This is the effect of **cumulative change**. Another variable that affects the need to respond to change is the degree to which individual changes impact a team's performance. This is known as **sensitivity to change**. Even in situations that are not very volatile, a single change may have a significant impact on a situation. A military sniper may lie in wait for hours or even days for the target to appear. In this situation, changes may occur only rarely, but the single change the sniper is waiting for is the one that can make or break the mission, depending on how the sniper responds.

Another point of the graph is to demonstrate that a point in time is only just that. A basketball team that is six points ahead is winning at that instant. However, if the team hasn't scored in the current quarter, yet the opposing team has closed from a 24-point deficit, things are not trending in their favor and the outlook is decidedly less favorable. Whether you're looking at metrics or some other qualitative measurement, historical trends tell you where you've been and where you may be likely to go next.

Identifying Change

For something to register as a change, it must differ from a baseline point of reference. That baseline may be what was recorded in a previous observation of the current situation or it may be a reference from a previous experience in a similar situation. If the sniper had previously noted no activity, then any activity would register as a change. On the other hand, if the sniper had been watching guard patrols following the same routine endlessly, any deviation from that routine would register as a change.

In the Jazz Process Cycle of Execution, we see that the principle "Listen for change" has a relationship to observing as well as orienting. As soon as the sniper observes something different, it registers as a change, even if he has not had the opportunity to orient to the new situation and decide what the change means. If the sniper is working with others, he might communicate to team members something like, "Stay alert—something is happening. I'm not sure what it is, but there's something going on." Upon orienting himself to the situation and processing the data into usable information, he may realize that there's nothing to worry about: "False alarm—it's not our target."

Having identified that change may originate from different sources, we can think about how we can make it easier to look for and identify change. Change from within a team is the easiest to manage because it originates from sources close to home that we should be able to trust. Figure 6.8 illustrates how multiple cycles of execution interact within a team. Each person's actions can be observed and considered by others in the course of deciding what actions they will each undertake. Not everyone will orient themselves to a given situation in the same way. We each have different criteria for our own actions that affect what we choose to observe and consider. For example, when the pianist plays a chord in a piano trio, the bassist is more likely to listen to the harmony suggested by that chord than is the drummer. This is because one of the most important responsibilities for any bassist is to help define the harmony. In jazz, most songs have a defined sequence of chord progressions that accompany the melody and over which improvisation takes place. Certain chords or sequences of chords are good candidates for substitution by others. For these substitutions to be effective, they often require that the pianist and bassist work together. A drummer is not so concerned about such things. What's important to note about change originating from within is that members of a team each have the ability to affect how quickly and accurately others will interpret their actions by acting transparently. In Chapter 4, "Build Trust and Respect," we briefly discussed how transparency helps build trust, which is essential to keeping a team unified. In Chapter 8, "Act Transparently," we discuss how openness and transparency improve execution.

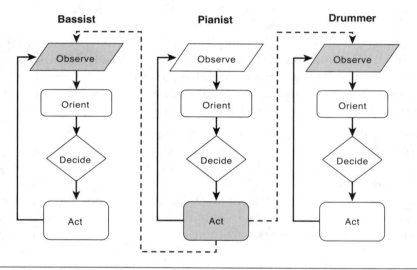

Figure 6.8 *Interaction between collaborators*

Identifying change from customers is important for teams whose livelihood depends on the purchasing behaviors of those customers. The earlier a team can recognize such change, the more time it has to react. It's better to hear that your best customer is seriously considering a switch to your strongest competitor's offering than it is to find out that they have already made the purchase and abandoned you altogether.

Not surprisingly, the hardest change to manage is that which originates from competitors. Just as you are trying to outmaneuver your competitors and get inside their execution cycles, they are trying to do the same to you. It stands to reason that part of their efforts involve hiding or obfuscating their actions as much as possible. Your competitors will purposely seek to maximize the impact of their changes, with the express intent of affecting the integrity and quality of your performance. This makes it even more important that you make a concerted effort to look for and identify their actions and determine their impact on your operations.

Recapitulation

- Observing is the act of acquiring data through various inputs or senses.

- Uncompromised observation begins with expanding one's field of view and being open to everything that is going on.

- Orienting is the act of making sense of data, turning it into information that can be used for decision making. Listening is a specific example of orienting.

- Personal awareness is observing your own actions.

- Team awareness is observing the actions of collaborators with whom you work.

- Situational awareness is observing consumers you work for and competitors you work against.

- The danger of receiving a lot of data is saturation. It's important to know how to filter the useful information from noise.

- Managing solely by numbers can lead to failure.

- It is important to understand how cognitive biases affect the way in which you observe and orient.

- To think outside the box, you must know the boundaries of the box and be able to observe and orient outside it.

- It is essential to recognize when the fog of war is making observation difficult and then try to see through it.

- Learn to identify change that requires a response.

CHAPTER 7

Lead on Demand

*"Do not wait for leaders; do it alone,
person to person."*
—Mother Teresa

Our Fascination with Leadership

If any singular aspect of organizational behavior engages people, it is leadership. Our history, present lives, and futures are greatly influenced by the actions of leaders. We are fascinated with the behavior of leaders in business, politics, science, sports, arts, religion, military, and other fields of endeavor. Think about some of the best known leaders of the last hundred years. Here's some that came immediately to mind:

Adolf Hitler	John F. Kennedy
Al Capone	Joseph Stalin
Albert Einstein	Madeleine Albright
Barack Obama	Mahatma Gandhi
Benito Mussolini	Margaret Thatcher
Bill Gates	Mao Tse Tung
Charles Manson	Martin Luther King, Jr.
Charles Taylor	Miles Davis
Duke Ellington	Mother Teresa
Dwight Eisenhower	Nelson Mandela
Fidel Castro	Neville Chamberlain
Franklin Roosevelt	Osama bin Laden
George W. Bush	Robert Mugabe
Gloria Steinem	Saddam Hussein
Grace Murray Hopper	Sigmund Freud
Henry Ford	Stephen Hawking
Hillary Clinton	Walt Disney
Howard Hughes	Winston Churchill

Some of these leaders are famous or infamous for their successes, and others for their failures. Some pursued goals of greater good, while others were seriously misguided in their quests. Some actively managed people, while others led by example or by simply declaring beliefs or opinions. Regardless of their missions, the path they took, or its eventual outcome, we continue to be intrigued by their exploits.

We read books, watch movies, and attend seminars to learn about leadership and improve leadership skills. By studying the actions, successes, and failures of other leaders, we learn what may or may not work for us as leaders. That knowledge is gleaned not just from studying publicly acclaimed leaders, but also by observing and sometimes receiving advice from the leaders in places where we live, work, play, and worship.

Despite our fascination with leadership and the wealth of material on the subject, I have always found two things surprising about our collective view of leadership:

1. No widespread agreement exists for the definition of leadership.
2. We tend to think that leadership is the sole responsibility of a select group or persons.

In the foreword to *The Leader of the Future: New Visions, Strategies, and Practices for the Next Era* (Hesselbein, Goldsmith, and Beckhard, 1997, xii), Peter Drucker wrote, "The only definition of a leader is someone who has followers." He added that leaders are highly visible and set examples, and that leadership is about responsibility and results. In *21 Refutable Laws of Leadership* (Maxwell 1998, 17), John Maxwell wrote, "leadership is influence—nothing more, nothing less." Warren Bennis is often quoted as having said, "Leadership is a function of knowing yourself, having a vision that is well communicated, building trust among colleagues, and taking effective action to realize your own leadership potential." Leadership is arguably all of this and more. I believe, however, that over the years, the concept of leadership has become way too complicated. Quite simply, one specific point defines leadership more than anything else: taking initiative.

Taking Initiative

To take the initiative is to take the first step without prompting. Anyone and everyone can and should be encouraged to take initiative; if everyone does so, it makes for a highly agile team. We can all take initiative within the scope of our roles and responsibilities. This doesn't require any specialized training, nor does it necessitate any innate ability. Initiative is not and should not be solely limited to those in obvious positions of leadership. If a team's performance is to remain in good health in the face of constant change, every member in the team must actively look for and identify change and then react to it individually or as part of a coordinated response.

Open source guru Linus Torvalds, who founded the Linux project, has been quoted as saying, "given enough eyeballs, all bugs are shallow" (Raymond 1997). This essentially means that the more people you have observing a software release for bugs and reviewing the proposed fixes to them, the easier it will be to find and fix those bugs. If you have enough people on the job, every bug will be found and fixed within a relatively short period of time. This is a principle that holds true in a more general sense: If every member of a team is observing and identifying the areas that require attention, the team is well on its way to delivering high-quality performance.

So far, we've focused mainly on reacting to external changes. Change also comes from within a team. Jazz musicians are masters of this kind of change. During the course of a performance, the change generated by external forces such as the response of the audience, the acoustics of an unfamiliar venue, and the behavior of temperamental instruments is not very substantial. For jazz musicians, the greatest source of change comes from within. In their quest to constantly create music that is unpredictable, exciting, and unique, the musicians are continuously and purposefully introducing change into their environments. They do this by changing personnel lineups, often introducing new musicians or musicians they know will be foils to one another. They do it during performances by initiating changes in musical elements such as harmony, rhythm, groove, time, and melody.

For jazz musicians, the greatest source of change comes from within. In their quest to constantly create music that is unpredictable, exciting, and unique, the musicians are continuously and purposefully introducing change into their environments.

Decentralizing Leadership

When asked to name leaders in an organization, most people tend to identify only a small group of people. Leadership can be present in many domains. Successful leadership in one domain does not necessarily guarantee equivalent success—or even any success—in other domains. This is immediately evident in a common problem that arises in many organizations: People who are strong practitioners in their field are promoted into positions of leading people without possessing the desire, knowledge, and skills to succeed in that very different role. This problem aside, often many leaders exist in practice, even though only one person owns the team's overall successes and failures. This is especially true in multidisciplined teams comprised of talented individuals who are expected to demonstrate leadership in their respective fields. High-performance teams may have many individuals who are both practice leaders in their respective fields and effective team or project leaders. Such a group of people may even be collectively engaged in simultaneous projects in which they each function as practice leaders or project or team leaders, as required.

This is precisely what happens in the jazz community when a group of musicians work together regularly. At different times, they may each lead gigs or recording projects in which the other musicians work as "sidemen." Take, for example, the bands of Miles Davis from 1955 to 1964. The period began with Davis's first quintet, which performed from 1955 to 1958. The band consisted of Davis (trumpet), John Coltrane (tenor saxophone), Red Garland (piano), Paul Chambers (double bass), and "Philly" Joe Jones (drums). This group is most famous for four classic recordings on the Prestige label that were released in 1956 as *Relaxin' with the Miles Davis Quintet*, *Steamin' with the Miles Davis Quintet*, *Workin' with the Miles Davis Quintet*, and *Cookin' with the Miles Davis Quintet*. In 1958, Davis added Julian "Cannonball" Adderley to record *Milestones* as a sextet. Shortly thereafter, he replaced Garland and Jones with Bill Evans and Jimmy Cobb, although Evans didn't stay long and left the same year, to be replaced by Wynton Kelly. Evans can be heard on the album *['] 58 Sessions*, and he also returned briefly in 1959 to record the classic *Kind of Blue*, in which he played on all tracks except one, "Freddie Freeloader," which had Kelly at the keys. Coltrane left in 1960 and was replaced by Sonny Stitt and then Hank Mobley; in 1963, Kelly, Chambers, and Cobb left, and that began the transition to what came to be known as Davis's Second Great Quintet, featuring a whole new lineup of sidemen.

During this time, Garland recorded with his own trio, featuring Chambers and Art Taylor (drums). They recorded the album *Groovy* in 1956–1957 and were double-billed with Coltrane on the 1957 album *Traneing In.* In 1959, Coltrane recorded his famous *Giant Steps* album with Chambers, Taylor, and Tommy Flanagan (piano). Between 1956 and 1959, Chambers recorded more than ten albums as a leader, usually with Philly Joe or Taylor on drums, although on the 1957 *Paul Chambers Quintet,* he had Elvin Jones, who later held the drum chair in Coltrane's quartet of the 1960s. Believe it or not, I've tried to keep all this simple for the sake of this example—I didn't even mention Cannonball's albums as a leader. To hammer home my point, Cannonball recorded *Somethin' Else* in 1958, with Davis as a sideman. All this clearly illustrates that jazz musicians are comfortable working as leaders or as sidemen, and they alternate between these roles frequently and regularly. Busy musicians who are both in-demand sidemen and leaders of their own projects may find themselves fulfilling both roles in the course of a week or even a day.

Jazz musicians simply cannot let leadership roles remain statically assigned if they want to create interesting, innovative music.

Jazz leadership changes not just between gigs, but also during the performance of a single piece of music. The leader of the gig might choose the tune and count it off, but at various times during the performance, different musicians take on leadership roles, and others follow as necessary. This happens most obviously when jazz musicians take turns performing as soloists and then provide accompaniment for another musician's solos. However, the reassignment of leadership occurs even more frequently and less obviously than that. Sometimes even for just an instant, a musician who is currently playing as an accompanist may take on a leadership role to direct a specific change in the music. For example, a bassist may switch between playing in two and playing in four, just as we discussed in Chapter 1, "Use Just Enough Rules." A musician may initiate a change even without knowing precisely where it will lead. The improvised endings we discussed in Chapter 1 are a good example of this. Musicians take a number of steps to completely wrap up a piece, and the precise steps or even number of steps is never known beforehand. Jazz musicians simply cannot let leadership roles remain statically assigned if they want to create interesting, innovative music.

Jazz musicians have been using decentralized leadership for almost a hundred years. We noted in the section "Essentials of Execution" that decentralized leadership, not overwhelming force, made *Blitzkrieg* tactics so successful. Why has the ideology of decentralized leadership failed to permeate mainstream thought? One reason may be that those with the ambition to obtain positions of leadership and authority generally do whatever they can to retain their power. When faced with failure, they are more likely to extend their reach of authority than share it with others. Citino noted this of the development of *Bewegungskrieg*, or "maneuver warfare" (Citino 1999, 16):

> *It was not, by and large, an innovation devised by Germany's military leadership. It was the German infantryman, faced with an impossible situation on the modern battlefield and saddled with old tactics that simply did not work, who instigated this tactical revolution.*

When leaders straitjacket people with restrictive command and reporting structures, they inhibit creativity and agility and limit their organization's ability to respond to change. They need to understand that the path to success lies in giving up control.

When leaders straitjacket people with restrictive command and reporting structures, they inhibit creativity and agility and limit their organization's ability to respond to change. They need to understand that the path to success lies in giving up control.

In recent years, a new wave of interest in decentralized leadership has emerged. In 2006, authors Ori Brafman and Rod A. Beckstrom released their book *The Starfish and the Spider*. Despite the subtitle, *The Unstoppable Power of Leaderless Organizations*, the book is not about organizations without any leadership; it's about organizations in which the leadership is decentralized. Brafman and Beckstrom's focus is not so much about how decentralized leadership enables agility and innovation, but how it enables redundancy. The book is named for the difference between cutting off a spider's head and cutting off a starfish's leg; the spider dies, whereas the starfish grows a new leg. The severed leg also can grow into an entirely new starfish because it has a decentralized neural structure that supports regeneration. The book references many examples in business, drawing attention to how Napster and peer-to-peer sites have impacted the music industry, how telephone companies have lost business to Skype, how Encyclopedia Britannica has suffered because of Wikipedia, and how Craigslist has devastated newspaper ad revenues. It also goes back in history to the Spanish army's failure to defeat the Apaches in North America and details the current challenges for the United States and its allies in defeating Al Queda. Not only is the book hot in business circles, but it has garnered considerable interest from senior U.S. military and intelligence leaders, who have also consulted with the authors in their attempts to better understand and fight terrorist organizations (Jones 2007). As further proof of the book's wide-ranging influence, Beckstrom was appointed in 2008 as the head of the U.S. National Cyber Security Center. Although Beckstrom has little experience in cybersecurity, the U.S. government believed that his understanding of starfish principles could help in the fight against the decentralized band of hackers and cybercriminals (Epstein 2008).

Although it may be unpleasant to acknowledge the success of modern terrorist organizations, such self-organizing networks demonstrate how common goals and passion, not hierarchical command structures, can fuel success. Margaret Wheatley, an acclaimed researcher and consultant in the field of organizational behavior, wrote (Wheatley 2007):

> *Although these groups appear leaderless, they in fact are well-led by their passion, rage, and conviction. They share an ideal or purpose that gives them a group identity and which compels them to act .... People who are deeply connected to a cause don't need directives, rewards, or leaders to tell them what to do. Inflamed, passionate, and working with like-minded others, they create increasingly extreme means to support their cause.*

Self-organization is a natural property of the world around us. On a cosmic scale, scientists have long been fascinated with the ever-evolving structure found among stars, planets, and galaxies. On a microscopic scale, we can study molecular self-assembly. It's a lot easier, however, to observe the behavior of insect colonies, flocks of birds, and schools of fish. A colony of as many as 200,000 virtually blind army ants can stage huge swarm raids in which they organize themselves into a column up to 20 meters wide and over 100 meters in length, with the capacity to transport more than 30,000 prey items per hour. Such raids are conducted within severe time constraints, as the ants must be in a position to move to a new nest site and foraging arena by the time darkness comes. The ants perform this amazing act of collaboration not through a chain of management, but simply by interacting with one another (Couzin and Franks 2003).

Helping the Team Navigate

Teams and organizations are often compared to ships, with the leader as the captain. To travel from one place to another, a ship must avoid collisions with other sea-faring craft, as well as steer clear of obstacles such as land masses, reefs, and bad weather. In some cases, the nature and behavior of these various obstacles is well-known. In other cases, they can be harder to predict because they are constantly changing or simply not well-understood.

As the captain of a ship, you have a few basic options to help you avoid known and unknown obstacles. You can alter the direction of the ship, or you can alter its speed. If commands such as "Right 5 degrees rudder, steady course 090" or "All engines ahead full" sound familiar, then you know what I'm talking about. If you're inclined toward science fiction, there's no reason you can't think of the ship as a space-faring vessel. In that case, the dialogue is more likely to be, "Come to heading 113 mark 5" or "Go to one-half impulse," and, of course, there's always "Maximum warp—engage!" for when things are rather urgent.

As with a ship, a team has the ability to make course corrections to successfully navigate the challenges and hurdles it encounters. We already know that one reason to issue a navigational command is in response to change. Change may be generated from outside a team or from within, such as when someone on a team creates a problem that requires a correctional response by another person. However, not all navigational commands are issued in response to problems. Similar to jazz musicians, high-performance teams don't just react to change; they generate it themselves because they are constantly seeking to innovate and create a unique offering.

The ability to issue a navigational command is one of the most vital and fundamental elements of leadership. Without a doubt, a very important consequence of issuing a command is seeing its implementation through to completion. Taking the first step along a different path, however, is also critically important. This responsibility cannot simply be left to the people who fulfill the more obvious, visible roles as leaders. This duty must be shared, particularly in multidisciplined teams. A single person may find it difficult to fully understand every discipline within a team. One person also may have a hard time unfailingly identifying every obstacle and challenge and determining the actions needed to navigate around or through them, let alone recognize the new paths that may help a team improve its outlook. When people in obvious roles of leadership insist on relying solely on their own initiative and spurn the suggestions and recommendations of others, they often fail. Even when they don't, they limit the possibilities for their team.

In many teams, a conscious effort must be made to ensure that people feel empowered to issue navigational commands. When people work as part of a team, they should each feel responsible for helping to steer the ship and maintain momentum. If any member of a team identifies a problem or has ideas about how the team can improve its performance, that member should feel empowered to share such findings with the rest of the team and, where appropriate, participate in formulating a response.

The problem, of course, is that if everyone issued navigational commands at the same time or without coordination, disaster—or, at least, downright confusion—would ensue. In any reasonably sized organization, it's hard for the average person to simply issue a navigational command and turn the ship around. Even when the ship is bearing down on an iceberg, many organizations simply cannot respond quickly enough. Especially when time is critical, it's important to have agile decision-making processes. But how do you avoid the chaos that would result from everyone trying to lead at the same time?

The Importance of Following

Jazz musicians constantly focus on the team and are guided by the team's rules. In Chapter 1 you read about the principle "Put the team first." In Chapters 11 and 12 we cover the rules "Maintain momentum" and "Stay healthy." These are all critical rules that good jazz musicians are always keenly aware of. In our study of "Put the team first," we looked at the trade-off between individuality and the team. In my experience, jazz musicians generally tend to have a much stronger sense of putting the team first than classical musicians do, although exceptions certainly exist. This is a potentially controversial statement, so let me explain.

In a symphony orchestra, musicians tend to focus on the music in front of them and on the conductor. In a jazz orchestra, the musicians tend to focus more on the ensemble, even when there is a conductor out front. This phenomenon is not simply a function of the size of the ensemble or the style of music being performed at the time. I've performed in and conducted small and large groups in which the musicians had to play the music as scripted on the page. In some cases, these groups have consisted entirely of classical musicians; in other cases, they were comprised entirely of jazz musicians. Sometimes the group included musicians who played with equal competence in either genre. I've also performed in all kinds of jazz groups where the music was improvised. In some cases, the music was entirely improvised, what some people might call "free jazz." In other cases, it was more typical jazz, in which we played specific tunes but improvised the specific notes and purposely played with and explored the limits of each song's melody, harmony, rhythm, and so forth. As I noted in Chapter 2, "Employ Top Talent," in most classical music ensembles, there tends to be a lot of doubling. For example, many violins play the same first violin part in even a small string orchestra. Yet quite often, many of those violinists are trying to play more as soloists than as a unified section. This notion is gleaned both from my own experience and from comments relayed to me by other musicians playing in such sections. The opposite tends to occur with jazz musicians. Even in large jazz orchestras, where everyone has an individual part, everyone seems to focus more on the entire ensemble.

Because jazz musicians are constantly switching between the roles of leading and following, they have a unique dyadic perspective that broadens their perception and makes them more empathetic to others in the group. This ultimately makes them both better leaders and better followers, with the ability to rapidly and fluidly switch between these roles. In military organizations, regular units rely on strict leadership and followership, whereas soldiers of elite commando fighting forces are encouraged to think more independently and lead individually as necessary. The command structure of the Special Forces Operational Detachment Alpha (ODA), or "A-teams," which we discussed in the Introduction, is well-defined. The soldiers, however, are always prepared to split into smaller groups or even handle objectives individually, if needed. This kind of shared governance can also work in organizations by replacing strict lines of hierarchy with more fluid and dynamic relationships that allow leadership to be shared and reallocated on demand.

In jazz, the musicians must cope with frequent and unknown change. For example, they often don't know who will solo next and for how long. They don't know exactly what the other musicians will play. Perhaps someone will change the groove or modulate to another key. In smaller groups, usually no single individual, such as a conductor, acts as a command and control center. All this contributes to a higher likelihood that the ensemble may lose stability and momentum. Jazz musicians must be highly attuned to the group's output and state if they are to ensure that doesn't happen.

Finally, jazz offers many opportunities for improvisation. This gives musicians an outlet for creativity and self-expression and makes it less likely that they will try to exert their individuality when it is not really called for. Think about all those virtuoso violinists or cellists playing together in an orchestra. Most of them rarely get an opportunity to shine or express their innate creativity. Is it really surprising that the odd violinist may at times try to stand out from the section or ensemble? This is especially likely when a conductor makes every decision, and it's made worse with a maestro who insists that he or she knows everything.

Jazz musicians must follow the principle of "Lead on demand," but as with any other real-time activity, there is simply no time or opportunity to make decisions by committee. If a musician wants to take the music to a specific place, he or she has to make that split-second decision and make it happen by communicating through the medium of the music, perhaps assisted by a glance or a nod of the head. Although this happens a great deal, it is also true that dialogues often arise. We've already discussed some of the interplay that can occur between a drummer and a bassist. We delve into this further in Chapter 13, "Exchange Ideas."

When I'm playing with musicians who are able to lead and follow, I feel empowered because I know that we can collectively take the music to new places and that we will be there for each other no matter what happens. This is the essence of a high-performance team. It's made possible through a shared desire to lead on demand while striving to adhere to the other principles of the Jazz Process.

Recapitulation

- The most important part of leading is taking initiative. Initiative is not and should not be solely limited to those in obvious positions of leadership. Every member in a team must actively look for and identify change and then react to it individually or as part of a coordinated response.

- When leaders straitjacket people with restrictive command and reporting structures, they inhibit creativity and agility and limit their organization's ability to respond to change. The path to success lies in giving up control.

- Jazz musicians avoid potential chaos and conflict that may result from decentralized leadership by balancing individual creativity and team stability. Their understanding of the critical need to do this is developed from the experience of constantly alternating between roles of leading and following.

CHAPTER 8

Act Transparently

"The spirit of jazz is the spirit of openness."
—Herbie Hancock

Transparency in the Execution Cycle

In most disciplines, sometimes it is vital for the rest of the team to follow through on one person's initiative—or, as I've referred to it previously, a navigational command. It might be a base hit with the score tied and two out in the late innings of the seventh game of the World Series. It could be a critical bid for a large contract that could save a company teetering on the brink of financial ruin. Success in such vital situations can depend greatly on transparency. Transparency can improve the strength and speed of execution. As we noted in Chapter 4, "Build Trust and Respect," transparency speeds up the process of building trust, which, in turn, gives a team the confidence to tackle challenges. In the context of the execution cycle, transparency affects what you ultimately communicate to others in these ways:

- Reducing the time required for others to observe your actions and increasing the likelihood that those actions will be observed
- Reducing the time required for others to understand and interpret the impact of your actions and increasing the accuracy of their interpretations

Figure 8.1 illustrates these effects and the resultant tightening of the feedback loop. Improving the speed with which feedback is identified, understood, and fed back into a system is an important concept in just-in-time manufacturing and concurrent engineering. Identifying problems earlier reduces overall cycle times and costs.

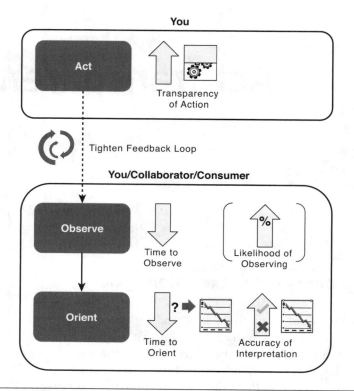

Figure 8.1   *Effects of increasing transparency*

Transparency is alluring.

Transparency has the potential to grow teams, communities, and customer bases by attracting people. A few reasons explain this. Transparency is alluring in the same way that passion is infectious. People appreciate honesty, openness, and authenticity. Most people have no desire to associate with someone who is phony or dishonest. Another reason is that people are naturally curious to know what goes on behind the scenes. Finally, transparency can give people comfort by alleviating any fears or concerns they might have about the unknown.

In developing its Jazz software platform and Jazz-based products such as Rational Team Concert, IBM is leveraging transparency. Dubbed Open Commercial Software Development, the approach is inspired by the practices of open source development but uses commercial licensing. All the software development is done on a public web site where anyone can see the team's plans, including the work they have committed to do for each release and how they are progressing. They can engage in discussions with the team through mailing lists and forums, report bugs and submit requests for feature enhancements, and read the minutes of the team's meetings. Most significantly, they can download new builds of components and products that are made available on a regular basis throughout the entire development cycle. Contrast this with traditional closed development models in which a team does all its development behind closed walls and issues a few alpha or beta releases toward the end of the development cycle to only a limited group of testers, who often must sign nondisclosure agreements. IBM's approach creates a tight feedback loop between the community and the development team. Customers can see everything as it happens, giving them the opportunity to provide input at the most appropriate times and the confidence to base their plans on a known set of features to be delivered on a known date. If the team is doing well, they may receive positive feedback. On the other hand, if they are doing badly, they may receive negative feedback that everyone else can see and comment on. This might seem like a bad thing, but by taking careful note of such negative feedback, IBM teams can improve their processes and products in a timely and continuous manner. More significantly, by establishing this level of openness in commercial software development, IBM is setting a standard for other companies.

How do we increase transparency? Figure 8.2 illustrates four vital elements of transparency. For many people, openness is the first element that comes to mind on this subject. Yet authenticity appears as the first element in our illustration. Let's explore this by explaining the different ways in which jazz and classical music are often performed and received.

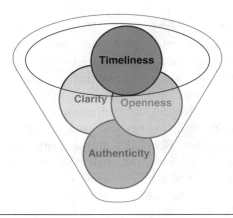

Figure 8.2 *Transparency*

Jazz pianist Herbie Hancock has been quoted as saying, "The spirit of jazz is the spirit of openness." When jazz musicians work together, they are always open about their actions and intentions. When one musician decides to take the music in a specific direction, that musician wants other members of the ensemble to note and respond to his or her action. The need for the rest of the team to respond in a way that strengthens the impact of the performance and reinforces its integrity may vary with the specific action. In some cases, the need may be critical, and a failure to propagate the initiative may push the performance right off the rails. In other cases, the change may be subtle; a lack of response from the other musicians might result in not a weaker performance, but simply one that follows a different path than desired by the musician who initiated the change.

The principle of acting openly in jazz is employed not only by collaborating musicians, but also by the consumers who listen to the music. Audiences at a live jazz performance provide authentic, timely feedback to the musicians. When I'm playing jazz, I can look out and scan the audience; quite often I see smiles, nodding heads, tapping feet, and snapping fingers. When jazz audiences are enjoying the music, they are physically demonstrative. Sometimes they even shout out their appreciation. When a musician finishes an improvised solo, they applaud—and then, of course, they applaud the entire band at the end of the piece.

Contrast this with classical music audiences. Their body language is often far less revealing. If I'm playing in a classical music concert or if I'm in the audience at such a performance, I notice that the expression on the faces of audience members is often very blank. I don't believe this has anything to do with the style of music, as I believe Bach "grooves" just as much as Ellington. One significant factor may be the etiquette that has evolved over the years for classical music performances. Classical music audiences never applaud during a piece of music, and, quite sadly, an unspoken rule holds that audiences should applaud only at the conclusion of the final movement of an extended work, not between individual movements. It wasn't always this way. The "applause rule" for classical music is a convention introduced in the twentieth century. In previous centuries, it was quite usual to applaud not only after individual movements, but even during the music, just as jazz audiences do today. Alex Ross, the music critic for *The New Yorker*, researched this topic in 2005 and noted that Mozart reveled in timely feedback from the audience in the 1778 premiere of his *Paris* symphony, while Brahms lamented the lack of it at the premiere of his "First Piano Concerto" in 1859 (Ross 2005). Ross also supplied his opinion of what Mozart might make of today's classical music conventions (Ross 2005):

Mozart here describes [in a letter about the success of his Paris sym-
phony premiere] an atmosphere similar to that of modern jazz clubs:
the audience demonstrates its sophistication not by remaining silent,
but by acknowledging the composer's best ideas with bursts of
applause. What would Mozart think of our modern concert culture?
I'm guessing he'd admire the precision of the performances, and he'd
appreciate the relative lack of chatter and noisemaking, but he might
well be disturbed by the generally passive, frigid demeanor of
audiences.

Fortunately for jazz musicians, their audiences have never developed such habits. By delivering timely feedback to the musicians, jazz audiences help improve the quality of performances as they evolve. It's a benefit enjoyed by both the producers (the musicians) and the consumers (the audience), and one that some classical listeners could well heed. Ross also claimed that some conductors are to blame for propagating the restrictive conventions of applause in classical music:

It's not surprising that conductors were intent on stamping out spon-
taneous clapping. To refrain from applause heightens focus on the
personality of the conductor. Silence is the measure of the unbreak-
able spell that Maestro is supposedly casting on us. A big ovation at
the end salutes his mastery of the architecture of the work, or what-
ever. Whereas a burst of applause after a first movement or a Scherzo
is probably inspired by a soloist's brilliant playing, or by a powerful
collective effort by the musicians, or by the infectious energy of the
music itself. Perhaps that's a cynical theory, but orchestra players
might be able to back me up.

I don't think this a cynical theory, and I know there are indeed orchestra players who would back up Ross if they felt free to speak their minds. Many symphony musicians put up with the absurd behavior of ego-centric conductors because there are very few positions in orchestras and they simply love performing the music. I feel strongly enough about the antics of maestros that I go out of my way to do the exact opposite, as I described in Chapter 3, "Put the Team First." The behavior Ross pointed out goes directly against the principle "Put the team first." It denies individual team members valuable direct feedback from consumers that could both motivate them and help them improve their performances. Ross also added:

By the way, I've noticed a new trend—Thoughtful Celebrity Conduc-
tors holding their arms motionless for ten or fifteen seconds after the

end of some vast construction by Bruckner or Mahler. "Do not yet applaud!" those frozen arms say. "Do not profane the moment!" If a truly wonderful performance has taken place, it's nice to savor the silence. But if it's only a mediocre run-through, then that priestlike call for silence becomes pretentious and absurd.

Ross is criticizing the lack of authenticity in such performances as a result of the conductor's behavior. For many people, certain experiences are fulfilling only if they are completely genuine. It takes only one fake element to mar that. By forcing audiences to withhold all applause until the end and then pressuring them into delivering a rousing hand when one may actually not be warranted, the conductors Ross describes are destroying what might otherwise be a genuine connection between the artists and the audiences.

Although transparency does require one to be open, it doesn't mean much if what you have to communicate is not truthful. That's why, in our study of transparency, authenticity needs to be considered before even focusing on openness. You must *act* openly, but you must first *be* authentic.

Authenticity

In the context of transparency, authenticity is a measure of truthfulness. Is something what it claims to be? In the context of the execution cycle, authenticity is not about whether a specific offering is real or fake because you can be absolutely honest in saying that something is totally fake. Some markets will always have fake products or services. Some people don't care whether a product or service is fake, or *faux*, as we often call legitimately known fakes. Other people simply can't afford the genuine article; in other cases, it's simply impractical to have the real deal. There's only one *Mona Lisa* painted by Leonardo da Vinci, and it hangs on a wall in the Musée du Louvre in Paris, France. However, there are thousands upon thousands of reproductions, none of which could be easily passed off as the original.

Authenticity is a measure of truthfulness.

What concerns us most is the case when something isn't real but people try to pass it off as such. These duplicitous people attempt to obfuscate their deceit by creating the perception of authenticity. This suggests that the perception of authenticity actually plays a greater role in the execution cycle than authenticity itself. Being truly authentic is more important, but problems can occur when one really is authentic but can't convince others that this is the case.

If an observer in the cycle of execution can't rely on the veracity of what he or she observes, the observations have no value. We look for and value authenticity in all our interactions with people and organizations. Precious time is wasted when we have to constantly question the authenticity of what others in our team say or do. Nobody is inclined to follow a leader who may not be fully on the level.

Not only relationships between collaborators are impacted by authenticity. The greatest demand for authenticity comes from consumers, whether they are retail customers, businesses, or government agencies. Whether it's a Rolex, a diamond ring, a genuine part for a computer, or a service for your car, knowing that something is the real McCoy is important, if that's what someone is expecting. On the other hand, countless industries produce reproductions, simulations, copies, and replicas and present them as such. Authenticity is about being truthful and honest, not about whether a product or service is genuine.

It's important to note that, regardless of whether an offering is genuine or a known fake, the need for quality always exists. If a violinist can't afford a real Stradivarius but can get a copy of one, the musician will, of course, prefer an instrument that is well made. Quality stands out as the most significant management imperative of the twentieth century, beginning in the 1920s, when Walter Shewhart applied statistical theory to quality control. His principles lived on in the work of W. Edwards Deming, who, along with quality gurus such as Joseph Juran and Kaoru Ishikawa, established a mid-twentieth-century quality movement in Japan that birthed concepts such as Total Quality Management, Total Quality Control, and Kaizen. Some argue that the quality movement has faded, but its demise is greatly overstated, and the quest for quality continues to live on in standards such as Six Sigma and ISO 9000. More significantly, quality management is no longer limited to manufacturing, but has moved into domains such as government services, healthcare, education, and environmental management. James Gilmore and B. Joseph Pine II, authors of *Authenticity: What Consumers Really Want,* claim that authenticity is the new business imperative, and businesses need to focus on being more original, genuine, sincere, and authentic (Gilmore and Pine II 2007, 1). If that's true, and a part of being authentic is being honest about problems and defects, then the quest for authenticity will encourage companies to improve the quality of their products and services.

So how does one create the perception of authenticity? Figure 8.3 includes some of the most important assessments.

Surprisingly, appearances can create a perception of authenticity. If two men explain the same financial investment, but one is dressed in a suit and the other in jeans and a T-shirt, which one are you more likely to think has given you accurate information? If you chose the man in the suit, then you're right, but only for you! Someone else may choose the other man. Social psychologists have come to understand that we render all kinds of **implicit theories**—or, as they are perhaps more appropriately called, naïve theories—based on stereotypes of personality traits, appearances, gender, sexual orientation, and other factors. For example, we may believe that someone is honest because he or she is warm and friendly. Although these kinds of associative judgments are highly subjective and not everyone will draw the same conclusions, they are precisely what marketing companies analyze. Endorsements by celebrities, testimonials from supposed experts, sex appeal, and respectable-sounding names or names that sound similar to those of respected products are all things marketers may employ based on how they believe they will affect their target market's perception of authenticity. The aim is to increase the perception of authenticity by *associating* the offering with something positive.

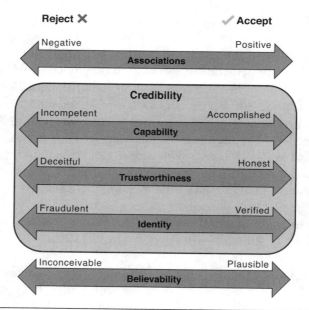

Figure 8.3   *Perception of authenticity*

Perhaps the most important determination in accepting a perception of authenticity is that of **credibility**. If we doubted every single thing we observed, our productivity would be impacted beyond measure. In many cases, we simply have to accept things at face value unless there is a reason to doubt them. We base such acceptance and assumption of authenticity largely on credibility. Three factors help determine credibility. **Capability** may be measured if a party representing something had a hand in producing it or evaluating it. Skill and experience are usually measures of capability. **Trustworthiness** is a measure of reliability, usually established with a positive track record. Finally, **identity** measures the validity of one's claim to be whom he or she professes to be. Someone may tell us that Bob Smith is responsible for a particular piece of work. You know a person named Bob Smith and find him to be capable and trustworthy, but he may not be the same Bob Smith as the one in question. In this age of identity theft, establishing someone's real identity may be vitally important, especially in online transactions.

Associations that are used to increase the perception of authenticity typically leverage credibility. For example, Bob has just joined a company and is eager to impress. After some careful analysis, he produces a report that indicates the company's performance will be dramatically impacted unless they make major changes to meet the threats of a new competitive offering. The report likely will be controversial, and Bob is not well-known in the company. He knows that Anne, a respected vice president, agrees with his findings, so he asks her to endorse the report by adding a foreword to it.

Unfortunately, some associations themselves lack authenticity. At the extreme end are completely fabricated associations that are dishonest, unethical, and fraudulent. Less obvious are the associations that stretch the truth. I have often observed that some musicians boast that they have played with a number of well-known performers. Upon investigation, it turns out that they were a member of a large ensemble such as an orchestra and played when the big-name musician was appearing as a guest soloist. The big-name musician never knew the musician's name and didn't ask to work with him or her specifically. Although the association is not completely false, it implies a personal association that doesn't exist. The association was really between the big-name musician and the orchestra.

Gilmore and Pine argue that, in today's economy, goods and services are no longer adequate. Consumers want experiences and "memorable events that engage them in an inherently personal way" (Gilmore and Pine II 2007, 1). Jazz is perceived as genuine music because it affords musicians a lot of room for personal expression. Although playing notes written by someone else undoubtedly allows for this, improvisation takes self-expression to another level. It gives audiences a much larger window into the musician's creativity and a chance to connect with him or her on a more personal level. The opportunity to connect personally is why blogging has become one of the most important tools for increasing transparency. Blogs are authentic not so much because of their content, but because they originate from identifiable individuals who write posts and respond to comments using their own words instead of those of some indistinguishable corporate mouthpiece.

Believability is an important consideration in determining authenticity. Even when we observe something from an accomplished, trusted, known source, if it's utterly inconceivable, we question its probability. On the other hand, if something is entirely plausible, we might be inclined to believe it even if the source is not particularly credible.

Openness

If an organization is akin to a black box, only those within that organization know its internal workings. People outside the organization know only what goes into the organization and what goes out. On the surface, this doesn't seem unreasonable. After all, as long as the organization gets its work done, does anybody really need to know how it goes about doing it?

Unfortunately, things are not so simple. Many companies are publicly listed, so thousands of shareholders share ownership and have a right to know what goes on inside their company. No organization is truly self-contained in its operation. Simply by hiring people, purchasing materials, or extracting them from the Earth and then producing and making available a service or product, that organization affects the world around it. The organization has an impact on individuals, suppliers, the environment, buyers, and a great many others. What if a company ...

- Employs people desperate for a job but doesn't pay them a fair wage or provide them with appropriate benefits such as health-care?
- Wreaks immeasurable environmental damage as a result of a construction or natural resources extraction project?
- Colludes with others to fix prices, thereby undercutting all the remaining competitors and driving them out of business?
- Uses political connections to win contracts without its competitors being given fair consideration?

These are examples of the kinds of concerns that drive consumers, businesses, government, and various stakeholders to demand that organizations and projects operate more openly. Such demands often culminate in the establishment or evolution of regulations and industry standards. In effect, they are a control mechanism in a negative feedback loop. For example, in reaction to corporate scandals involving companies such as Enron, Tyco International, and WorldCom, the Sarbanes-Oxley Act was enacted into United States federal law in 2002. Also known as the Public Company Accounting Reform and Investor Protection Act of 2002, and commonly called Sarbanes-Oxley, Sarbox, or SOX, the act requires that companies be more open with their financial operations.

If openness is optional and your competitors are acting openly, you may be suspected of hiding something if you're not following suit.

When openness is mandated, all affected must comply. Noncompliance usually leads to fines or criminal charges and damages an organization's reputation. If openness is optional and your competitors are acting openly, you may be suspected of hiding something if you're not following suit. This highlights another benefit of raising the transparency bar: It can be an effective strategy that helps differentiate you from the competition, while also requiring other organizations to expend effort playing catch-up.

Openness within an organization is just as important as openness beyond its borders. It can increase the effectiveness of collaboration by reducing the chance that a colleague will misinterpret an action or take too long to observe and interpret it. We should never presume to know precisely how observers will view what we do. Everyone observes differently and looks for different things, depending on their own unique perspectives. Leaders sometimes assume that employees will require only certain information. This is a somewhat arrogant assumption to make. James O'Toole and Warren Bennis, authors of *Transparency: How Leaders Create a Culture of Candor*, polled 154 executives and found that 63 percent of them described their own corporate culture as opaque. The remaining 37 percent felt that they were still not being fully transparent (Bennis, Goleman, et al. 2008, 57). They wrote:

> *In all groups leaders try to hoard and control information because they believe it's a source of power. Managers sometimes believe that access to information is a perquisite of power, a benefit that separates*

their privileged caste from the unwashed hoi polloi. Such leaders apparently feel that they're smarter than their followers, and thus only they need, or would know how to use, sensitive and complex information. Some even like opacity because it helps them to hide embarrassing mistakes.

Employees all too often feel that they're being kept in the dark. Leaders should develop openness inside their organizations so that people feel empowered to always speak out if they believe problems exist or the organization could do some things better. Groupthink is more likely to occur when a lack of openness exists within a team. In such situations, contrarians, who are often discounted for their opposing views, frequently do not feel as if they can speak up.

When we discussed Col. John Boyd's research into execution loops, we noted that it grew from his study of the behavior of lone pilots in single-seat jet fighters. A related field of study, known as *cockpit resource management,* has developed since the late 1960s in response to investigations into aircraft accidents. Cockpit resource management focuses on the teamwork that takes place in large aircraft with multiple people in the cockpit. This is a particularly important field of study because approximately 80 percent of all large jet aircraft accidents result from poor management in the cockpit (Carroll and Taggart 1987, 40). More significantly, although the ratio of aircraft accidents to flying hours has decreased in past decades, mainly as a result of better-built and -maintained aircraft (Keyes 1990, 1), the percentage of accidents attributed to pilot error has increased (Yamamori 1987, 75–76).

U.S. Air Force cockpit resource management researcher Maj. Ricky J. Keyes noted that cockpit communications are greatly enhanced when inquiry and advocacy are both present. **Inquiry** is the process of seeking information from all sources, and **advocacy** is the obligation to speak in support of alternative courses of actions while remaining open to opposing viewpoints (Keyes 1990, 11). Leaders, who are usually the captains of flight crews, play an important role in ensuring that both forms of communication can exist in a cockpit.

Researchers at NASA's Ames Research Center studied the underlying causes of pilot-error accidents in the mid-1970s. Their research involved interviewing airline crew members and observing flight crews exposed to potential accident situations in simulator experiments. The NASA researchers learned that leaders are far more likely to make mistakes when they rush to action instead of waiting to obtain more information, which they often can get from other team members. In the 1980s, management theorists Robert Blake and

Jane Mouton did further research on the results of NASA's findings. They concluded that the pilots in the study who made the right choices routinely had open exchanges with their flight crew members. On the other hand, crew members who worked regularly with leaders who didn't promote an open culture were unwilling to intervene in potential accident situations even when they had information that could have prevented the disaster (Bennis, Goleman, et al. 2008, 56).

Openness in teams is important not only between leaders and their reports, but among all team members. Especially in geographically distributed teams, people can easily lose awareness of what others are doing. Retaining and increasing that awareness helps reduce the likelihood of duplicated efforts. It also helps everyone in a team understand the problems and issues impacting their colleagues. That's especially important when people may be feeling frustration or resentment toward other team members because of failures or lower-than-expected performance. The reverse is also true: It's good for people to know about the successes and accomplishments of their colleagues.

It's important for people to believe that openness given can lead to openness received. This openness must extend to admitting mistakes when necessary. Remember our discussion of Warren Buffett's straight talk in Chapter 4? When people admit to mistakes, others in a group are more apt to do so as well. It's always better to know about mistakes earlier than later. Being open about them has the added benefit of giving critics less ammunition.

It's important for people to believe that openness given can lead to openness received. This openness must extend to admitting mistakes when necessary.

Timeliness

A basic level of transparency may be achieved with authentic and open behavior, but that may not be enough to achieve the desired level of success. As I described earlier in the discussion of feedback at classical music performances, feedback is most beneficial when it is delivered in a timely manner. Sarbanes-Oxley forces companies to be more authentic and open, and it also requires that the disclosure of information be issued on a "rapid and current basis," as specified in Section 409 of the act. The need for timely reporting is especially important in today's fast-moving world, where global transactions can happen in the blink of an eye. If disclosures aren't made available in a timely manner, the information they provide may be obsolete, regardless of how authentic and open it once was. This is very true in jazz, where musicians must communicate their actions and intents in real time as a performance proceeds. Jazz audiences are also apt to express their appreciation (or displeasure) in a timely manner, and this helps tighten the feedback loop.

If disclosures aren't made available in a timely manner, the information they provide may be obsolete, regardless of how authentic and open it once was.

Timeliness of interactions is important in software development. Sometimes a software development project must be partitioned into one or more subprojects to make it easier to manage. This may happen at the outset of a project or later, as the project evolves. Factors that may lead to such subdivisioning include the size or complexity of the project's work effort, the size of the team, and geographic or technical boundaries. Fortunately, software development systems are modular in nature, and multiple modules can be developed independently. If dependencies exist between the modules, it becomes important to synchronize their schedules. Software developers have ways of minimizing the impact of dependencies and the problems introduced by scheduling delays. For example, if module A is dependent on module B but module B is not ready, it may be possible for module A to use "scaffolding" code in place of module B until module B is ready. Regardless of the techniques used, all the real parts have to come together and be fully tested and delivered. On a larger scale, the focus is on not on modules, but on projects. Thus, if you have multiple interdependent projects, they typically form a "release train" in which projects are completed, tested, and declared done so that other projects that depend on them can do likewise.

Each year, the Eclipse Foundation and thousands of open source developers who work on the Eclipse projects around the world deliver a release train of software based on the Eclipse Project. This includes, among other things, a set of frameworks and common services known as the Eclipse Platform. When IBM delivered the first open source release of the Eclipse Project in 2001, before the Eclipse Foundation even existed, the Eclipse Platform was used primarily to create software development tools. It has since become a foundation for many other types of applications. In 2009, the Eclipse release train, codenamed Galileo, consisted of 33 projects with a combined codebase of more than 24 million lines of code. In the Galileo project schedule, each participating project specified its delivery delay in relation to the Eclipse Project. For example, the Eclipse Data Tools Platform had an offset of one day, while the Rich Ajax Platform had a delay of two days. None of the 33 projects was more than three days behind the Eclipse Platform. Such tight schedules left little room for delays. If one project was delayed by even one day, it would delay all the projects that depended on it.

In release trains such as Galileo, tight offsets between interdependent projects are necessary not simply to avoiding prolonging the release date of the last project in the release train, but also because the quality level of each project relies on timely feedback from the projects that depend on it. As new milestones of a project are delivered during the development cycle, they are adopted by their dependent projects. By adopting quickly, they increase the likelihood of identifying problems earlier and having those problems addressed by the projects on which they depend. At the very end of the schedule, if a project is too slow to adopt the project it depends on, it may be too late to address any problems discovered in the adoption because the project that owns that code may already have shut down and declared its release done. Alignment of interdependent schedules does not necessarily have to be tied to the provision of feedback, although that can often simplify issues. For example, let's say that Team A is working toward A 2.0, and Team B is working toward B 1.1 but won't even begin working on B 2.0 until after A 2.0 is done. B 2.0 depends on A 2.0. If Team B allocates enough resources to specifically adopt, test, and report feedback on A 2.0 while it is still in development, Team B can ensure that it will meet Team A's needs even while it continues to focus on B 1.1.

Clarity

When jazz musicians are performing, they often have only fractions of a second in which to signal their intent. Sometimes it's a particular note played and emphasized with a lifting and dropping of the head or the horn, or it may be a glance or a hand signal or perhaps even a quick word to direct the other musicians to a specific place in the musical form or to play specific harmony. Being clear about these signals is important to the musicians. It's not important that the audience be able to understand these directives, and it doesn't particularly matter if they are able to decipher them.

Being clear about an intent or action helps to minimize the time people need to orient to an action they observe. What makes clarity difficult is that obfuscation is often necessary to prevent actions from being clear to competitors or sometimes even customers. Jazz musicians rarely use obfuscation, but other fields do so extensively.

In baseball, participants use many forms of hand signals on the field. Base umpires signal whether runners are safe or out. The home plate umpire has additional responsibilities, such as signaling balls and strikes. Meanwhile, the first and third base coaches relay signals from the manager. Should the batter hit and run, bunt, or swing away? Should the base runners attempt to steal? The catcher signals to the pitcher to indicate what pitch to throw. Although everyone, including all the players and the fans, must understand the umpires' signals, most of the signals the players and coaches use must be obfuscated so that only the players on their respective teams can decipher them. Basketball players are constantly dodging and feinting to confuse the players on the opposing team, yet the players on their own team must be able to decipher their actions. If you've ever seen the Harlem Globetrotters in action, then you've seen an exaggerated display of such techniques of obfuscation. Although the Globetrotters focus on entertainment and comic routines, they still play serious basketball; in more than 80 years, they have notched up an impressive win record of 98.5 percent, with more than 23,000 victories and only 345 losses.

Military and police operations and espionage also use obfuscation extensively. Examples include hand signals for close-range combat engagements, cryptography and coding for communication, and camouflage of physical objects and disguises. This obfuscation is necessary, but it must be clearly decipherable for those with a need to know. Any confusion may put lives and critical operational objectives at risk.

In business, valuable trade secrets such as designs, formulas, or processes must be protected at all costs. In most cases, the processes that produce the products must obfuscate the nature of these secrets. People have tried to reverse-engineer the formulas for Coca-Cola and KFC's Original Recipe of 11 herbs and spices, but no one has yet succeeded. For this inherent obfuscation to work, these companies must protect the recipes and formulas at all costs. The formula for Coca-Cola, allegedly kept in a bank vault in Atlanta, Georgia, is known to only a few people, who have undoubtedly signed nondisclosure agreements. Until 1991, Coca-Cola was not sold in India because, until that time, Indian law required that trade-secret information be disclosed. The FDA even tried to force the Coca-Cola Company to disclose the ingredients in 1909, but it was unsuccessful after nine years of litigation. The formula for KFC's recipe of 11 herbs and spices exists on only a single sheet of notebook paper signed by the company's founder, Col. Harland Sanders. It is apparently kept in a safe with limited access by no more than two executives at a time, and multiple suppliers are used to ensure that no one supplier is aware of all the ingredients. In software development, one of the most valuable trade secrets is the human-readable source code written by software developers. Although the software has to be made available for users, the source code is often obfuscated by compiling it into a machine-compiled binary form that is generally impossible to reverse-engineer back to the original source code. Tools can be used to specifically obfuscate certain kinds of software that are not traditionally compiled into binary form.

Obfuscation is also used in politics and is typically referred to as "doublespeak." Politicians sometimes say one thing when they actually mean something else. Even doctors may engage in obfuscation by using medical jargon to keep unpleasant diagnoses from patients.

For something to be clear, it must be intelligible.
If it has to be obfuscated, it must be readily decipherable
by those who need to know about it.

These are all examples of a need to conceal the real meaning or substance of something while ensuring that it is clear to others. For something to be clear, it must be intelligible. If it has to be obfuscated, it must be readily decipherable by those who need to know about it. When performing an action or disclosing something, always ask yourself who the observers are and take the appropriate steps to ensure clarity or obfuscation, as required.

Considerations

Transparency brings rewards, but it also introduces risks. Being totally transparent doesn't always make sense. In some cases, you have to be selectively transparent and decide when it makes sense to be authentic, open, timely, and clear, and when doing so would be detrimental. One of the first concerns for teams that are thinking about developing software in the open is that everyone will be able to see all the defects and not-yet-implemented enhancement requests filed against their products. In this case, transparency may cast them in a negative light. At the same time, it keeps them honest and forces them to lift their game. Sometimes privacy laws and policies must be considered, and, of course, protecting intellectual property and other confidential information is paramount. To further complicate matters, many companies today engage in open source development, consuming open source code and even contributing to or maintaining open source projects. So on one hand, they may be working in the open on some projects, while working behind closed doors on others. In these cases, it's even more important to be aware of what you are doing and which hat you are wearing at any given time. It may even be necessary to separate duties and construct "Chinese walls" to delineate boundaries more clearly.

Of course, being selectively transparent does not mean that you should hide anything that really should be visible and open. Some things should never be hidden. Even when organizations do their best to conceal information, the truth often finds a way to surface. This is especially true in today's Internet-empowered world. In June 2009, massive protests erupted in Iran, with citizens there claiming electoral fraud in the re-election of incumbent Iranian President Mahmoud Ahmadinejad. The Iranian government attempted to block all communication out of the country, jamming cellphones and text-messaging services, and blocking access to social networking sites such as Facebook. Despite their efforts, microblogging site Twitter escaped their reach and was successfully used to communicate events to the outside world.

If organizations or individuals do attempt to hide something that should be communicated, they inevitably pay the price. Think about these people:

- Kenneth Lay (Enron)
- Bernard Ebbers (WorldCom)
- Bernard Madoff (Madoff Investment Securities)
- Nick Lesson (Barings Bank)
- Conrad Black (Hollinger International)
- Barry Bonds (baseball player)
- Ben Johnson (sprinter)
- Milli Vanilli (pop music)
- Diego Maradona (soccer)
- Tonya Harding (ice skating)

All of these individuals were accused of committing some kind of fraud and were eventually discovered. On a smaller scale is the story of Zipatoni and Sony.

Around Christmas 2006, fans of the Sony PSP discovered a blog entitled "All I Want for Christmas Is a PSP." Detailing the exploits of Charlie, who was trying to help his friend Jeremy get a PSP for Christmas, the blog featured posts of pseudo-hip-hop-speak and supposedly amateur videos. The domain was soon discovered to belong to a marketing agency called Zipatoni that was trying to create an online viral marketing campaign for Sony. Zipatoni and Sony's duplicity was soon the subject of a growing consumer backlash. Yet even when people posted comments on the blog claiming it was a total fraud, the site's maintainers continued to foster the illusion in their faux hip-hop replies. Consumers didn't buy it, and eventually the issue developed into a storm of controversy. In mid-2007, Sony admitted to the scheme in a genuine, straight-worded post signed "Sony Computer Entertainment America." Although the site is gone, Sony's faux pas is recorded for eternity: Just Google "Zipatoni" or the title of the blog. It simply doesn't pay to be two-faced.

I mentioned before that people appreciate honesty, openness, and transparency. People also appreciate vulnerability and self-deprecation and often rally for the underdog or those in need of assistance. In 2006, Glenn Kelman was hired as the CEO of Redfin, an online brokerage firm that was, in his own opinion, "the ugly red-haired child" in the real estate industry. Redfin tried to differentiate itself by refunding two-thirds of the commission that agents usually charge. Customers loved this. Agents, however, were upset and began to blacklist Redfin, refusing to sell any houses listed with the service. Initially, Redfin tried to keep this a secret. Kelman said, "We were really ashamed that our customers were getting pushed around, so we tried to keep it this dirty little secret." When things didn't improve, he decided to try a transparent approach. He set up a blog and started an open discussion about the practices of the real estate business, lamenting what he saw as its eventual downfall: "If we don't reform ourselves, and take out all the sales baloney, too, people will come to hate real estate agents the way they hate tobacco companies or Big Oil." Agents responded by attacking Kelman in comments to his posts, and a storm of intense discussion erupted on the blog. Customers loved it, and business turned around as a result. Kelman told *Wired* journalist Clive Thompson, "Instead of discouraging customers, being open about our problems radicalized them." He said, "They rallied and started pulling for us" (Thompson 2007).

Consistency is vital when you're trying to be transparent. Changing the rules about what is transparent or having different rules for different groups of people is confusing for consumers and collaborators. Failing to explain why the differences exist is to be inherently opaque—that is, not very transparent at all.

Recapitulation

- Transparency can improve the strength and speed of execution by reducing the time taken to observe actions and increasing the likelihood that important actions will be observed.

- Transparency is alluring and can help attract people to a team or project. People appreciate honesty, openness, and authenticity and are curious about what happens behind the scenes.

- Transparency is enabled by authenticity, openness, timeliness, and clarity.

- Authenticity is a measure of truthfulness. The perception of authenticity is based on associations with positive things or people, believability, and credibility, which, in turn, is based on capability, trustworthiness, and identity.

- Openness provides insight into how things get done. It can increase the effectiveness of collaboration and assure consumers. However, it also may provide competitors with an advantage.

- If disclosures of transparency aren't made available in a timely fashion, the information they provide may be obsolete, regardless of how authentic and open it once was.

- Clarity minimizes the time needed to orient to an observation. For something to be clear, it must be intelligible. If it has to be obfuscated, it must be readily decipherable by those who need to know about it.

CHAPTER 9

Make Contributions Count

> *"Always count the cost."*
> —American proverb

Contributing in Collaborative Scenarios

In many fields, subjective or quantitative judgments compare the contributions of multiple individuals or organizations and single out the highest ranked. In sports, the Most Valuable Player award is given to the individual who is deemed to have made the greatest contributions. The National Academy of Recording Arts and Sciences uses the same term for annual awards in instrumental categories. Microsoft has a much lauded Most Valuable Professional award that is given for contributions in technical fields. Salesperson of the Year and Employee of the Month are typical of similar awards in business, and the military bestows countless awards for distinctive service.

Recognizing valuable contributions can be rewarding for those who are acknowledged and can motivate others to improve their efforts. However, if metrics are the primary basis for such judgments, it's important that they be widely accepted as a fair measure of a contribution.

Sometimes people say that all contributions are valued. Such statements are often made to express appreciation or to motivate people to continue their efforts. Although these intentions may be good, it's important to accept that some contributions can have a negative value. You've probably been in a situation in which someone could do nothing right. Every time the person tried to "help," he or she not only failed to add value, but the person's efforts required other people to redo the work—and possibly even undo damage.

Figure 9.1 illustrates four people working together: A, B, C, and D. They could be engaged in any team activity you can think of, including software development, a sports game, a jazz performance, or a military operation. The activities of each person are represented by the various symbols explained in the legend. Each person is engaged in an individual execution loop in which they observe and orient to their own actions, the actions of others, and the result of everyone's contributions that affect both the collective value and the health of the team. Before acting, each person must measure his or her contribution as follows:

- The effort required to create that contribution and integrate it with the collective value
- The value of the contribution
- The impact of integrating the contribution with the collective value

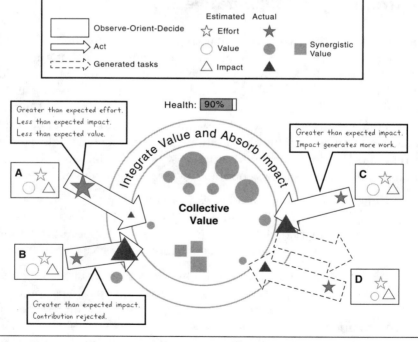

Figure 9.1 *Measuring contributions in collaborative scenarios*

The size of the symbols represents the relative magnitude of each measurement. After a person acts, the actual effort, value, and impact of the contribution is realized. Each of these measurements can be determined in any number of ways. For the purposes of this discussion, we consider them to be fair and accurate assessments.

If I could show this illustration as an animation, you would see that the impact of making a contribution is transient: After a contribution has been integrated and its impact has been absorbed, the impact disappears. You would also see in an animated diagram the "act" arrows disappearing and the instances of effort disappearing or being moved somewhere else, where they could measure each person's total effort over a period of time.

The result of integrating all the contributions is measured by the collective value in the center of the illustration. It consists not only of the value derived from each integrated contribution, but of the synergistic value that is created as a result of combining multiple individual contributions. See the Introduction for a discussion of synergy.

If we look at this illustration and note what happens for each person, A, B, C, and D, and think about other possibilities and variations for individual contributions in a collaborative situation, we can draw a number of conclusions:

- Not everyone requires the same amount of effort to produce a given measure of value. Skill and experience play a part in this.

- In collaborative scenarios, the value of a specific contribution is a function of many things, including the other contributions. What might be of great value in one situation may be of lesser or even no value in another situation. Two people might contribute precisely the same thing at the same time. Depending on the nature of the activity, this might mean that one person's efforts were wasted, although there may be some consolation in the experience gained.

- Never underestimate the impact of integrating a contribution into a team's activity. The impact is often a function of the number of people involved in the activity. As you increase the size of the team, it becomes more difficult to integrate each person's contribution. Sometimes the impact of one person's contribution generates more work. In this particular case, we see that the impact of integrating C's contribution is that D had to expend effort. Impact may also affect the health of the activity. We look at this more specifically in Chapter 12, "Stay Healthy." In the context of this illustration, let's consider that sometimes people must act with the sole purpose of restoring the health of the activity without adding any value to it.

Thinking in this manner can help people consider how they interact in collaborative situations. Of course, this must be done by considering the characteristics of any specific activity. Let's look at a few examples.

In jazz, the collective value and health of a live performance is always readily apparent to the audience. Small group jazz performances comprised almost entirely of improvisation are very organic. Unknowns at any moment may take the music on a path none of the musicians expected. The real-time nature of a live performance demands that contributions be integrated immediately. A contribution is inherently delivered by virtue of a musician playing or singing the notes of his or her musical expression. These contributions often require a response from other musicians. When one musician's contribution lowers the health of the performance or detracts from its value, the others must respond immediately to regain lost ground. Perhaps a musician gets lost or confused and ends up at a different point in the musical form or in a different key than the rest of the band. Or perhaps a musician decides to take the music to a place that the other musicians are not willing to go, such as doubling the tempo to a pace that is too fast for the drummer or bassist. On the other hand, if a musician contributes something that is valuable, responses from the other musicians can add synergistic value, but only if they respond quickly. In jazz, intensity and interest are two qualities that undoubtedly are considered when measuring the collective value of a performance. These qualities often result from one musician expressing a musical idea and another reacting with either a development of the idea or a response to it. However, this can work only if the reaction is immediate. Any delay results in a weakening or total loss of the effect, along with the synergistic value that it could add to the performance.

A software development team works in a different way than a group of jazz musicians does. Most software development projects are far more complex than jazz performances, and they usually engage many more people. Contributions are typically combined by running an automated build that integrates all of the team's software components. Features of the software add value, whereas defects reduce value and often impact the health of the software. Builds are usually run continuously or according to a schedule. In some environments, individual developers can run personal builds that enable them to measure the value and impact of their contributions before they deliver it to the team build. Teams working together on specific components or features may run their own builds, enabling them to evolve and stabilize their collective contributions locally before unleashing them on the greater team. Contributions may break a build, preventing the team's software artifacts from being produced. If this happens, the team must determine which contributions caused the breakage and make a decision to either roll back the contributions or contribute further changes to resolve the issues. Even if a build is successful, the resulting software may contain defects as a result of recent contributions. These might introduce minor problems or completely break critical functionality. Manual and automated tests can help determine whether features are working and performing as specified and whether any known or expected defects might be present. Software teams often have the luxury of determining the timeliness of transparency by choosing which builds will be made available to consumers. Even in transparent software projects such as the Jazz projects hosted by IBM at jazz.net, or in open source projects such as those hosted by the Eclipse Foundation, Apache Software Foundation, or SourceForge, builds are typically made available to consumers no more frequently than once per week.[1] This gives a development team time to resolve problems generated by contributions submitted during that week. This doesn't mean, however, that it is okay to deliver problematic contributions. They still waste time and effort that could be spent adding value.

Workers in political campaigns include a candidate and perhaps a running mate who are the face of the campaign, and hundreds or even thousands of paid staff and volunteers who are engaged in all manner of supportive activities. One might think that the collective value of the campaign is the benefits it brings to the candidate's constituents. That value actually does not come until the candidate is in office. During the campaign, the most important focus is winning the election. Ideally, that is determined by the candidate's platform, but as we all know, politicians don't always deliver what they promise. Many politicians also have been elected without having much of a platform at all. During a campaign, the opinions of voters and the size of the campaign's coffers ultimately determine votes. Contributions to a political campaign are many and varied and include speeches and interviews given by candidates, as well as interactions between the candidates and constituents, statements by aides, promotional efforts, and anything else that increases the goodwill of the campaign. Because political contests are so competitive and typically adversarial, valuable contributions can include anything that decreases the value of an opposing candidate, such as a successful effort to dig up dirt. Many campaigns have been ruined and candidates forced to

---

1   Some projects make nightly builds available, but these are not typically expected to be stable.

retire from a race after a negative revelation developed into a scandal. Imagine a campaign that has compiled or even falsified negative information about an opponent. The campaign might have a number of stories to release over a period of time or perhaps stories kept in check and used only if needed. Regardless of whether you agree with such tactics, they are used; sadly, they add value to a campaign because they often do affect the outcome of elections. On the flip side, problematic contributions can include gaffes by a party's own candidate and various missteps, such as failing to gain the support of someone or some group that turned out to have much more influence than previously thought. In 2008, Hillary Clinton's campaign for the Democratic nomination in the United States presidential election lost to Barack Obama. During and after Clinton's campaign, the press documented missteps such as the inability to execute on strategy, faction infighting that sometimes led to staff losses, constantly changing themes and slogans, and gaffes made by both Clinton and her husband, Bill Clinton, as well as the inability to recover from them (Vandehei and Kuhn 2008; and Green 2008). It's easy to be critical in hindsight. However with 935 employees, countless volunteers, and constant scrutiny from around the globe, it's not hard to imagine the difficulty of managing so many contributors and integrating their contributions.

Measuring Contributions: Saying More with Less

Regardless of the activity, contributions must be carefully considered. We must always ask ourselves these questions:

- How much *effort* will it take to perform this action?
- How much *value* will it add after it has been integrated into the team's activity?
- What will the *impact* of my action be? What other work will it generate, and who will have to do that work? How will it affect the health of the activity?

In many cases, the answers to these questions are obvious and our experience enables us to derive the estimates in split-seconds, allowing us to react immediately and play a note, pass a ball, or fire at an enemy, as warranted. However, not every contribution can be initiated as a result of a preprogrammed reaction. We must often perform more careful analysis and seriously think before acting.

If we could quantify effort, value, and impact, we could calculate efficiency with a simple formula, such as Efficiency = Value / (Effort + Impact). As you might expect, quantifying these variables and formulating a precise equation for efficiency is not always practical or even possible. In basketball, the number of points, rebounds, and assists provides a useful measure of the value of a player's contributions. Yet when a player assists in the formulation of strategy, boosts morale, or encourages or discourages others to take risks in a way that benefits the team, such actions add value that is less quantifiable. Similarly, the precise scoring of an ice skating competition includes a subjective element in the judging. Although there are no scores to measure the contributions of jazz musicians, the improvised solos in three different performances of the same tune can be compared and ranked relative to one another, with subjectivity also playing a part.

Numbers aside, what's most important is that contributors understand the benefits of adding value, the cost of wasting effort and other resources, and the problems of impacting a team's activity. Contributors should seek to maximize the value they add while minimizing effort and impact. The impact of a contribution may create problems. To fix those problems, others may need to expend additional effort. We delve further into this topic in Chapter 12, when we discuss the principle "Stay healthy." When we expend effort, we may not only burn human time and energy, but deplete other resources as well. In many situations, constraints limit the effort that may be expended. As a result, we must often improvise. In jazz, a time constraint forces jazz musicians to improvise. When they must participate in the creation of an ending, respond to the reharmonization of chords, or react to harmonic or temporal modulations, the need to perform in real time demands that jazz musicians observe, orient, decide, and act immediately. In India, one of the fastest-growing economies in the world, people must cope with many constraints. The World Bank has estimated that, in 2005, 42 percent of India's population fell below the international poverty line of $1.25 a day (World Bank, n.d.). A 2007 study of 20 cities by the Asian Development Bank showed that the average duration of water supply was only 4.3 hours a day, with no city having a continuous supply (Asian Development Bank, n.d., 3). According to research by *The Economist* in 2008, an estimated 700 million people had no access to a proper toilet, and only 13 percent of the sewage was treated. Power outages are a common occurrence, and some 600 million people have no access to power. Only half of Indian school teachers show up for work ("Creaking, Groaning" 2008). Corruption is rife. India has been ranked one of the 5 highest bribe payers among 22 countries, according to Transparency International's Bribe Payers Index (BPI) in 2008. Transparency International's "India Corruption Study 2007" estimated that Below Poverty Line (BPL) households paid about $212 million to obtain the basic public services to which they are entitled (Transparency International India, n.d.).

To deal with such a multitude of constraints, people in India have become experts in improvisation. *Jugaad* is a Hindi slang word that refers to a minimalist approach to execution and innovation in which necessity is the mother of improvisation. Examples of *jugaad* are everywhere in India, demonstrating what people can do with a bit of creativity and whatever scant resources are available: footwear made from old car tires; old washing machines used to churn *lassi*, a yogurt-based drink; recycled plastic bottles used for drip irrigation; and vehicles jury-rigged from bicycles parts and farm carts with diesel water pump motors and makeshift steering and braking mechanisms. With the Indian government unable to guarantee even the most basic services, many citizens and private organizations have taken matters into their own hands, demonstrating *jugaad* on a larger scale. Indian cities had no ambulance service before a group of entrepreneurs established Dial 1298, a private ambulance service. *Sukrupa* is a charity that has established schools to educate underprivileged children and help them escape poverty and life in the slums. Aravind Eye Care Hospital provides ophthalmological services to people who might not otherwise have access to eye care. In the Indo-Pakistani War of 1971, Indian military commanders were in a bind. They had T-54 and T-55 Russian-made tanks already deployed on the western border, but more than half of the tanks were crippled as a result of the government's inability to buy replacements for defective firing pins. In a race against time, an elderly Sikh in a nearby village concocted a *jugaad* solution in the form of a replacement pin that proved to be as good as the original and less than one-tenth the cost of the imported item (Talukdar, n.d.). In the culture of *jugaad*, there is always a way to get things done, even if the result is just a temporary solution. This can-do attitude has helped India survive and grow, despite its considerable burdens. American companies, slammed by the recession, are now looking at *jugaad* to learn how to operate more efficiently—but what are they really trying to learn? As Robert C. Wolcott, executive director of Northwestern University's Kellogg Innovation Network, said, "Having a consulting industry built around *jugaad* is almost anathema to the word itself" (Jana 2009). People simply need to develop a mindset of carefully measuring the effort, value, and impact of their actions.

Of course, skills of resourceful inventiveness are not unique to India. They transcend all cultures and disciplines. Americans have long referred to such improvisation as Yankee ingenuity or the do-it-yourself approach. In France, the term is *bricolage*, from the verb *bricoler*, meaning "to fiddle or tinker." Studying the way in which people with such skills imagine possibilities where others fail to see solutions, Diane Coutu, writing for *Harvard Business Review*, noted (Coutu 2002):

Bricolage in the modern sense can be defined as a kind of inventiveness, an ability to improvise a solution to a problem without proper or obvious tools or materials. Bricoleurs are always tinkering—building radios from household effects or fixing their own cars. They make the most of what they have, putting objects to unfamiliar uses. In the concentration camps, for example, resilient inmates knew to pocket pieces of string or wire whenever they found them. The string or wire might later become useful—to fix a pair of shoes, perhaps, which in freezing conditions might make the difference between life and death.

The ability to make the most of whatever resources are available is a skill that enables teams and individuals to develop resilience. This is the ability to weather adverse conditions and events, including change, loss, and setbacks. People are frequently encouraged to do their very best. But what does it really mean to give it your all? It's all too easy to say "Put in 110 percent effort" or "Mistakes aren't tolerated," but such platitudes ignore the complexities of many activities. Leaders often resort to such simplistic goals in an effort to motivate people, but as we observed in Chapter 5, "Commit with Passion," if you follow the principle of "Employ top talent," such people are highly self-motivated and will instinctively do their best in any situation. Experienced and capable individuals know that sometimes it's necessary to make a less substantive effort to meet a greater goal. They may even knowingly make mistakes and forego an opportunity to correct them, to avoid the associated effort and impact. Although mistakes or defects can be problematic, their impact is usually measurable and sometimes tolerable. Effective people and teams generally know when they are creating problems, and as we noted in Chapter 4, what's most important is that they are aware of these problems and understand their impact. Details are important, but sometimes they can be compromised. It's great to strive for perfection, but perfection should not be mindlessly pursued at the cost of all else. In reality, many software products are released with known defects. Some defects are tolerable because their impact is negligible or can be worked around; other defects are critically serious. Zero defects is a meaningful target, but it is far more important for a missile guidance system than for a word processor. Mistakes in sports are common, but defeating your opponent is usually more important than simply playing an error-free game.

There is possibly no greater example of how to act with economy than that of jazz great Miles Davis. Davis rose to prominence in the mid-1940s when he replaced Dizzy Gillespie in Charlie Parker's quintet. This was a great opportunity for the young trumpet player, but it presented him with a considerable challenge. Gillespie, to whom he invariably was compared, was a masterful improviser who exploited with flair his ample virtuosity on the trumpet. Furthermore, bebop, the style of music Gillespie had a strong hand in developing, was characterized by instrumental virtuosity, complicated harmony, sophisticated rhythms, and fast tempos.

Jazz musicians typically base their melodic improvisations on notes from scales that sound "right" with a chord. In bebop, chords typically changed every two beats. This was not new. Many bebop chord changes were based on older songs. For example, **rhythm changes** is the term given to a sequence of chord changes based on George Gershwin's 1930 song "I've Got Rhythm." Rhythm changes were the basis for many other songs during the swing era, as well as bebop classics such as Parker's "Anthropology" and "Dexterity." The difference in bebop was that the pieces were typically played at breakneck speeds, and the changes often featured sophisticated altered chords or substitutions. Bebop melodies were characterized by certain melodic elements that were partly suggested by the more sophisticated harmony. Over time, they became a part of the bebop sound. Bebop lines often featured odd intervals and a lot of chromaticism where the melody moved in small steps. Unwritten rules even determined what kinds of intervals should follow other intervals in a melodic line. Accents were often used in unusual places to emphasize syncopation. All this required bebop improvisers to thoroughly understand the bebop vocabulary and grammar.

Bebop was partly a reaction to the approachable, danceable swing music of musicians such as Benny Goodman and Glenn Miller. Eager to reassert ownership over jazz, the architects of bebop developed a style that sounded frenetic, nervous, and often fragmented with melodies that were unpredictable and exciting. This was music that was virtually impossible to dance to and, if it had any words, could be sung by only a few. When there was any singing in bebop, it was usually fast scat that emulated the saxophone or trumpet. The complexity of bebop made it inherently unapproachable—audiences needed an understanding of the music to fully appreciate it, and certainly not just any jazz musician could play it.

Davis did not possess Gillespie's level of technical facility on the instrument, and he knew there was no sense trying to emulate or match Gillespie's dynamic style of playing. Instead, he developed his own contrary style characterized by sparse, lyrical playing, with lines that contained less notes. He made great use of space/silence/rest in his playing, making it a feature of his improvisations and melodic variations. In essence, Davis's goal was to say more with less. He went further by exploiting a style of jazz that became known as modal jazz. Davis did not invent this style—its origins are frequently attributed to composer and bandleader George Russell, who hung out with Davis, Parker, and many other jazz musicians at the New York apartment of composer and arranger Gil Evans. Evans later collaborated with Miles on famous works such as *Birth of the Cool, Miles Ahead,* and *Sketches of Spain.*

Modal jazz was a strong reaction to the complexities of bebop. Whereas bebop musicians used unusual scales that enabled them to deal with sophisticated chords changing every two beats, modal jazz challenged the musicians to improvise over scales or modes that might be employed continuously for many bars. Unlike bebop, no esoteric rules or expectations covered for how melodies were to be constructed. This gave the musicians a great deal of freedom. Davis wasn't the first to perform modal jazz, but he brought it to the fore by basing almost an entire album on it. That album was the famous *Kind of Blue,* recorded in 1959. "So What," probably the album's most famous track, uses only two modes. Soloists must improvise through choruses in which one mode is used for 16 bars (64 beats) and another for 8 bars (32 beats). They must then return to the original mode for another eight bars. The title, "So What," was Davis's way of saying, "So what if you have all those chords and scales? Listen to what we can do with just two of them!" The modal approach was not just about the chords and the scales. The modes and their resulting sounds were based on musical concepts that Western music did not widely use; they were more common in music from the East and actually originated in European medieval music and Gregorian chant. These exotic sounds explain the title of one of the album's most moving pieces, "Flamenco Sketches." During the recording sessions, producer Irving Townsend gave "Flamenco Sketches" the temporary title "Spanish"; he used the title "African" for the piece that eventually became known as "All Blues." As pianist Bill Evans reminded members of Davis's sextet at the *Kind of Blue* recording sessions, the aim was to play the sound of the scales and not necessarily just the scales themselves. The minimalist approach extended beyond the harmony to the number of notes, the rhythms, and the song forms.

Davis's approach to performance and composition teaches us that a handful of well-placed notes can count for just as much, if not more, than a flurry of note-intensive runs, such as John Coltrane's sheets of sound, which we discussed in Chapter 6, "Listen for Change." We each have to contribute in a way that makes sense for us individually. Often when I am playing jazz, my chance to improvise a solo may follow that of a saxophone player or pianist or guitarist who has just played a solo crammed full of notes. My instinct may be to try to match that level of activity or at least to maintain the same level of intensity, by also playing lots of notes in my solo. The trouble is that I play bass, and the physical limitations of the instrument make it hard to play lots of notes as a saxophonist might. I actually have to avoid getting "sucked into" repeating what another musician just did. So, inspired by Davis, the first thing I might do when it comes my time to solo is begin with silence. This has a few benefits for me:

- It gives me a moment to let my hands switch from a mode in which I am pounding out notes on the beat and playing bass lines as loud as I can to accompany the other musicians, to one in which I play more lightly and melodically.
- It grabs the attention of listeners because suddenly there is no bass, and quite possibly no sound at all while the other musicians follow my cue. People look up and wonder what is going on.

As I proceed through my solo, I may be inclined to leave a lot of space. This contrast in style between solos can actually create more interest and, hence, add more value to the performance. In the same way, Davis chose note-intensive players such as Coltrane to provide contrast to his own sparse style of playing.

By focusing more on the quality and less on the quantity of our contributions, we gain the added benefit of being able to spend more cycles in the observation phase of our individual execution loops. This gives others greater opportunity to submit their contributions and reduces the "noise," making it easier for team members to observe and orient to the team's collective activities. Most collaborative efforts are a dialogue, whether it's performing jazz, conducting a legal negotiation, or playing baseball. We examine this more in Chapter 13, "Exchange Ideas." When one person continuously dominates the conversation, it creates all kinds of problems, and the activity becomes less of a collaborative effort and more of an individual one. It is often too easy to get sucked into contributing even when it is not necessary, just as when one feels pressured to fill an awkward silence by conversation in a social setting.

In the same way that varying the density of notes can increase the strength and value of a statement, varying the dynamics can have the same effect. When playing in an ensemble, inexperienced or insensitive musicians often play louder when they want to be heard. The problem is that when one person plays louder, others may respond in turn so that they, too, can be heard. Everyone ends up competing against one another, and the entire ensemble plays too loudly. Instead, each member of the ensemble needs to play more softly, to ensure that those who need to be heard more prominently can do so with less effort. With a greater range of dynamics at its command, an ensemble can emphasize interesting parts of the music with very soft and very loud dynamics. A sensitivity of dynamics needs to be realized not just generally, but with each contribution. When playing long notes, instead of simply attacking the note and sustaining it at the same volume, good musicians immediately drop back on the volume, to allow the instruments with the moving parts to be heard more easily. In this way, the nuances of the music are more likely to come out.

Often, less is more.

The ability of any team to perform in a similar manner is predicated on the presence of trust and respect. Every person must have respect for the contributions of others and help ensure that important contributions will be noticed. Those with important parts to contribute must trust that others will exercise restraint and sensitivity. Without such trust, they may automatically assume that they must compensate. Ultimately, the most fundamental requirement is that people listen to others and understand enough about the team's collective efforts that they can identify and support the important contributions. Every contribution is important, but not every member of a team is contributing something of the utmost importance at precisely the same time. In music, important contributions include solos, noticeable statements of a theme, and notes and phrases from which others must synchronize the timing of their contributions. In a basketball game, important contributions might include any possession of the ball and a defense against a particularly strong player or one with a shot at scoring.

In music, the greatest dynamic range is often heard in large orchestral performances. A symphony orchestra can invoke the power of 50 to 100 instruments at full voice. Yet the composition may also call for a single soft sounding instrument. The presence of a conductor can provide direction to the musicians, encouraging them to make the most of loud and soft dynamics and ensuring that the blend of dynamics is balanced and nuanced, to bring out the important parts of the music. In ensembles with no conductor, in which leadership is more decentralized, everyone must exercise leadership to achieve the same effect.

In software, what matters is not how much code you write, but what it does. In fact, longer and more complex code only consumes more memory and storage, is slower to execute, and is more likely to have bugs. Often, less is more.

Timing

When people are able to measure their contributions in terms of value, effort, and impact, they can develop a better understanding of the need to time contributions. Precise timing is important when actions must be coordinated with other team members or when they must coincide with specific events in the surrounding environment, such as the actions of consumers and competitors. A racecar driver approaching a corner must time his or her braking and gear selections with respect to the car's distance from the corner. A sniper must carefully time a shot with an enemy's movements. Precise timing is also important to ensure the success of contributions that must be coordinated among multiple team members. A pick-and-roll (also called a screen-and-roll or screen-roll) is an offensive play in basketball in which two players work together against a single defender. The exact outcome of the play may vary, depending on how the defender reacts. The ball handler and teammate must be prepared to move quickly and precisely. A flanking maneuver is a military tactic in which one attacking unit pins down an enemy with suppressive fire while another attacking unit (known as the flanking unit) then advances to attack the enemy's flank at close range. If the flanking unit moves before the enemy is correctly pinned down, it could be exposed to an unexpected counterattack. If the unit takes too long to move in and engage, the enemy may have time to prepare for the attack. In a jazz performance, precise timing is constantly important. The musicians must continuously listen to the other members of the ensemble as they play their own parts, to maintain the tempo and groove. Something as simple as playing one note on each beat can be problematic when precise timing is disregarded. For example, most musicians know that if they all play too close to the front of the beat, the tempo tends to rush.

The timing of a sequence of contributions should consider how effort, value, and impact are distributed over time. This avoids problems such as running out of steam too early or having to absorb a lot of impact at the end of a schedule and running out of time. This is obvious in physical activities such as athletics, but it applies to other disciplines as well. When a composer writes a piece of music or a jazz musician improvises a solo, he or she generally tries to impart a shape to the musical form. If the climax happens too early, there's no room for further development. Similar consideration to timing must be given in political or marketing campaigns, especially when they are based on deadlines such as an election or product release. Campaigns often tease people with small tidbits of information and then release a steady stream of details, developing core themes and leading to a well-timed climax. Releasing too much information at once may confuse people or cause them to tire of the concept. It may also deplete resources, leading to a lull in communications. Although it's important to go beyond the limits when needed, it's even more important to know how to temper contributions and to understand the value they will bring and the impact they will have. Many teams must work with limited resources and have to make tradeoffs to deliver on what's important. Software developers often do a quick-and-dirty initial hack, with the intent of doing it right later. That can be okay, as long as they deliver the real solution before the temporary one creates problems. Can you imagine an improvised solo in which the soloist does nothing for a whole minute and then unleashes a torrent of activity in the final seconds? That might be an interesting expression, but the lack of any contributions in that first minute could confuse, frustrate, and perhaps even bore the audience and other musicians. More significantly, the audience and the other musicians may find it very difficult to cope with the impact caused by such a large contribution being delivered at the last possible moment. When contributions are distributed more evenly over time, the impact of each contribution can be more easily absorbed. This is especially true if the action or its impact is new, requiring people to adjust to it. Delivering smaller contributions over time gives consumers and collaborators a chance to make that adjustment gradually. Iterative software development methods work in this way, whereas the traditional waterfall method of development delays the delivery of contributions until later in the cycle. This is often referred to as a big-bang effect. Working in this way can significantly increase risk. In the worst case, a team or stakeholders may fail to absorb the impact of these late deliveries, and the project schedule may slip, or budgets may be exceeded.

Location and Proximity

When people collaborate, they operate together within a shared space. It may be a physical space, such as a battlefield or a basketball court. It may be a virtual space, such as a software project represented by a collection of software modules, or a sonic space that musicians fill with sound. When people work in any space, they must consider their location within that space because it may affect their performance as well as that of their team.

When soldiers are organized into "fire teams" or squads, formations are employed, such as the wedge or single-file formation, skirmish line formation, or squad column. Each formation describes the arrangements of the soldiers in relation to each other and with specific soldiers such a rifleman, grenadier, or automatic rifleman assigned to specific places in the formation. The formation doesn't specify distance between the soldiers; this may vary with terrain, visibility, and presence of enemy forces. In this way, the various situational factors have a strong bearing on the proximity of the soldiers to one another. Formations and distance between soldiers are also determined by the need to have adequate fire coverage on an enemy while minimizing the chance that the soldiers will fire on each other. When soldiers are in a single-file formation, they can fire immediately to the flanks but have limited coverage of fire to the front and rear. If they spread out in a skirmish line, where they are abreast, the team vastly increases coverage of fire to the front.

In basketball, different systems provide defensive coverage of an opposing team. In the NBA, man-to-man defense is the primary defensive scheme. It requires players to guard a specific offensive player on the opposing team. In doing so, players must maintain proximity not to one another, but to the players they are guarding. The system is not completely rigid and gives players the opportunity to temporarily suspend the rules of the scheme for good reason. For example, two defensive players might switch the offensive players to which they are assigned or might work together ("double-team") against one offensive player. As with a military formation used by a fire team or squad, man-to-man defense doesn't necessarily mandate the distance that a defensive player should be from an offensive player. That is determined by such factors as the location of the ball and the strength of the offensive player versus the defensive player. If a defensive player is too close to the offensive player he or she is guarding, it will be harder to intercept a pass directed to the offensive player. An alternative to man-to-man defense is zone defense, in which players are assigned specific areas of the court and then engage any offensive player who enters the zone.

In software development, the architecture of the software and the organization of a team help determine the proximity of developers to one another within the project they collectively develop. People or groups of people are assigned ownership of specific modules within a project. This enables them to work independently on their modules while other work proceeds elsewhere in the project. This organization minimizes the contention that may occur if multiple people attempt to simultaneously modify the same code. This saves wasted time and effort and helps to avoid confusion. More important, it maximizes quality by ensuring that only those familiar with the intricacies of a specific module can make changes to that module, while still allowing others to make suggestions. A scheme of ownership also ensures that when a change of a specific nature must be made to all modules, there is complete coverage to do so everywhere at once.

In the Introduction, I described the team of Barack Obama and Joe Biden as an example of synergy because their differences helped them appeal to and address different segments of the political vote. It was vital, especially with just a team of two, for them to coordinate their locations. By being in different places at the same time and addressing different demographics, they maximized the value that their respective efforts added to their campaign.

Jazz musicians always strive to remain aware of where they and others in their team are at all times. Think about a single musical element, such as pitch. The bass usually plays the low notes, the guitar or piano usually plays in the middle-to-high range, and the horn plays above that. However, jazz musicians have a lot of freedom and are not bound to these conventions. They often depart from them, with the goal of generating tension and interest in the music. Because they can do this at any time, they need to be even more aware of their locations in the frequency range, to ensure that the combined effect works as desired.

When no specific rules affect proximity between team members, a good general rule is that they be close enough to interact but not so close that they get in one another's way.

If you're involved in an activity where physical or virtual location matters, aim to be constantly aware of your own location and that of your team members and ensure that you understand how these locations influence your individual and collective efforts. When no specific rules affect proximity between team members, a good general rule is that they be close enough to interact but not so close that they get in one another's way. If they are too far apart, they may lose track of one another. If they are too close, they won't have the freedom to innovate and respond to the unknown. Additionally, they risk compromising the team's coverage in an attempt to be in two places at one time. If you're encroaching on someone else's space, you may not be covering what was assigned to you or meeting your team's expectations.

Recapitulation

- Every intention to contribute to a collaborative activity must estimate the effort required, the value to be added, and the impact of integrating the contribution.

- An activity may develop synergistic value as a result of combining individual contributions.

- Miles Davis was a master of making contributions count by saying more with less. Efficiency is greater when the value of contributions is increased and the effort and impact are reduced.

- Making a less substantive effort, or even making mistakes, may enable a team to meet an important goal.

- Each person in a team must understand which contributions are most important at any one point in time and help ensure that those contributions are successful.

- Precise timing of contributions helps ensure success when coordinating with other team members or synchronizing with external events such as the actions of consumers and competitors.

- The timing of a sequence of contributions should consider how effort, value, and impact are distributed over time. This avoids problems such as running out of steam too early or having to absorb a lot of impact at the end of a schedule and running out of time.

- When no specific conditions affect proximity between team members, a good general rule is that they be close enough to interact but not so close that they get in one another's way.

PART III

Executing

In this section, we discuss three principles for high-performance execution. By applying these principles, teams can improve efficiency and ensure timely delivery even in the face of unforeseen challenges.

10. Reduce friction
11. Maintain momentum
12. Stay healthy

CHAPTER 10

Reduce Friction

*"Friction, as we choose to call it,
is the force that makes the apparently easy so difficult."*
—Carl von Clausewitz

Concepts of Friction

Have you ever had an experience when you've wanted to purchase a product but, try as you might, you can't figure out how to complete the transaction? The web site doesn't accept your credit card, yet you know that it works fine, and you've checked with your bank to be sure. Your calls to the customer service number require you to navigate a labyrinth of automated voice messages. After 30 minutes of listening to recordings of "Please hold, as your business is important to us," and maybe even getting cutting off once or twice, you're no closer to success. You go to the store, only to be told by the salespeople that they've never heard of the product, yet it's on their web site and they're advertising it on television. You're incredulous that, despite so wanting to spend your money with this company, they can't seem to work out how to sell you their product.

Or perhaps you were wronged by a company and your attempts to get things corrected required you to spend unreasonable amounts of time traversing the company's bureaucracy and constantly harassing them to acknowledge the issue, locate the source of the problem, and correct it. If you've dealt with a large corporation or a governmental department, you've no doubt been frustrated by bureaucracy. Perhaps, much to your chagrin, you've even been part of such a bureaucracy yourself. You're faced with a frustrated customer who has been challenged at every step by nonsensical processes, but try as you might, you can't get the processes changed because they've been like that for a very long time, and changing them would require moving mountains. You can only apologize to the customer for your organization's ridiculous policies.

These are all examples of friction. The most obvious concept of friction is defined by the laws of physics. If you roll a ball along a flat and level surface, it will eventually stop as a result of rolling friction. A ship sailing through a body of water is slowed by friction caused by the movement of the hull in the water. An aircraft flying through the air is slowed by the friction of air resistance. Even in space, friction acts on a moving object. Although space is generally described as a vacuum, it is not a perfect vacuum, but one in which small frictional forces are at work (Scherer and Fahr 1998).

Friction plays an important role in sports. Swimmers, cyclists, ice skaters, and skiers are just some of the athletes for whom friction is of great concern. For others, friction is an important factor even though they might never think about it. A field hockey ball on the ground doesn't move because of static friction between the ball and the grass. Once the ball is hit, both sliding and rolling friction may resist its motion, causing it to eventually come to a stop. At the 1968 Summer Olympics, records were broken because the high altitude of Mexico City imposed less air resistance on the athletes.

In *On War*, Carl von Clausewitz, wrote in a chapter entitled "Friction in War" (von Clausewitz, Heuser, and Howard 2007):

> *Everything is very simple in war, but the simplest thing is difficult. The difficulties accumulate and end by producing a kind of friction that is inconceivable unless one has experienced war ....*

> *Countless minor incidents—the kind you can never really foresee— combine to lower the general level of performance, so that one always falls far short of the intended goal ....*

> *Friction is the only concept that more or less corresponds to the factors that distinguish real war from war on paper ....*

> *Friction, as we choose to call it, is the force that makes the apparently easy so difficult.*

General von Clausewitz was making the point that, in war, even the simplest of tasks can be difficult due to a multitude of small, unaccountable things that can be collectively referred to as "friction."

In social situations, friction describes the tension and possible conflict that may exist between people as a result of their interactions. It's even possible for tension to be present between people without interaction. Someone can react negatively toward another person simply upon hearing his or her name because of a negative stereotype about that person. Personal interaction also can generate substantial tension even between people who might normally get along fine. The medium of communication can play an important role in social interactions. For example, research has shown that e-mail can increase friction in negotiations because it impedes the personal, contextual conversation that can create rapport and foster trust and cooperation (Morris, et al. 2002).

In his book *The Inmates Are Running the Asylum: Why High Tech Products Drive Us Crazy and How to Restore the Sanity*, Alan Cooper coined the term **cognitive friction** to describe "the resistance encountered by a human intellect when it engages with a complex system of rules that change as the problem changes." Cooper observed that software interaction is high in cognitive friction because the meaning of pressing the keys on a computer or using the mouse can change. In contrast, he rates playing a violin as low in cognitive friction because the violin's response to manipulation is predictable and subject to physical laws, even though a violin is actually extremely difficult to control (Cooper 2004). Cognitive friction can be present when we interact with seemingly simple everyday objects. How many times have you tried to push a door when it can only be pulled open? Have you ever had difficulty programming a microwave oven to simply reheat something?

In business, friction in markets can be thought of as any force that makes it difficult for sellers and buyers to connect and complete a transaction. Wharton management professor Olivier Chatain and INSEAD strategy professor Peter Zemsky explored this concept in their paper "Value Creation and Value Capture with Frictions." Think about your own buying experiences and how you choose among various competitors. Why did you pass on one or more vendors? Perhaps a store was too far away. You may have visited a web site and found it difficult to navigate. Maybe you placed a phone call and gave up after you had trouble navigating the vendor's automated phone system. Or perhaps you connected with someone on the phone or in person and found that person incompetent or rude. These are all examples of friction. In low-friction markets, such as those in which the offerings are highly commoditized, buyers don't have to obtain much information to arrive at a buying decision. Buying gasoline doesn't require much research. Gas stations are everywhere, people know that gas is virtually the same regardless of where they purchase it, all the sellers clearly advertise their prices, and consumers don't need to be aware of any extras or hidden fees. In high-friction markets, buyers must expend effort to arrive at a buying decision. Complex products and services require research to determine whether an offering fits a buyer's needs and to assist in ascertaining the offering's value (Chatain and Zemsky 2009, 3–4). Buying a cellphone and getting it connected to a network is surprisingly difficult. Different kinds of phones have varying features, and the packages for airtime have different services and price levels. You must also figure out the savings or cost associated with locking in with a cellular provider because often a cost is associated with switching vendors, especially if your contract hasn't run its full course.

Firms may experience friction from within their own organizational boundaries. Friction within a firm is costly—and the greater the friction, the greater the cost. Some internal friction is unavoidable and is part of the cost of doing business, or what economists refer to as *transaction cost*. Friction can also arise from inefficiencies such as unnecessary reviews, checkpoints or approvals, and difficulties with communication. The greatest friction of all results from making mistakes. This is why Deming and other quality gurus have advised companies to build in quality throughout the production process instead of relying on downstream testing to identify problems later.

Reducing Friction

Friction is resistance that can increase the difficulty or time taken to complete a task. Some causes of friction don't seem like a problem until you have to perform that task frequently. Many of the principles of the Jazz Process can help reduce friction. For example, friction can be generated if rules are too numerous or too strict. Focusing on the principle "Use just enough rules" helps reduce friction. It's easy to see how principles such as "Build trust and respect," "Commit with passion," and "Maintain momentum" can also assist in reducing friction. Adhering to these and other best principles doesn't necessarily guarantee that you can reduce friction to an appropriate level, but it certainly helps. Reducing and changing processes and implementing best practices takes time, especially for large organizations or those set in their ways. When the effects of friction have been felt, applying best practices doesn't necessarily rectify the existing problems; however, it does reduce the likelihood of friction in the future.

Imagine a machine with moving parts. When the parts in the machine are turning, friction is generated. As friction increases, the machine's efficiency decreases as energy is transformed into undesirable side effects such as heat and noise. Increase the level of friction further, and the machine not only may fail to work, but may sustain damage. It might be possible to redesign the machine to operate with reduced friction, but that might take time and money and fundamentally might not be a financially viable decision. A simpler way to reduce friction is to apply lubrication to the machine. Lubrication reduces friction and improves efficiency.

Lubrication can be applied to an activity in the same way it can be applied to a machine. Researchers at Stanford and Northwestern Universities studied *social friction* in the context of e-mail negotiations. Negotiations always involve some degree of friction as a result of the disagreement that may result from conflicting interests. When this friction increases, negotiations can potentially overheat and break down. The inevitable friction in negotiations makes them a particularly flammable type of discussion. E-mail negotiations are even more problematic. Although e-mail may be good for communicating complex information, its asynchronous, mostly text nature makes it a poor medium for communicating the subtle nuances that are usually conveyed through inflection, facial expressions, and gestures. Thus, e-mail negotiations are a good candidate for researching very specific means of reducing social friction. Using the term **social lubrication** to describe the ways in which social friction can be reduced, the researchers identified multiple methods for lubricating a negotiation (Morris, et al. 2002, 4, and 8–11):

- Background conversation or "schmoozing" about personal or unrelated issues to "break the ice" at the beginning of a negotiation or to relieve tension during a negotiation
- Responsive expression to create a feedback loop that compensates for the difficulty of conveying nonverbal nuances through e-mail
- Explicit statements that affirm the value of the relationship
- Clarification to avoid and repair misunderstandings

Although this study specifically focused on e-mail negotiations, the lubricants are applicable to any social interaction, regardless of the medium. Other social lubricants include these:

- Apologizing for or accepting blame for a mistake
- Acknowledging facts
- Making substantial change that demonstrates a willingness to immediately address a problem

- Giving credit where it is due
- Downplaying mistakes others make

A lubricant helps things proceed smoothly. This is precisely what is meant in metaphoric expressions such as "She greased the wheels, and everything went fine" or "He accepted some grease to fix the outcome of the race." In high-friction scenarios, stopping or altering the source of the friction may be beyond your control. However, you may be able to reduce the impact of the friction. Let's say you have a product that is difficult to install and configure for correct, optimum performance. It could be a software package or a device of some sort. Simplifying the installation and configuration might not be possible because of cost or time restrictions, but you can reduce friction for customers by providing such lubricants as these:

- Easy-to-follow instructions
- "Recipes" for a variety of standard configurations that will suit common usage scenarios
- A trouble-shooting guide to assist in solving problems
- Customer support via telephone

If friction is causing you to lose sales, you need to find ways that make it easier for potential buyers to discover your offerings and then analyze and obtain them. We're all familiar with those feature comparison tables that appear in brochures and on web sites. They frequently differentiate various editions of a vendor's offerings or compare the offerings of two or more vendors. Another similar mechanism is the quizzes or "wizards" that can suggest a specific, suitable offering based on answers to a series of questions. When you visit the supermarket, the "eight items or less" checkout lane helps speed everyone's exit from the store by reducing the friction associated with waiting in a queue. Amazon.com reduced the friction associated with purchasing when it implemented the infamous 1-Click purchasing system. This allows customers to expedite their online purchases by using a previously supplied address and credit card number. If a customer is purchasing a single item, he or she can complete the transaction with 1-Click without even having to put it in a virtual shopping cart.

Optimizing Friction

If friction is bad, avoiding it entirely seems logical. As it turns out, this is often an undesirable goal. In music, friction is tension that is manifested through such musical elements as harmonic dissonance, melodic chromaticism, and rhythm syncopation. Musical pitches that don't sound "good" or "right" together or that sound "clashing" are dissonant. The music of Bach is not very dissonant, whereas the music of Stravinsky is highly dissonant. Chromatic melodies may be harder to sing, with awkward and angular intervals and unexpected notes. Rhythms that are always squarely on the beat, even when subdivided into shorter notes, are easy to follow. Highly syncopated rhythms, such as those used in jazz, are constantly against or off the beat, creating tension. When there's a great deal of syncopation, such as when a drummer plays a complex drum solo, even accomplished musicians can find it difficult to follow along. Listening to music with too much tension can be tedious. On the other hand, if there is too little tension, the music lacks interest.

Improvised jazz gives musicians the freedom to choose the specific notes played. Consequently, the musicians also have the freedom to generate friction. As a bassist, my primary responsibilities are to help define the time and the harmony. Let's look at this in detail. In the rhythm changes that we discussed in Chapter 9, "Make Contributions Count," the first four bars of chords might look something like this when the chord changes are played in the key of B flat:

| Bb | | G- | | C- | | F7 | | D- | | G7 | | C- | | F7 | |

Each chord covers two beats, with two chords per bar. In a basic two-feel groove, I could just play the root of each chord and simply play the following notes:

| Bb | | G | | C | | F | | D | | G | | C | | F | |

If I wanted to play in four with a walking bass line, I would add notes between each chord:

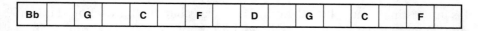

| Bb | D | G | B | C | E | F | Eb | D | F# | G | D | C | E | F | A |

I could play a huge number of possible permutations just within these four bars of music—and that's without varying the rhythm. With each chord, some notes are consonant, or "inside" the chord, and others are dissonant, or "outside." If I play largely inside and clearly define the notes of each chord, I minimize friction. The problem is that this can become overly predictable and boring for the listener and the other musicians. If I stray further away and play more notes outside each chord, I generate more friction, tension, and interest.

One of the specific harmonic devices in the bassist's bag of tricks is the pedal. This is where the bass maintains a specific note even while the chords are changing. For example, I could play a dominant pedal. To explain this, let's talk about what **dominant** means in musical terms. At the end of many classical music pieces, you hear two chords. Together these chords form what is known as an authentic cadence. The first of these chords is a dominant chord, so called because it's a strong-sounding chord. In fact, the only chord that is stronger sounding or more rooted to the music's key is the second chord in an authentic cadence, which is called the tonic chord. At the end of the Beethoven's Fifth Symphony, you hear, in the key of C, an authentic cadence repeated 15 times as the music moves alternates between G7 and C chords. Beethoven uses the same cadence 24 times in succession at the end of his Eighth Symphony. Each time a dominant chord is played in a cadence, the listener fully expects the tonic chord to follow. A pedal occurs when the bass maintains a note even while the harmony is changing. In our rhythm changes example, I could play F, which is the dominant note in the key of B flat throughout the entire four bars of chord changes. F is the root of chords such as F7 and part of other chords such as B flat and G7 and D-; therefore, it sounds very inside those changes. Yet it sounds outside and, therefore, more strained when played against the remaining chords in our four-bar example. The listener expects to hear the harmony defined by the chords of the music, but the pedal alters that harmony and creates tension and friction. Additionally, when an audience hears a dominant note in the bass, they expect to hear a resolution to the tonic soon thereafter. Delaying that resolution generates further tension and friction.

It's interesting to note how the other musicians handle this friction. The tension generated with a prolonged pedal often inspires a soloist to play more intensely. The soloist responds to the tension the bassist creates by hooking into the idea and creating his or her own musical tension. A less experienced player may be thrown off by the use of this musical device and lose his or her place, especially if the pedal is prolonged. If that happens when I am playing bass, I'm always prepared to lubricate the situation. I do this by playing something obvious and leading that fits with the chord changes. This helps take the soloist back to familiar territory.

What's interesting about friction is that although it generally creates difficulties when present in large quantities, eliminating it entirely can create a whole different set of problems. Rolling friction slows a rolling ball, but without static friction, the ball would slide and not roll at all. Adhesive friction between tires and the surface of a road allows the tires to maintain traction on the road, thus enabling the driver to accelerate, slow down, and negotiate turns. Without traction, the wheels would spin, and the vehicle would go nowhere. Static friction ensures that objects such as those sitting on your shelves and your desk stay put on surfaces that aren't perfectly level. Static friction also allows all of us to walk by converting a backward push of feet along the ground into forward motion. Without that friction, people would fall over as if they were walking on slippery ice. The machine with the moving parts I mentioned previously? Without friction, all the parts would slip against one another, and the machine simply wouldn't work.

In economics, **perfect competition** describes a market that is the opposite of a monopoly. Many buyers and sellers exist, all with similar and uniform offerings, and the barriers to entry and exit are low so that sellers can come and go without penalty. All information, including pricing, is readily available to all the buyers and sellers so that buyers can easily compare offerings and shop around. A perfectly competitive market has no friction, but it is a theoretical model. No known market truly meets all the requirements. However, some markets approach the model. In the old world, agricultural markets approached the perfect competition model, with many suppliers all providing perfectly substitutable goods. Today this is less true, as government subsidies and protective tariffs provide advantage to certain suppliers. In the modern world, eBay exhibits some of the characteristics of a perfectly competitive market. Anyone can buy or sell on eBay, and often large quantities of similar goods sell for nearly the same price. In a perfectly competitive market, buyers don't favor any particular sellers. Consequently, many sellers exist, all with a small share of the market, so no one seller ends up doing better than any other. Sellers earn only enough profits to keep them in business. If any seller earns excess profits, other sellers enter the market or expand, thus increasing supply and driving the price back down to a uniform level. This is effectively a negative feedback correction to help maintain equilibrium in a self-regulating system. It is an example of what economists refer to as the **invisible hand**, a metaphor coined by Adam Smith in his 1759 book *The Theory of Moral Sentiments* and referred to in his later works, including the 1776 classic *The Wealth of Nations*.

Not surprisingly, most businesses with capitalist goals have no interest in participating in such a model of perfect competition. Chatain and Zemsky found that although profits can suffer when friction in a market is too high, the same is true when friction is too low. Chatain noted, "When you reduce friction, one would usually think it must be good for the strong firm. But it's not always the case. We found that stronger firms want to have less friction than weaker firms, but they don't want to eliminate frictions." On the other hand, the researchers found that increased friction leads to decreased rivalry because sellers do not need to compete so directly with one another. Consequently, weaker firms may benefit from high levels of friction because they may get the opportunity to capture buyers in small niche markets where larger sellers might not have an interest (Wharton School of the University of Pennsylvania 2009).

In "Essentials of Execution," following Part II, I described how Norbert Wiener and Julian Bigelow observed the behavior of *hunting* in the servomechanisms of anti-aircraft guns when a lack of friction existed. If you try to walk on slippery ice without traction aids on your shoes, you will slide back and forth. Even if you're fortunate enough not to fall down, the only way you can follow the path you desire is to move extremely slowly, to maximize whatever friction you have. If you slide, you will try to compensate, and you may end up sliding a different way; then you may try to compensate again, and so forth. Of course, this is hunting in a negative feedback loop. If there's too little friction, an action can fall into a mode of hunting, which can cause delays or damage to an activity.

As it turns out, friction is a necessary evil. Too much friction is bad, but too little is also a problem. As I mentioned earlier, when there are too many rules, the resulting friction can slow people or even stop them from progressing. Yet people can also get stuck when not enough rules help guide them. It's hard for people to know how to think outside the box when they don't know where the box is! The optimal amount of friction varies for each activity. When a group of people try to solve a problem, a degree of healthy debate is important. Without it, groupthink results. Later you'll see how divergent thinking is essential to innovation. On the other hand, an excess of social friction can lead to all kinds of problems between people. Other forms of friction are needed in greater amounts, such as the friction that jazz musicians generate. The trick is to identify the optimal level for each specific form of friction and learn how to adjust it. This is usually done by controlling the mechanism or process that generates the friction and by using specific techniques to apply lubrication.

Recapitulation

- Friction is resistance that can increase the difficulty of completing a task or the time needed to do so. Some causes of friction don't seem like a problem until you have to perform that task frequently.

- The greatest friction of all results from making mistakes. Deming and other quality gurus have advised companies to build in quality throughout the production process instead of relying on downstream testing to identify problems later.

- Changing processes to reduce friction can take too long, especially for large organizations. An alternative may be to apply a lubricant.

- Too much friction is bad, but too little is also a problem. With too little friction, an action can fall into a mode of hunting, which can cause delays or damage to an activity.

- Adjust the amount of friction by controlling each mechanism or process that generates friction and by applying specific lubrication.

CHAPTER 11

Maintain Momentum

"It does not matter how slow you go,
so long as you do not stop."
—Confucius

Concepts of Momentum

Any system must expend resources to advance or move in a specific direction. Energy that a baseball pitcher transfers to a ball, fuel that a car consumes, and a team's united intellectual efforts to solve a problem are all examples of expending resources in pursuit of a goal. When resistant forces such as friction are present, making progress is harder, and additional resources must be expended. The pitcher must exert more energy when throwing into a strong wind. If you add parts to a car's exterior, such as a roof rack, or if you open one of the car's windows, the vehicle's wind resistance increases. If the car's tires are underinflated, it increases their rolling resistance. Each form of resistance, also known as *drag,* increases fuel consumption. As we've learned, sources of friction in business, such as politics, excessive bureaucracy, lack of trust, poor communication, and frequent mistakes, all require people to spend more time and energy.

Momentum is the tendency or impetus to continue in a specific direction. When momentum is present, fewer resources need be consumed to advance. If you're driving a car and you take your foot off the throttle, the vehicle's momentum causes it to continue moving, despite various forms of friction. You must apply the brakes and create substantially more friction to slow the car more quickly. If velocity is a measure of how quickly a team is progressing, constructive momentum makes it easier to continue at a constant velocity—and also makes it easier to increase velocity. **Constructive momentum** can make it easier to establish positive feedback loops such as economies of scale that build on previous results to produce increasingly greater future results. **Destructive momentum**, on the other hand, is negative progress. Repeated mistakes or problematic behavior can generate destructive momentum, fueling costly and dangerous negative feedback loops that waste precious time and resources. In our further discussions, references to momentum refer to constructive momentum unless otherwise noted.

In physics, momentum is calculated as the mass of an object multiplied by its velocity. A truck has greater mass than a car, but the car can have equal momentum to a truck if it is moving fast enough. This concept of momentum applies to teams as well. For any given velocity, a larger team or organization has more momentum than a smaller one. In theory, a smaller team can have equivalent momentum to a larger team if its velocity is high enough.

Getting started, or "getting the ball rolling," to quote an often-used metaphor, can be one of the hardest things to do. **Critical mass** is a sociodynamic term for a state in which there is sufficient momentum to enable an activity to be self-sustaining. To reach this state, considerable resources may need to be expended, especially if resistance must be overcome. In social situations, this can happen when introducing a new idea, a new practice, or new people. People have resisted change for as long as humans have been able to establish routines that they can take comfort in. Comfort is largely the result of emotional connections that are established over time, and severing such connections can be difficult. In any transition, it's important to acknowledge both the good and the bad about the things people are familiar with, while helping them connect with what they are being asked to adopt. In Chapter 8, "Act Transparently," we identified how associations can help establish a perception of authenticity. Similarly, associations can help people establish connections with new ideas, practices, or people. Execution champions, used in large companies, are an example of employing such associations by having people act as advocates for something new. Their clout can often enable them to lubricate situations, easing the inevitable friction that can be generated in the course of a transition.

The single most important element of momentum is regularity. People are naturally drawn to the predictability of regular cycles. The "theater" exercise described in the Introduction is an example of how a group of people instinctively fall into a regular cadence when they read together, just as a church congregation does when reading liturgy. This is a manifestation of a physics concept known as **entrainment**, wherein two or more interacting oscillating systems fall into the same period. Momentum can be maintained by managing four operational elements that leverage people's affinity for regular cycles: form, tempo, pulse, and groove. Let's look at each one in turn.

Form

Most activities that require committed efforts in the pursuit of specific goals are organized with some kind of form. This is true regardless of the duration of the activity. It could be a 10-minute jazz performance, a 3-hour hockey game, a 6-month software development project, an 18-month political campaign, or a 5-year military operation. Consider some examples of form:

- The minuet is an eighteenth-century dance that originated in France. The music of the minuet had a basic ABA form, meaning two different sections of music, with the A section played at the beginning and the end, and the B section between them. In practice, both sections often repeated with many variations. In turn, the minuet was often part of a larger work, such as a dance suite, which also contained other musical dance forms, such as the courante, allemande, gigue, Gavotte, and Bourrée.

- Many jazz songs are based on the AABA form, with 8 bars given to each section and 32 bars total. The B section is often referred to as a bridge. Examples of AABA tunes include "Take the 'A' Train," by Billy Strayhorn; "Round Midnight," by Thelonious Monk; and "So What," by Miles Davis. Another common form is ABAC, used in George Gershwin's "A Foggy Day" and Jerome Kern's "My Romance." Sections may not necessarily be eight bars in length. Gershwin's "Summertime" is ABAC, with each section comprised of four bars. Kern's "All The Things You Are" has an ABCD form with 8-8-8-12 bars, and "Stablemates," by Benny Golson, is ABA with 14-8-14 bars. The entire song is repeated multiple times, with at least one iteration of the melody at the beginning, followed by multiple iterations for each improvised solo and at least another iteration of the melody at the end.

- A basketball game consists of four quarters. In the National Basketball Association, each quarter is 12 minutes long. Overtime periods are five minutes long. There's a 15-minute break between the two halves; there's 120 seconds between the first and second quarters, between the third and fourth quarters, and before overtime periods.

- In software development projects that use an agile methodology, iterations (or sprints) typically last from one to four weeks. In the Eclipse projects at eclipse.org and the Jazz projects at jazz.net, projects often have three to nine milestone iterations. The goal of each iteration is to produce a stable build of software that demonstrates new functionality or defect fixes. These are typically denoted as M1, M2, M3, and so on. During each iteration, tasks such as gathering requirements, designing, coding, verifying new functionality, and fixing defects may all be performed. At the end of the last milestone, a project usually declares a feature freeze and then enters a series of shorter test-and-fix iterations to improve quality and stability. These are typically referred to as release candidates because the goal is to produce a releasable product at the end of each iteration. They are typically denoted as RC1, RC2, and so on.
- The structure of a political, marketing, or military campaign typically includes the following phases:

  1. **Assessment**—Setting goals and evaluating conditions and restrictions.

  2. **Planning**—Defining specific objectives, scope, and cost, and allocating resources by staffing and equipping. In a political campaign, fund-raising may begin in this phase.

  3. **Execution**—Mobilizing resources and executing on specific objectives—for example: raising funds, connecting with voters, running advertisements, and carrying out orders. Throughout this phase, the results of the execution must be constantly monitored so that actions can be controlled and adjusted or cancelled, if necessary.

  4. **Conclusion**—Assessing the outcome of the campaign and cleaning up with specific tasks such as thanking donors, supporters, and volunteers; resolving any campaign debts; bringing home troops; and so on.

People use the predictability of form to help them set goals, time their deliveries, and shape their contributions. For example, a jazz musician who knows that he has 32 bars in which to improvise a solo may define a musical riff or motif, develop it with a climax, and then wind down the solo with an ending that assists the band's transition into another musician's solo or a restatement of the song's melody. A software developer may plan to deliver a new feature or fix a defect before the end of a specific iteration. This allows her to plan specific activities such as design, modeling, coding, testing, reviewing, documenting, and so forth.

A form helps a team coordinate its efforts and increase synergy. The degree to which the team can reap those benefits depends on its ability to navigate a form. Such a form must define more than just the beginning and end of the activity. Sections, phases, and iterations are all examples of subdividing an activity. These subdivisions reduce the activity to more manageable chunks and give teams checkpoints against which to synchronize. It's important to use a form that works for each situation. If too few checkpoints are spread too far apart, the coherency of a team's efforts may suffer. Too many checkpoints occurring too frequently may add unnecessary overhead and reduce productivity.

The way in which an activity is subdivided is also important. It's interesting to note how the form for software development projects has evolved over the decades. In projects that employ the waterfall model of development, the form defines four or five long phases for the project, with each phase focusing on one specific task. This means that all the requirements must be determined before moving on to the design, all that work must be completed before writing all the code, and so forth. In contrast, the form for a project using an agile methodology is more finely subdivided, with each iteration featuring a compressed cycle of all the software development activities to produce usable software.

Proponents of agile software methods tout them as vastly superior to the waterfall method. Indeed, they have many advantages. Agile methods can be particularly effective when a lot of change is expected or when, as is often the case in software development, many factors are not entirely known or understood. Does this mean that all activities can benefit from an iterative method? If you look back at the form of a political or military campaign, you will notice an uncanny similarity to the waterfall method. A similar form also is used in the construction of a building. Software development is a very different type of activity than hardware development or warfare or building construction. The cost of making changes is far lower, and the likelihood of unexpected changes is greater. When an aspect of a project involves substantial cost, it is critical to mitigate risks and get things right the first time. If you're deploying 20,000 troops into enemy territory, you can't simply drop them in there and then start iterating. It can be helpful to iterate if an initial plan goes awry, but the overwhelming bulk of the planning must be done up front wherever possible. Agility is a capability predicated on a mindset of responsiveness and flexibility. You should feel entirely comfortable using the waterfall method or some form of it if it provides sufficient agility yet enables you to effectively manage risks and costs. It's far more important to follow the rules "Maintain momentum and "Lead on demand" and to heed other useful principles than it is to subscribe to specific methods.

Tempo

Tempo is the overall pace of an activity. It sets the speed at which individuals must deliver their respective contributions. When people must follow rules that dictate the specific content and method of their contributions, they may have trouble keeping up with a pace that is too fast. On the other hand, freedom from such rules can allow them to meet objectives while altering their contributions as required. For example, when I perform in a large ensemble with 13 to 30 musicians of the Impressions in Jazz Orchestra, most of what each musician plays comes from written parts. There's an expected range for the tempo for any given tune we play. Duke Ellington's "Stevedore Stomp," for example, is typically played with a tempo of 260 beats per minute. If I count it off faster than that, either deliberately or by accident, the entire band has to maintain the pace I set, playing all the notes written in their parts at that tempo. If the tempo of the performance is significantly faster than the pace to which people are accustomed, and if they can't play all their notes well at that speed, the performance will suffer. At best, it might weaken the presentation, with some notes being dropped or tentatively played. At worst, it might result in a total train wreck as people stumble over their parts and lose track of their place in the music. The effects can be cumulative, as one person's loss of stability affects others who depend on him or her. Just as a tempo that is too fast can lead to problems, a too-slow tempo can also be problematic. For example, the duration of each note is increased and wind instrumentalists must blow for a longer time. For many pieces of music, the piece "sits" right and feels comfortable at a certain tempo range.

In improvised passages within predominantly prescripted music, or in small-group jazz performances in which there is little sheet music to read and most of the notes are improvised, the musicians can cope with a much larger variation in tempo. A simple jazz standard such as "My Funny Valentine" can be played at any tempo, from a really slow ballad at 60 beats per minute to a fast burner at 300 beats per minute. Individual musicians alter their contributions to suit the tempo, while still meeting objectives such as stating the melody or improvising a solo.

In music, variations in tempo typically come at the discretion of the musicians, or at least the leader or conductor of the ensemble. The tempo contributes to the character of the music. A jazz standard played as a slow ballad has a very different feel compared to when it is played at a medium tempo. It's very different again when played as a burner. Miles Davis's first quintet played many jazz standards on the classic 1956 Prestige albums *Relaxin' with the Miles Davis Quintet, Steamin' with the Miles Davis Quintet, Workin' with the Miles Davis Quintet,* and *Cookin' with the Miles Davis Quintet.* If you listen to performances of the same tunes by the second quintet, such as those on the 1965 Columbia recordings, available as a boxed set called *The Complete Live at The Plugged Nickel 1965,* you'll find that the second quintet almost always employed faster tempos. The character of each comparative performance is poles apart.

Listen to the Difference

Listen to the performance of "If I Were a Bell" on *Relaxin' with the Miles Davis Quintet,* recorded by Davis's first quintet in 1956. Then listen to the 1965 performances by Davis's second quintet at the Plugged Nickel: One performance was recorded in the first set on the first night, and another even slightly faster performance was recorded in the first set the following evening. For further comparison, listen to a performance from the *Saturday Night at the Blackhawk* recording of 1961, which features Davis with a transitory band between his first and second quintets. There's also a great performance by the second quintet in Tokyo in 1964 on the album *Miles in Tokyo,* which is now also available in the boxed set *Seven Steps—The Complete Columbia Recordings of Miles Davis (1963—1964).* To be fair, there's a great deal more going on in the recordings of the second quintet than just the faster tempos. The musicians are far more daring and evolve the music in all manner of ways. However, it's also arguable that the faster tempos on the standards facilitated their approach to the music. As a special bonus, if you listen to the performance in Tokyo, pay attention to how the band halves the tempo for Davis's solo at the end (time reference 7:35). This can be seen as a nod to the first quintet and brings the musical development full circle.

In other domains, where variations in tempo occur for different reasons, the effect on team members is the same. In a software project, a team may be tasked with delivering a new feature in three months. The only problem is that they had estimated it would require six months. They've just learned that a competitor's product will include a similar feature in a release that will be made available next month. The team's ability to respond to such a dramatic difference in tempo depends greatly on the freedom they have to act on their goals. They may have to drop specific elements of the feature or reduce its performance to get the feature delivered in time. They may not be able to deliver the product on all the platforms that the product supports, or the user interface and documentation may not be translated to all the languages they usually target. Perhaps the documentation will have to be very lightweight, and they will need to compensate with articles and tutorials that will be delivered at the company's website after the release of the software. Perhaps they can deliver the feature exactly as originally proposed, but they will have to drop or compromise another feature. If the company's processes are so rigid that they can't tolerate these kinds of tradeoffs, delivering the feature by the required date simply may not be possible.

It is sometimes said in music that there's no part that is too hard—there are only tempos that are too fast. This is indeed true. Yet even when musicians must stick to the script and play all the notes on the page, when the tempo is fast enough that they have difficulty with their parts, I encourage them and work with them, where necessary, to simplify the parts. Sometimes notes can be intentionally left out, or *ghosted,* a technique in which the note is only implied, not fully sounded. The difference to listeners may be negligible. Sometimes playing all the notes at a faster tempo can actually sound worse because the music becomes too dense or too heavyweight and loses the intended character. In these cases, simplifying the part is the right answer both technically and artistically. Thus, even when it appears that the rules may make it impossible to deliver on time, you may be able to make subtle but highly effective optimizations to turn an impossible task into a possible one.

In agile software development, much has been made of the timebox in which the end date of an iteration is fixed. This is an important concept because a large proportion of software projects are late in delivering. In a timebox, instead of moving a date to accommodate a deliverable, the deliverable—or, at least, the way in which it is implemented—must be altered. In music, as in most real-time activities, timeboxes are always in effect. In basketball, when mere seconds are left on the clock and a team is down by one point, the players don't have the luxury of extending the available play time. By the way, this is one of the many reasons Michael Jordan is one of the greatest basketball players ever. He won no less than 25 NBA games in the final moments of the game. In 24 of those games, he made his move in the final 10 seconds; the other was in the last 22 seconds. Eight of the game-winners were right on the buzzer (Mitchell 2001).

Self-organizing, agile individuals and teams can respond to unexpected tempos when they have freedom to determine how they will achieve their goals.

When a tempo is set for any given activity, it must take into account the goals of the activity, the abilities of the individual team members, and the flexibility of the processes that guide them. Self-organizing, agile individuals and teams can respond to unexpected tempos when they have the freedom to determine how they will achieve their goals.

Pulse

A musical pulse is just like the heartbeat of a person. It's a constant, regular event that drives the music and helps the musicians maintain synchronicity with respect to the tempo. The pulse is always a function of the tempo. In jazz, the tempo is communicated by the drummer more than any other musician. The bassist, however, is the primary communicator of the pulse. The drummer and bassist must "lock in" together and maintain the same tempo. Most music maintains the same tempo from the beginning to the end of the piece. Longer, complex pieces may change the tempo in different sections or temporarily slow down or speed up in specific sections such as transitions or endings, but generally the tempo stays constant for extended periods of time. In contrast, a bassist can alter the pulse, and the drummer and the other instruments must usually follow along. If they choose to go specifically against the pulse set by the bassist, it introduces tension into the music. This may actually be a desirable thing, and a bassist may set up such a situation purposely. However, for the most part, the pulse is felt consistently throughout the band, just as it is felt in all the arteries of a person's body.

In Chapter 1, "Use Just Enough Rules," I described how a bassist may play in two by playing two beats per bar, or in four by playing four beats per bar. This is an example of a musical pulse. The pulse is significant because improvising musicians play to the pulse, not the tempo. When a small jazz group plays a slow ballad, they may occasionally play one or more sections of improvised soloing in a double-time feel. This is often done to introduce some variety into the character of the piece. In double-time feel, the tempo doesn't change; neither does the rate at which the chords in the song's harmony are traversed. The musicians create the *illusion* of doubling the tempo by doubling the pulse and effectively playing in eight. Although the pulse is communicated throughout the band by the bassist, he or she may take direction from others in setting that pulse. You may sometimes hear a saxophonist play a run of notes in the preceding beats to a section as a signal that he or she wants to move into a double-time feel, and the bassist often responds and completes the transition. Alternatively, the bassist may resist the urge for a while, which creates tension and, thus, interest in the music that is resolved when either the bassist moves to playing in the double-time feel or the saxophonist abandons the push to go there.

In a general sense, the pulse is a mechanism a team can use to cope with a tempo that is too fast or too slow for their liking. Instead of synchronizing directly with a tempo, they lock into a pulse that is related to the tempo but may be changed even while the tempo must remain constant. To some degree, external constraints, such as the actions of competitors, dictate the tempo. In companies, senior management may set the tempo of business or a particular project, but the leaders of the teams can set the pulse. The leader of a military squad might double-time the pace of the squad's march, to get to a certain location to rendezvous with another squad or avoid an encounter with an enemy or with bad weather. The leader of a software development team faced with multiple critical issues might increase the number of team meetings for a two-week period to resolve the problems. At the same time, the leader might increase the number and type of approvals required to deliver changes to the codebase. This would slow down the rate of change to the codebase and minimize the possibility of further destabilization.

Although a pulse is communicated to the greater team and to consumers, experienced contributors don't pay attention to every pulse. For example, a fast four-beat jazz piece might be perceived as having a rapid pulse that pulsates on every beat. However, many experienced jazz musicians will feel an internal pulse at a quarter of that rate, coinciding with the first beat of every bar. In some cases, when the form of the song defines sections with multiples of 4 bars, such as 8 or 16 bars, a musician will actually think in 4-bar chunks. Similarly, a jazz waltz, like a classical waltz, has a three-beat feel with three beats to a bar. Examples include "Waltz for Debby," "Alice in Wonderland," "Jitterbug Waltz," "Bluesette," "Someday My Prince Will Come" (popularized in jazz by Miles Davis), and "My Favorite Things" (introduced into the jazz canon by John Coltrane). If the bass walks and plays a note on every beat in a jazz waltz, the pulse might seem rapid, but experienced musicians focus only on the first beat, ignoring the other beats and feeling the pulse *in one*. When the tempo is fast and the pulse is fast, experienced musicians know that the only way to realistically manage things is to focus less on the details and think more generally. For musicians, that translates to thinking more about the shape and overall story of a solo and less about the specific notes. For a racecar driver, it's about thinking of the path through a series of turns instead of overly focusing on each specific turn. When we get bogged down in the details, we increase the likelihood of destabilizing the performance.

Groove

The groove is a function of the pulse; therefore, it's also a function of the tempo. Musically, a bassist can play a song with a variety of grooves, such as Latin, bluegrass, and funk, with each groove based on a two-beat pulse. Abstractly, a groove is a specific set of essential, fundamental activities that are repeated with respect to the pulse. As an example, the Rational Team Concert development team typically operates with a tempo and form that dictate four-week iterations. The pulse is weekly, with the groove as follows:

Monday	Integration build (a.m.)
	Meeting of Project Management Committee (90 minutes)
	Teams deliver new functionality and fixes for defects
	Integration build (p.m.)
Tuesday	Integration build (a.m.)
	Meeting of all team leads and interested stakeholders (60 minutes)
	Teams deliver new functionality and fixes for defects
	Integration build (p.m.)
Wednesday	Integration build (a.m.)
	All-hands testing
Thursday	Integration build (a.m.)
	Meeting of all team leads and interested stakeholders (30 minutes)
	Teams deliver new functionality and fixes for defects
	Integration build (p.m.)
Friday	Integration build (a.m.)
	Teams deliver critical fixes if Thursday p.m. build is not usable (stable)
	Optional integration build (p.m. or earlier) to incorporate critical fixes
	Distribute build

In the last (fourth) week of an iteration, which is called a milestone week, the groove varies slightly, with the addition of team leader meetings on Wednesday and Friday. The additional meetings are needed because there is a specific focus on delivering new functionality for the milestone while ensuring a stable build that interested consumers can adopt and the development team can use for self-hosting. Self-hosting is synonymous with **dogfooding**, a term used in the software industry that comes from the phrase "eating one's own dog food" and refers to the practice of using the products that you build. Dogfooding is especially effective if you use early builds of your own products as valuable feedback on functionality and defects can be given as new features evolve. Looking at this set of activities in our groove with a little less detail, we have this:

	Week 1	Week 2	Week 3	Milestone Week
Monday	Build	Build	Build	Build
	Code	Code	Code	Code
	90-minute PMC meeting	90-minute PMC meeting	90-minute PMC meeting	90-minute PMC meeting
	Build	Build	Build	Build
Tuesday	Build	Build	Build	Build
	Code	Code	Code	Code
	60-minute TL meeting	**60-minute TL meeting**	**60-minute TL meeting**	**60-minute TL meeting**
	Build	Build	Build	Build
Wednesday	Build	Build	Build	Build
	Test	Test	Test	**30-minute TL meeting**
				Test
Thursday	Build	Build	Build	Build
	Fix	Fix	Fix	Fix
	30-minute TL meeting	**30-minute TL meeting**	**30-minute TL meeting**	**30-minute TL meeting**
	Build	Build	Build	Build

	Week 1	Week 2	Week 3	Milestone Week
Friday	Build	Build	Build	Build
	Fix	Fix	Fix	**30-minute TL meeting**
	Optional build	Optional build	Optional build	Fix
	Distribute build	Distribute build	Distribute build	Optional build
				Distribute build
				Self-host on build

Can you see the groove in this table? Let's try a rhythmic exercise. With your fist or open hand, lightly hit the desk or your thigh, as if you're simulating a drumbeat. Hit the "drum" at a rate of approximately once per second, and keep it going continuously. Each beat of the "drum" represents a weekly pulse. Now with each pulse, say "BE-bop," giving equal time to each of the two syllables and stress the first syllable as you hit the drum. Repeat that three times, and then on the fourth pulse, say "BE-bop-bop-bop," but say that twice as fast to keep in time with the pulse. "BE" corresponds to a 60-minute meeting, and "bop" corresponds to a 30-minute meeting. So you've got this:

Lyrics:	BE-bop	BE-bop	BE-bop	BE-bop-bop-bop
Pulse:	Beat	Beat	Beat	Beat

Repeat the four-week sequence a number of times, and you'll be feeling the groove of a software development team!

A groove invites everyone to participate and align their contributions with it.

When you listen to music with a pulsating beat and an infectious groove, you enjoy it and feel like joining in. You may find yourself repeating elements of the groove to yourself or improvising little rhythmic or melodic elements that complement the existing parts of the groove while fitting right in alongside them. A groove invites everyone to participate and align their contributions with it. A groove is most effective when it is simple and clear to everyone.

Momentum in an Organization

I mentioned at the beginning of this chapter that destructive momentum can be a problem. Yet even constructive momentum can cause problems if it is not effectively managed. To begin with, all contributors should be aware of the process by which form, tempo, pulse, and groove are defined. In a jazz ensemble, the form is typically set by the composer of the music to be performed. The leader of the group sets the tempo, and the rhythm section plays an important role in helping the ensemble maintain that tempo. The rhythm section is also largely responsible for defining the pulse and the groove, although those musicians may follow a composer's directions, if any are given. The bassist often takes the lead in defining the pulse and the groove, although this can vary with different ensembles. The drummer, if there is one, is the primary communicator of the tempo. It's natural for this responsibility to fall to the drummer because everyone in the ensemble can clearly hear the unique timbre of the drums. Short, sharp sounds such as the click of a hi-hat or the snap of a snare allow the drummer to clearly delineate the time. Both the drummer and the bassist play repetitive parts, and this provides the predictable regularity that others in the ensemble can hook into. In software development, a project manager or release manager may set the form, tempo, and perhaps pulse and overall groove, with component team leaders setting specific grooves within their own teams. The assignment of responsibilities can vary greatly. What's important is that everyone understand where the responsibilities lie and stay willing to help build and maintain momentum. Just one person working against the effort can render it ineffective.

The idea that specific grooves may exist within the framework set by a more general groove is important. In Cuban music, the efforts of a multiperson rhythm section are defined first by a pattern known as the clave (pronounced "CLA-veh"), which is played on a pair of wooden sticks known as claves. All the other rhythm section instruments, including the timbales, congas, bongos, maracas, guiro, piano, and bass, each play their own specific rhythms that lock into the clave.

In large teams or organizations, or in complex projects, there may be multiple independent but related efforts that each benefit from momentum. For example, a software development team may define an annual cadence of product releases and updates as follows:

Jan	Feb	Mar	Apr	May	Jun	Jul	Aug	Sep	Oct	Nov	Dec
					MAJOR						
								FIX			
											MINOR
		FIX									

This cadence defines four deliveries, as follows:

- A major release in June (such as 4.0), with fixes and substantial new features
- An incremental maintenance fix-pack in September (such as 4.0.0.1), with fixes for defects
- A minor release in December (such as 4.0.1), with fixes for defects and a few new features
- Another incremental maintenance fix-pack in March (such as 4.0.1.1)

July and August are vacation months, and one of the fix-packs must be delivered while the work for the major release is underway. The momentum associated with such a schedule is very important because it affects customers; they may need to know when new features or defect fixes will be delivered so they can plan rollouts of software updates in their organizations. This schedule implies a monthly tempo and a pulse in which there is a release every three months. The groove is Fix–**Major**–Fix–**Minor**. Say it to yourself a number of times rhythmically to feel the groove, with a stress on the releases in bold. The annual form, evident in the table, is this:

- Six months of intense work
- Two months of vacation
- One month of fixing
- Three months of relatively intense work

The development schedule for each of these releases employs its own form, tempo, pulse, and groove to help maintain momentum for the delivery of its release. The tempo and pulse could be weekly, whereas the form for a major release might look like this:

Iteration	Duration
M1	6 weeks
M2	6 weeks
M3	6 weeks
RC1	3 weeks
RC2	2 weeks
RC3	2 weeks
RC4	1 week

The groove might define builds, team meetings, and testing and fixing efforts, as described earlier.

Maintaining Momentum

Looking ahead for potential issues and addressing them before they become problems helps avoid a loss of momentum. This outlook can be seen as a strategic perspective more than a tactical one, but that's not to say that you should look only strategically. Strike a balance between planning and simply reacting. Both extremes have their own problems. It is possible to plan too much and become overly confident as a result. On the other hand, you simply cannot plan for some things, such as aberrational events. This is why it is essential to maintain a state of readiness in which you can react and improvise. When a team must respond to change, each member of the team must react quickly enough that momentum is not lost.

The combination of tempo, pulse, and groove defines the rate at which the participants in an activity generate change. If jazz musicians play a slow ballad, the tempo will be slow, with typically no more than 60 beats per minute. To get a feel for this tempo, tap or clap once per second. The bass often plays in two, which essentially means the pulse is half the tempo. To feel that pulse, tap or clap once every two seconds. If you can, keep playing that pulse while you read on. Now what about the groove? Ballads are usually introverted, with a solemn, melancholy, or reflective disposition. The groove must be very simple; for that reason, it is usually the same as the pulse, with no additional complications. Even a soloist playing over the top of this will often play sparsely, with very few notes. As a result, the overall velocity is low. You can stop the pulse now if you managed to keep it going through those last few sentences. Everything we've discussed—the slow tempo, the two-beat pulse, the simple groove, and the simple playing over the top—creates

temporal tension. The listener must patiently wait for each change to materialize, and the result is dramatic. Imagine a small group, perhaps a trio or a quartet, playing a ballad. Recalling that momentum is a function of mass and velocity, we would expect the momentum to be very low because the velocity is low and the group is small. When the momentum is this low, a real danger of losing stability arises. This can happen in any task in which a small number of people are producing a low rate of output.

Jazz musicians do two important things to prevent a loss of stability from low momentum. First, they impart greater weight to specific notes. They do this by choosing the notes carefully, placing them with extreme precision, and stressing the note or playing it for its full duration. When playing fewer notes, the importance of each one increases. Second, specific notes are set up by playing one or more short notes immediately preceding the expected note. This has the effect of preparing the listener and the other musicians for the expected note. To get a feel for this, let's perform a number of exercises in rhythm.

Begin by tapping out a slow pulse like you were doing previously. Once per second, tap your hand on a table or on your thigh and say "DUM" at the same time. Once you've gotten a feel for the regular pulse, begin to precede the occasional note with "ba" as in "ba-DUM" but make sure "ba" is short so you maintain a regular pulse. Do you feel the difference when you prepare the note? To get more sophisticated, say "ba-pa-DUM" and always make sure that "DUM" falls with the tap of the hand on the expected regular pulse. The use of these preparatory notes effectively increases the velocity and momentum for a short period of time, leading up to one specific, expected contribution. To make the benefit of these preparatory notes more obvious, let's slow down the pulse so that is extremely slow. Tap and say "DUM" and leave nine seconds between each pulse. To do this and actually maintain a regular pulse, you will have to subdivide the time in your head by counting silently between the pulses. Say "DUM" followed by "2, 3, 4, 5, 6, 7, 8, 9, 10," but count the sequence of numbers silently. Perform this slow version of the exercise for someone else. They will find it extremely difficult to predict when the next pulse falls. However, if you set it up with a preparatory note, then they have an idea that the pulse is coming. You can also speed the exercise up and tap out the pulse at, say, 120 beats per minute or two taps per second. If you listen to a jazz performance, pay close attention to the sound of the bass and you will occasionally hear the bassist adding these preparatory notes to impart more momentum into his or her bass line. It's important to note that the technique of giving weight to notes and the technique of preparing notes both help to maintain or increase momentum at any tempo. It's just that they can be critically effective at a slow tempo.

What Is Swing?

People often refer to the concept of **swing** when they refer to jazz. People often ask what swing is. Swing is many different things, including a particular style of jazz and dance, a somewhat intangible feeling of movement and momentum and a specific rhythmic device. It is the rhythmic device that can help give the music that feeling of movement and make it swing, so to speak. In music, a note that is one half of a beat in duration is known as an eighth note. If you tap "1, 2, 3, 4," you are tapping quarter notes. If you simply add "and" after each beat and maintain the same tempo, then you have eighth notes. So you would say "1-and-2-and-3-and-4-and" with equal time given to each syllable. To employ the rhythmic device of swing, make each number longer and each "and" shorter. If each beat is divided into thirds, you would give about two thirds of the time to the number and one third to "and." It's a little bit like the rhythm you'd get if you were skipping or like what you might have gotten when you were saying "DUM" above with preparatory beats. So you would say "DUM-ba-DUM-ba-DUM-ba-DUM-ba" (don't forget to tap) and so forth. The rhythmic device of swing is yet another method of imparting momentum to the music of jazz.

There is an interesting poetic equivalent to the rhythm of swing. **Iambic pentameter** is the meter that William Shakespeare typically employed when he wrote verse. In poetry, a **foot** is a group of syllables. Iambic refers to two syllables, the first unstressed and the second stressed. An example is the word "tra-PEZE." Iambic pentameter is five feet or five pairs of alternating unstressed and stressed syllables. Here is the first quatrain from Shakespeare Sonnet 128 with the stressed syllables in bold:

> How **oft** when **thou**, my **mu**-sic **play'st**

Or more plainly:

> ba-DUM-ba-DUM-ba-DUM-ba-DUM

You may notice this is the reverse from "DUM-ba-DUM-ba" etc. It doesn't matter how you begin; once the rhythm is in use, the effect comes into play. What's interesting is that the lilt of the meter is very much like the rhythmic device of swing. As you can see, Shakespeare swings, too, and this is perhaps one reason why his poetry is so entrancing.

How does the use of these techniques play out in other activities? It should be possible to give more weight to a specific contribution in any activity. For example, in a business or software development team, you can have additional people lend their help. Senior people especially can make a difference. The idea is to not only help ensure the success of those specific contributions, but to communicate their importance to everyone. Similarly, you can increase the momentum leading up to a specific contribution by setting it up with a smaller preparatory effort. People do this all the time. If a team has an important monthly meeting, the chair of the meeting might send out one or more reminder notes in the days leading up to the meeting. This ensures that people don't accidentally miss the meeting. The chair might also send out an agenda and any preparatory materials to ensure that people will be effective at the meeting.

You can increase the momentum leading up to a specific contribution by setting it up with a smaller preparatory effort.

There is one other important technique that jazz musicians use to maintain momentum, and that is **syncopation.** This is a completely independent technique from the rhythmic device of swing. The two can be used separately or together. In Latin jazz, straight eighth notes are employed just as in classical music but syncopation provides the momentum.

Syncopation is quite simply the technique of deviating rhythmically from a regular pulse. One way to do this is to alter the timing of notes. If you say "DUM-DUM-DUM-DUM" evenly, then there is no syncopation. You can suspend or delay the second note by pausing for two-thirds of the note (we're also using the rhythmic device of swing at the same time) and then filling in the last third with a preparatory note. So you would say "DUM-[pause]ba-DUM-DUM," and of course don't forget to tap. Your second tap will be right on the pause. Repeat this a few times and you'll notice that the suspension of the second note creates momentum simply because the pause causes people to feel or imagine the missing note. Of course, the note is not actually missing but simply delayed. Let's try syncopation another way by anticipating the second note. What we will do is begin the second note where the last third of the first note would be. We will then hold that note until we get to the third beat. So we say "DA-ba-aa-DUM-DUM" and make "DA" short (two-thirds of a beat) and "ba-aa" one continuous note. If you tap at the same time, the second tap will coincide with "aa." Anticipating the note generates momentum by creating the illusion that the tempo is increasing.

Suspension and anticipation can be used to increase momentum by altering the timing of contributions with respect to a regular pulse. These techniques of syncopation give people freedom in the timing of their contributions. Here's one final example to illustrate a third way to syncopate. Notice the emphasis on the first word at the beginning of one of Shakespeare's most famous lines:

Now is the **win**-ter **of** our **dis**-con-**tent**
DUM-ba-ba-DUM-ba-DUM-ba-DUM-ba-DUM

Rather than changing the timing of words, Shakespeare simply alters the placement of the emphasis. The technique of displacing accents is employed in almost all music, and jazz musicians use it frequently.

There are two important points to keep in mind when syncopation is employed. The first is that you must always respect the pulse even when the syncopation is extended or constant. If you lose track of the pulse then you will lose momentum. The second point is that when you contribute in a way that deviates from the pulse, you should do it with total commitment to avoid the deviation being misinterpreted as a mistake. If you listen to jazz musicians, they will regularly accent syncopated notes to make them a rhythmic feature. If you had a regular Thursday meeting and then one week you had to move the meeting to Wednesday, you would try to reschedule the meeting in a way that avoids any confusion. When competitors come into play, then obfuscation, discussed in Chapter 8, "Act Transparently," should be employed. If your regular product cycle is to make available a major release of a product in June but then one year you want to get the jump on the competition, you might want to communicate this syncopation clearly to your team but not to your competitors.

It's important to understand that when people interact together in support of momentum, there may be variances with respect to the tempo, pulse, and groove. Many new jazz musicians practice with "play-along" recordings because they don't have easy access to other musicians. This is quite difficult to do, and many people believe it doesn't help develop the correct sense of tempo and groove. One reason is that a recording cannot respond to a live musician. The reality of being human is that our timing can't always be exact at a high resolution. An electronic or mechanical drum machine might be able to play in perfectly exact time, but we prefer the sound of a good human drummer because a human can do creative things and respond in ways that a machine cannot. Although the drummer is the primary communicator of the tempo in a typical jazz context and the bassist is the primary communicator of the pulse, the reality is that everyone in a band is responsible for the tempo, the pulse, and the groove, and everyone has the ability to weaken and strengthen them. It's interesting to study some of the famous pairings of drummers and bassists. Some jazz musicians are well-known for playing on the front of the beat; others are known for playing on the back of the beat and others squarely on the beat. By analogy, in any activity, certain people will be more gung-ho, with a tendency to move quickly, and others will be more cautious, often waiting for others to move first. No style is better than the others, but it can be useful to understand the subtle nuances of each. A well-balanced team should have a mix of both styles. If too many people in a team want to rush in, the team may take unnecessary risks. If the team's thinking is too conservative, the team may not be competitive.

Recapitulation

- Momentum is the tendency or impetus to continue in a specific direction.

- If velocity is a measure of how quickly a team is progressing, momentum makes it easier to continue at a constant velocity and also increase velocity.

- When momentum is present, fewer resources need be consumed in order to advance. Momentum can make it easier to establish positive feedback loops such as economies of scale.

- The rule in physics that momentum is a function of velocity and mass can be applied generally. For example, for any given velocity, a larger team or organization will have more momentum than a smaller one.

- Getting started, or "getting the ball rolling," can be one of the hardest things to do. To reach critical mass, considerable resources may need to be expended, especially if resistance must be overcome.

- The single most important element of momentum is regularity. People are naturally drawn to the predictability of regular cycles.

- Momentum can be maintained by managing four operational elements that leverage people's affinity for regular cycles: form, tempo, pulse, and groove.

- *Form* is a structure that organizes an activity. People use the predictability of form to help them set goals, time their deliveries, and shape their contributions.

- Teams use checkpoints to coordinate their efforts and increase synergy. If too few checkpoints are spread too far apart, the coherency of a team's efforts may suffer. Too many checkpoints occurring too frequently may add unnecessary overhead and reduce productivity.

- *Tempo* is the overall pace of an activity. It sets the speed at which individuals must deliver their respective contributions. Using just enough rules can give people the freedom to keep up with a tempo that is very fast by altering their contributions as required.

- A *pulse* is a constant, regular event a team can use to cope with a tempo that is too fast or too slow for their liking. Instead of synchronizing directly with a tempo, they lock in to a pulse that is related to the tempo but may change, even while the tempo must remain constant.

- A *groove* is a sequence of scheduled events that are repeated continuously. It is a function of pulse and, therefore, a function of tempo. A groove invites everyone to participate and align their contributions with it. Within a team, many specific grooves may work synchronously within the framework set by a more general groove.

- Maintain momentum by adding weight to a contribution to give it greater significance. This is particularly helpful at slower tempos.

- Maintain or increase momentum by preparing a contribution with a preceding smaller contribution.

- Increase momentum and take liberty in the timing of your contributions by employing syncopation to either anticipate or suspend a contribution. You can also syncopate by altering the placement of emphasis within a stream of contributions.

- When people interact together in support of momentum, there may be variances with respect to the tempo, pulse, and groove. In any activity, some people will be more gung-ho, with a tendency to move quickly, and others will be more cautious, often waiting for others to move first. A well-balanced team should have a mix of both styles.

CHAPTER 12

Stay Healthy

"Health is not valued till sickness comes."
—Thomas Fuller

The Importance of Health

It's often said that people take good health for granted, and today this is probably truer than ever. Increases in life expectancy might be one reason. In England, life expectancy was an estimated 35.5 years between 1541 and 1871, with an average low of 27.7 years between 1561 and 1565. In France, the life expectancy between 1740 and 1790 ranged from 24 to 28 years for males and 26 to 30 years for females (Riley 2001, 32–33). The numbers improved dramatically by the twentieth century. In the United States, life expectancy in 1900 was 47 years. It increased to 68 years by 1950 and hit 77 years in 1998 (Moore 2001, 27). Of course, these are simply statistics. Who among us has not had a close friend or family member die prematurely from a chronic illness or disease? Coronary heart disease, stroke, respiratory infections, HIV/AIDS, and tuberculosis all ranked in the top 10 causes of death across the world in 2004, according to the World Health Organization (World Health Organization, 2008). In the same analysis, traffic accidents are listed as the only non-health-related cause of death (ranked number nine), and premature birth and low birth weight was the tenth cause of death.

Even moderate cases of poor health are of great concern because they compromise the ability to function effectively. Poor health can degrade to a point at which recovery is impossible. Our discussion about health pertains not only to the health of individuals, but also to the health of projects, activities, teams, and organizations. Health should be of particular concern to high-performance individuals and teams because they are more prone to develop health issues. Have you seen an Olympic-caliber sprinter pull up out of the starting block and then retire due to injury? At first thought, it seems incredible that an athlete could be injured in the first few steps of the race; children competing in school athletics rarely encounter this problem. Similarly, Formula One cars often have mechanical problems, despite having access to a team of mechanics and full engine rebuilds between races; most of us, on the other hand, get by with our cars with far less maintenance. High levels of performance increase the strain and stress on a system, making it more susceptible to health problems. This is true whether the machine is the human body, a vehicle, an organization, or a type of activity.

High levels of performance increase the strain and stress on a system, making it more susceptible to health problems.

In previous chapters, I used the word *stability* when referring to the health of an activity or team. I now illustrate this in more concrete terms, with one example involving cars and another involving aircraft.

In high-speed auto racing, the mechanical health of the vehicle is important. However, another important aspect of a racing vehicle's health is controlled directly by the driver. I'm referring to the stability of the car, which is potentially compromised each time the driver engages with the vehicle's controls. Imagine an everyday driver in a manual transmission vehicle. He is driving briskly along a straight section of road and approaching a corner. As the car nears the corner, the driver begins to apply the brakes. As the speed of the car decreases, he then shifts down through the gears, easing the clutch out slowly with each downshift, to let the engine speed adjust to the new gear. Eventually, the driver reaches the apex of the turn and applies throttle to accelerate out of the corner. This is not a difficult maneuver—most of us do it countless times every day without compromising the vehicle's stability. However, if you make that maneuver significantly more difficult by requiring that you execute it at three or four times the speed, different techniques are needed to maintain a stable footing.

When a racecar driver in a high-performance vehicle approaches a similar corner, he uses a complicated set of footwork called heel-and-toe double-declutching. These are actually two separate operations. **Double-declutching** is used primarily in vehicles with unsynchronized manual transmissions, such as heavy-duty trucks and race cars. However, it can be used with any kind of manual transmission to ensure a smooth downshift. Instead of simply depressing the clutch, changing to a lower gear, and then releasing the clutch, a double-declutch involves depressing the clutch, shifting into neutral, releasing the clutch, and then depressing it again to shift into the lower gear before once again releasing. When this is done quickly, it appears to be a single shifting operation, but it's essentially performed in two parts. **Heel-and-toe** is a separate technique that involves depressing the brake with the toe of the right foot while using the heel to "blip" the throttle to increase the engine speed when selecting a lower gear. Depending on the placement of the pedals, it's also possible to use the left and right halves of the right foot and rotate the foot to the right, which is what I find myself doing in most mass-market cars. When double-declutching and heel-and-toe are combined, the blip of the throttle happens as the clutch is released for the shift into neutral. The blipping of the throttle with the heel-and-toe is why you hear that characteristic "vroom-vroom-vroom" sound as a racecar is approaching a corner. The advantage of this fancy footwork is that a driver can simultaneously brake while shifting down through the gears, sometimes skipping gears if the speed is decreasing rapidly. The correct engine speed is always selected to ensure smooth downshifts. When a car is braking heavily from a very high speed to the low speed necessary to negotiate a tight turn, any sudden movements transmitted through the drive train could upset the vehicle and cause a loss of stability. In modern racecars with computer-controlled automatic clutches, double-declutching is not needed, but heel-and-toe is still used to ensure the correct engine speed. This leaves the left foot free to operate the brake. That can be very useful because it decreases the reaction needed for sudden braking, as there is no need to transfer the right foot back and forth between the two pedals.

In the sport of rallying, drivers race against time from point A to point B. Rally drivers must be experts in improvisation because they rarely encounter the same section of road more than once and must be prepared for the unexpected. Rally drivers often drive on unstable surfaces such as dirt, gravel, and ice, and there is pressure to complete each rally stage in the shortest time possible. Consequently, a high likelihood of losing stability arises. You can see how "out-of-control" rally cars get when you watch them in action. One important aspect of a rally car's stability is the pitch or weight distribution between the front and rear sections of the vehicle. Perhaps you recall our brief discussion of trailing throttle oversteer in "Essentials of Execution." Most people don't think about weight distribution in everyday driving. In fact, it's easy to think about weight distribution as generally fixed and dependent on the design of the car and the placement of objects inside it. However, because the tires and the suspension of a car can be compressed, weight can be transferred to different parts of the vehicle during driving maneuvers. Rally drivers use all kinds of techniques to ensure that the car remains stable even in the wildest of maneuvers. Left-foot braking is one such technique. It is especially useful for rally drivers when they must drive front-wheel drive cars that tend to *understeer*—that is, the cars tend to run wide on a turn when the driver applies too much power. If you could see the footwork of a rally driver using left-foot braking, you would see him not only switching between brake and throttle as everyday drivers do, but also applying brake and throttle at the same time! This sounds crazy to most people and increases wear on certain parts of the vehicle, but the technique allows a driver to smoothly modulate the power and braking. For example, if a rally driver is driving a front-wheel drive car through a turn and the car begins to oversteer, with the rear of the car sliding around more than the driver wants, he can decrease the pressure to the brake and increase the throttle, thus smoothly transitioning between oversteer and understeer.

These forms of competitive motorsports are examples of inherently unstable activities. The drivers could easily make the activities more stable by reducing the speed at which they drive, but then they wouldn't be pursuing the highest levels of performance. The drivers use a variety of special techniques to maintain the health of the activity.

One measure of the design of an aircraft is **static stability**. This is usually defined as the initial tendency of an aircraft following a perturbation from a state of steady flight. In other words, it describes what happens when something (usually input from a pilot) creates a change to the aircraft's flight path. Most aircraft are designed with *positive static stability,* which means they are inherently stable, with built-in dampening mechanisms that return them to a state of equilibrium after a change or disturbance is introduced into the flight path. This built-in correctional behavior functions like a self-balancing negative feedback loop. Much like the average car, the operator actually has to work against the system to cause a loss of control. The problem is that such stability limits maneuverability. The F-16 was the first aircraft designed to be slightly aerodynamically unstable. This design goal is known as relaxed static stability; in the case of the F-16, it resulted in negative static stability. In such designs, instability is intentionally built into the system to increase maneuverability. The tendency of the aircraft is to continue in the direction away from equilibrium after a change has been introduced into the flight path. As you've probably guessed, such behavior is a positive feedback loop. The downside of such aircrafts is that they cannot be flown by human input alone. They can only be controlled with the assistance of computer systems that constantly dampen potentially dangerous positive feedback loops in flight behavior. Without these systems, which usually have multiple backups, aircraft such as the F-16, F-117 Nighthawk, and Eurofighter Typhoon would be impossible to fly.

It is often necessary to build instability into a team to enable high levels of performance. An example of this is a team of extremely talented people with problematic personalities. In this case, you would trade the rule "Put the team first" for "Employ top talent." One such person on a team might be bad enough, but having multiple people like this further increases the likelihood of problems. We see this kind of "design" all the time in sports teams, when a franchise tolerates a talented player with highly publicized negative behaviors in the hope that the added talent will propel the team to a winning record. The trick is managing the instability so that it doesn't lead to unrecoverable or permanently damaging situations.

It is often necessary to build instability into a team to enable high levels of performance. The trick is managing the instability so that it doesn't lead to unrecoverable or permanently damaging situations.

Stability is just one example of health in a system or activity. Another obvious one is quality. I mentioned in the Introduction that with the United States Postal Service processing and delivering 667 million pieces of mail each day in 2008, a defect or error rate of just 0.1 percent would mean losing 667,000 packages daily. Each organization, team, and activity has a different degree of tolerance for problems. Quality is often a tradeoff. It may be possible to increase quality, but at the expense of increased cost, delivery time, or reduced functionality. In the same way that instability may be built into a system, it may be necessary to accept a certain level of defects to fulfill other criteria. You then must be careful that such defects do not lead to irreversible or uncontrollable problems.

Causes of Injury

The robustness of a system is its capability to handle changes that may compromise its health. We already know that any change applied to an activity may have an impact. The health of the activity depends on the ability of its participants to absorb such impacts. In simple activities, corrective actions as part of negative feedback loops can usually absorb impacts completely and avoid any impact on health. However, in complex or inherently unstable systems negative feedback corrections can often be difficult to apply with success. It can be difficult to fix a complex software bug on the first attempt, just as it is can be difficult for a rally driver to regain control of a vehicle in excessive oversteer at high speed. When multiple attempts are required to correct a problem, hunting, such as that described in "Essentials of Execution," may ensue. In the worst case, a negative feedback loop can degrade and become a positive feedback loop in which any attempt to further manipulate the situation only makes it worse. In general, poor health can lead to a positive loop because any initial sickness compromises operational efficiency, which reduces the ability to absorb impact, which then results in further sickness, and so forth.

When is the impact from an action or contribution a simple part of everyday activity, and when does it lead to an injury that compromises health? The answer lies in the nature of feedback loops as we previously studied them. If an action takes place within a damaging or dangerous positive feedback loop that's spiraling out of control, or when a correction is attempted within a negative feedback loop that has fallen into or is about to fall into a mode of hunting, then it's an action that is harmful to the activity's health. Figure 12.1 illustrates this.

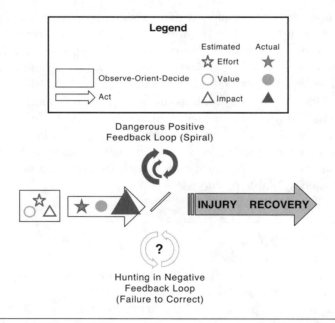

Figure 12.1 *How actions lead to injury*

Poor health has an effect on people's impressions of a team or project and is one example of the positive feedback loop just described. If sickness sets in and is left untended, people within a team may be less inclined to address what they sense others don't care about. Health may degrade further, which leads people to care less—and so the loop goes. At some point, this begins to have a serious effect on morale, and people start to abandon the sinking ship. This same perspective infects consumers, partners, and customers, who will be less likely to take interest in something that is not well-maintained. If someone walks down a street and sees one house that is immaculately kept and another with long grass, broken windows, and bad graffiti, they form instant perceptions regarding the content of the house and its residents. In fact, a specific theory in sociology is referred to as the **Broken Window Theory**. The name comes from an article that appeared in the March 1982 edition of *The Atlantic Monthly,* although the authors, George L. Kelling and James Q. Wilson, noted that others had done research on this theory decades earlier. The authors wrote (Kelling and Wilson 1982):

> *Social psychologists and police officers tend to agree that if a window in a building is broken and is left unrepaired, all the rest of the windows will soon be broken.*

Open source projects, including Wikipedia and software projects such as Linux and those hosted by the Apache Software Foundation, Eclipse Foundation, and SourceForge, rely significantly on the efforts of unpaid volunteers. To attract volunteers, they must promote a well-run, well-maintained, active, healthy project. People are less inclined to jump onto a project that presents major challenges and a likelihood of resource constraints, let alone a project that appears to be doomed.

Prevention

Prevention is often said to be better than cure. The adage holds true for virtually any system or activity. The sicker you are, the more effort and time it takes to recover. During that time of illness, operational efficiency is compromised, resulting in an additional opportunity cost for work that you were unable to do. Prevention requires proactive efforts to mitigate the potential that health may be compromised. Doing so necessitates knowing the kinds of health problems that might arise. For example, in any team of people, serious personality conflicts can compromise social stability, resulting in frustration, needless arguments, and even destructive behavior that sabotages the work of others. Valuable team members who aren't involved in the conflicts might depart the team. I have lost track of the number of artistic groups I've known that have disbanded over their inability to resolve personality conflicts. Preventive measures that can avoid such problems might include these:

- Researching the history and background of candidate employees
- Identifying different personality types and understanding how they might interact (such as through Type A/Type B personality theory, Myers-Briggs, Keirsey Temperament Theory, and so on)
- Coaching, counseling, and providing other activities to relieve tension, anxiety, or frustration as a result of personal interactions within a team
- Reassigning roles within the team

A software development team might attempt to prevent the introduction of bugs in code using these practices:

- Implementing conventions for programming style and technique
- Using development methodologies that assist in or encourage sound architecture, design, and implementation
- Using analysis tools that check for specific problems, such as memory leaks
- Performing proofs of correctness or conformance (for example, against a specification)

Software testing is not strictly the work to prevent bugs—rather, it is the proof of their existence. If software testing is done before the software is distributed outside the team, it can prevent potential impact to customers.

Many of the principles in the Jazz Process depend on one another. We previously discussed the need to follow the rule "Maintain momentum," and we explained how regularity contributes to that effort. A regular, predictable pulse is like a heartbeat. Just as it does in a medical context, an arrhythmic or absent project heartbeat may indicate that a project is in poor and waning health. A failure to listen for change or to reduce friction might similarly have adverse affects on a team's ability to operate effectively. In this case, paying attention to the relevant principles might prevent problems.

Chronic Conditions

Some health conditions are acute and treatable, but chronic conditions are long-lasting and often incurable. Just as some people have lifelong or long-term medical conditions such as asthma, diabetes, allergies, cancer, and various kinds of disorders, any activity or organization can have permanent or pervasive problems. In software, some bugs manifest themselves only in rare conditions and cannot be easily reproduced. A **heisenbug**, named after the Heisenberg Uncertainty Principle, is a computer bug that disappears or changes behavior when an attempt is made to debug or analyze it. A **mandelbug**, named after Benoît Mandelbrot, who coined the term *fractal* to describe a class of often complex geometric shapes, is a bug that is extremely complex or seemingly chaotic in behavior. These kinds of bugs can live for a long time and elude detection or fixing. This is the unfortunate reality of complex software development and limited budgets: Most commercial software programs today have hundreds or thousands of defects.

Elusive bugs affect software as long as that software is used. Other activities may be shorter in duration but still be afflicted with health problems that are classifiable as chronic because they are in effect for the duration of the activity. A military unit deep in hostile territory might lose the ability to use a critically important piece of equipment, or one of its soldiers serving a role without backup might be killed or permanently injured. Without any support from home, the unit might have to deal with that condition for the duration of the mission—that might be days, weeks, or months. A racecar driver might have to deal with a mechanical condition such as a misfiring engine for an entire race. In business, suboptimal operating conditions are often the result of practical and commercial realities and may be uncorrectable. Sometimes circumstances are simply beyond one's control.

The severity of a chronic condition may vary greatly and ultimately. What matters is how the condition impacts operations. Does it make sense to continue operating? Should the condition simply be noted and declared to all relevant stakeholders? As an example, consider that a team meets it goals year after year, even though repeated requests for more staff fall on deaf ears. Is that team simply a bunch of high performers, or do they have a health issue? If the high efficiency is not simply the result of synergy, but is due to individuals continuously working beyond their capacity, then the team is suffering a chronic lack of resources in the same way a person with a respiratory condition may suffer a chronic lack of oxygen. If the team continues to operate in that way, it will eventually begin to suffer other health issues, such as loss of morale, loss of staff, and burnout. If someone were to study the team and exclaim, "That is not healthy!" then it is clearly not! One of the primary methods of dealing with a chronic health condition is to admit that your capabilities are compromised and reduce your work effort.

Recovery

How does an entity recover from a bout of poor health? Major injuries demand specific attention and effort, just as you would rush to a hospital if you were badly hurt. Minor injuries can be handled by mechanisms or processes that respond automatically, just as your body heals a small cut on your arm. Regardless of the effort involved, any recovery consists of a combination of regeneration and repair. A small cut on your arm will heal through regeneration; after the process is complete, you won't be able to see any evidence of the original cut. However, a major wound requires repair and leaves scar tissue that never goes away. In some organisms, regeneration seems to be particularly advanced, although the truth is that, in general, the more highly evolved an organism is, the less capable it is of regeneration. If you lose a fingernail, it will grow back. If you lose a finger, you're out of luck. In contrast, if you cut a planarian flatworm, one of the simplest organisms to possess a central nervous system, into many pieces, each piece will grow into a whole worm, complete with a new head. We previously discussed Ori Brafman and Rod Beckstrom's reference to the regenerative capabilities of starfish in their book *The Starfish and the Spider*. One arm and about one fifth of the body of a starfish can regenerate completely to the original dimensions.

If someone was doing something harmful to you or you saw someone harm another person, your immediate reaction would be to tell that person to stop immediately. That's the kind of reaction people within a team (or others within an organization who are observing the team) should have upon observing actions that can damage the health of the team or its activity. If you remember our previous discussions about feedback loops, the solutions to terminating such behavior are as follows:

- If you're in a harmful positive feedback loop, do everything you can to break out of the loop by stopping the actions causing the loop. Think back to the description of howling audio feedback with a microphone and P.A. system described in "Essentials of Execution."

- If you're hunting, either increase the speed of your reactions and respond more quickly or increase friction (see "Essentials of Execution") by slowing down, relaxing, and choosing the right solution more deliberately.

Figure 12.2 illustrates different types of recovery efforts. The equivalent of innate, automated biological mechanisms, such as those that automatically heal your body, are the preprogrammed reactions that are selected and carried out in an execution loop in response to an injury. If a team within an organization loses one or more people, the organization automatically moves to fill those gaps. The extent to which it can do this solely through regeneration depends on the complexity of what has been lost. If other people with the necessary skills are readily available, it's simply a matter of assigning people. When jazz musicians are performing and one of them is rushing and pushing the tempo too aggressively, the other musicians instantly and automatically take steps to rein in that person. If a musician begins a phrase early or later, or otherwise ends up in a different place than the rest of the band, the other musicians take steps to synchronize everyone. This might involve accommodating the musician who was at fault, or it might require one of them to signal the musician to jump to the right place. If a basketball player fumbles a ball or misses a catch, the other players instantly take steps to repair the situation. If a software developer delivers code that causes her team's build to fail with a compilation error, the developer immediately fixes the problem and delivers the fix. These kinds of reactions to minor problems happen all the time. The damage done can be restored entirely through an internal regenerative process that leaves no permanent effects, and often little decision making is needed to rectify the situation.

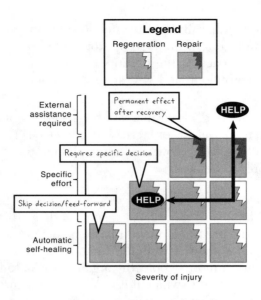

Figure 12.2 *Types of recovery efforts*

More serious recovery efforts require specific forethought, even though they might be entirely regenerative. In these cases, a decision must be made after careful observation and orientation. External assistance may sometimes be useful. For example, medication can help aid the recovery of the body. Similarly, a loss of staff may require that you bring in temporary help from an outside firm until internal staff can acquire the necessary skills. The most problematic recovery efforts are those that leave long-lasting effects or scars. If a person who is a core part of a team departs, the team may eventually recover, but things may never quite be the same. Scarring and irreparable harm can occur in almost any situation. Damage to a reputation or relationship, for instance, may be irreversible.

If a political candidate makes a major blunder in a campaign that harms his or her reputation, the time spent recovering siphons energy that could be spent debating issues and winning votes. In a software project, time spent fixing defects is time that could otherwise have been applied to developing new features. Any substantial recovery effort must be given the appropriate resources to ensure that it succeeds, and one must recognize the impact that the recovery effort will have on regular operations. The cost of not recovering and continuing to limp along with an injury is usually great. Not only will productivity or output continue to be compromised, but further injury may occur.

Shock

Occasionally, an event occurs for which we are totally unprepared. We discussed such aberrational events in Chapter 6, "Listen for Change," and noted that they are extremely difficult to prepare for or predict, despite beliefs to the contrary. In a rally car, the navigator or co-driver helps prepare the driver for what lies ahead by reading off "pacenotes." Yet no pacenotes can offer foresight about aberrational events. A perfect example is the time Federico Villagra and his co-driver, Jose Diaz, were driving their Ford Focus RS WRC 08 in the first stage of the World Rally Championship Portugal Rally (April 3, 2009). Racing through the Patagonian hills, they rounded a turn, crested a small hill, and drove straight into a herd of wild horses crossing the road. In business, a similar event could be the sudden appearance of a new competitor that has the ability to completely outclass all existing competitors. The entrance of Google into the Internet search engine business is such an example. Such aberrational events can shock a system and render it incapable of responding. Events of a catastrophic nature can produce similar shock. Think about how the terrorist attacks of September 11, 2001, had a sudden, dramatic effect on economics and on people's lives around the world. These kinds of events are simply outliers. They are not part of any hunting or dangerous amplifying behavior—or, at least, none that can be detected at the time. In cases of shock, due consideration should be given to determining the true impact on operations and the effort necessary for recovery. In some cases, recovery is impossible. Nick Leeson's fraudulent trading single-handedly brought down the Barings Bank in 1995 and, in doing so, wreaked indescribable carnage on thousands of people's lives.

Monitoring Health

It is impossible to maintain good health without the ability to measure health. Every activity and system has characteristics and qualities that can be considered when determining the overall state of well-being and fitness. The indicators we are particularly interested in are the indicators of integrity and stability. We're also interested in indicators that reflect performance, especially because poor performance often degrades health. When a team performs poorly, its morale may decline, and the team's mental health then is damaged. When musicians play wrong notes or play out of time or out of tune, the performance may become unstable. Compromised stability or integrity, or poor performance as a result of mistakes or failures, indicates problems. Software development build processes produce user-consumable software artifacts from development artifacts such as source code authored by software developers. A build process may involve many steps, such as compiling, linking, packaging, and running automated tests. Any of these steps may contain errors, such as compilation errors or test failures. A healthy build is one with no errors. Some errors are tolerable and categorized as simply warnings; others might be severe enough that they prematurely terminate the build process.

Compromised stability or integrity,
or poor performance as a result of mistakes or failures,
indicates problems.

It should be possible to create a useful measure of general health for any activity or system by considering multiple facets of fitness and well-being. For example, the health of a software project could be determined by the number of unresolved defects, the number of incomplete features committed in the plan, performance test results, and so forth. The health of a company might consider its liquid assets, liabilities, tracking against sales targets, sales in the pipeline, results of customer and employee satisfaction surveys, and more. Companies have traditionally used processes such as scorecards to report such across-the-board health. The problem with such reporting, as I noted in Chapter 6 in our discussion of "Measuring Success," is that metrics can be misused and misinterpreted, especially when they are reduced to simple red, yellow, or green indicators. Instead of focusing solely on specific issues, it's important to take a strategic view to ensure that fundamental problems, not mere symptoms, are addressed. Solutions must be long-lasting. They must also address the entire organization, not just the silo in which a problem might be apparent. Finally, just as you wouldn't drive a car by looking solely in the rear-view mirror, you must look forward and try to predict problems instead of waiting for them to occur. If there's one thing you can predict for a high-performance team, it's that the team will push its limits—and sometimes even go beyond them. It can do this for short periods, but sustaining such levels of performance or even indulging in short spurts too regularly can eventually take its toll. Top athletes time their peak condition to coincide with important performances and then follow this with recovery time. Similarly, teams should plan for downtime after a major effort so that they have an opportunity to decompress and regain lost health, whether it's the physical or mental well-being of people, or repairs, or system improvements.

Recapitulation

- Poor health can compromise the ability to function effectively.

- High levels of performance increase the strain and stress on a system, making it more susceptible to health problems.

- It is often necessary to build instability into a team, to enable high levels of performance. The trick is managing the instability so that it doesn't lead to unrecoverable or permanently damaging situations.

- The robustness of a system is its ability to handle changes that may compromise its health. The health of a team depends on the ability of its participants to absorb the impact of contributions. This can be difficult to achieve completely in complex or inherently unstable systems.

- Health can be compromised when multiple attempts to correct a problem result in hunting in a negative feedback loop. In the worst case, a negative feedback loop can degrade and become a positive feedback loop, in which any attempt to further manipulate the situation only makes it worse.

- Poor health has an effect on people's impressions of a team or project and can become a positive feedback loop.

- Prevention is better than cure. The sicker you are, the more effort and time it takes to recover. Prevention requires proactive efforts to mitigate the potential that health may be compromised.

- Poor health can be restored through recovery, but if poor health is left untended, it can degrade to a point at which recovery is impossible. Recovery from poor health is a combination of regeneration and repair. The latter can leave long-lasting effects or scars.

- Some health conditions are acute and treatable, but chronic conditions are long-lasting and often incurable. One of the primary methods of dealing with such a condition is to admit that your capabilities are compromised and reduce your work effort.

- Occasionally, an aberrational event may occur that is so significant that it leaves a system in shock. It is extremely difficult to prepare for or to predict such events, and they may have dramatic effect on health. In some cases, recovery is impossible.

- A method for measuring the health of activities and teams is essential.

- Look for indications of problems, such as a loss of stability or integrity, or poor performance as a result of mistakes, errors, or failures.

- Plan ahead and follow major efforts with downtime so that teams have an opportunity to recover.

PART IV

Innovating

In this section, we discuss two principles that help teams deliver unique and innovative solutions, performances, services, and products.

13. Exchange ideas
14. Take measured risks

CHAPTER 13

Exchange Ideas

"If you have an apple and I have an apple and we exchange these apples then you and I will still each have one apple. But if you have an idea and I have an idea and we exchange these ideas, then each of us will have two ideas."
—George Bernard Shaw

Creativity and Innovation

I previously mentioned that people are fascinated by leadership. Quite possibly, the second-most-popular topic in the business section of any bookstore is innovation and creativity. You will undoubtedly find many variations in the definitions, but **creativity**, the process of creating new ideas, can be thought of as a subset of **innovation**, the process of creating new ideas and applying them to a specific situation. Necessity is not necessarily the mother of creativity. One can be creative simply for its own sake. Innovation, on the other hand, is usually undertaken to solve a specific problem.

Creativity can be a difficult and frustrating process for some and an effortless, liberating experience for others. Creativity has many facets and has been studied by many people. It's well beyond the scope of this book to discuss the study of creativity in detail. Of note, however, are the contributions of Joy Paul Guilford, an American psychologist who served in the U.S. Army during World War II. Beginning as a lieutenant colonel and serving as Director of Psychological Research Unit No. 3 at the Santa Ana Army Air Base, Guilford eventually became Chief of the Psychological Research Unit at the U.S. Army Air Forces Training Command Headquarters in Fort Worth and was discharged as a full colonel after the war. He then joined the faculty at the University of Southern California, where his financial supporters included the Office of Naval Research and the National Science Foundation. In all of these positions, Guilford sought to understand individual human intellect and capability. He is noteworthy in the study of creativity for a number of reasons, including the galvanizing presidential address he gave at the 1949 convention of the American Psychological Association. In that speech, he called for psychologists to focus on the study of creativity, pointing out that it had been largely ignored until then. This was an important turning point in the study of creativity, and a lot of important research was conducted in the 1950s after Guilford gave his speech (Kaufman 2009, 11).

Guilford's own contributions to the study of creativity included his claims that creativity could not be measured with traditional intelligence tests and that personality was an element of creativity (Weisberg 2006, 450). Most important, he defined two types of thinking: convergent and divergent, noting that most people tend toward one type. **Convergent thinking**, generally associated with mathematics and science, is the process of selecting a single solution to a problem. Logic plays a strong part in convergent thinking; hence, most aptitude tests, such as those that assess intelligence quotient (IQ), ask for singular answers to a problem. **Divergent thinking**, generally associated with the humanities and the arts, is the process of generating many possible solutions to a problem. This type of thinking answers problems such as "How can we do this better?" or "How many different uses are there for this product?" Guilford associated divergent thinking with four main skills:

- **Fluency**—The ability to quickly produce large number of solutions to a single problem
- **Flexibility**—The capacity to simultaneously consider many solutions to a single problem
- **Originality**—The tendency to produce solutions that others have not thought of
- **Elaboration**—The aptitude for adding to or developing existing solutions

If personality does indeed play a part in creativity, then curiosity, spontaneity, free thinking, and risk taking are some of the useful personality traits in divergent thought. Playfulness is another useful trait, as evidenced by children, who often possess ample ability to think divergently.

If pure creativity can be thought of as mostly divergent thinking, then innovation is the combination of divergent and convergent thought, in which new ideas are generated and then tested for suitability and success. If one looks at creativity/innovation across multiple domains, it becomes obvious that different forms of creativity require different proportions of divergent and convergent thinking. Scientific creativity depends more on convergent thought, whereas artistic creativity relies more on divergent thinking.

Benefits of Innovation

Creativity and innovation are the pursuit of ideas, concepts, and methods that are new and unique. Throughout most of the world, patents protect processes or products that provide a new way of doing something or offer a new solution to a problem. The types of things that can be patented may vary according to specific patent types and laws, but for anything to be patentable, it must demonstrate an element of novelty, such as a new characteristic that is not already known in the body of existing knowledge in which the invention exists. Intellectual property laws aside, uniqueness is a critically important characteristic in many offerings. Although it alone doesn't guarantee that people will want access to a product or service, a lack of uniqueness greatly reduces the appeal of an offering if all other factors are constant.

The value of uniqueness is not limited to business and science. If a basketball team can string together a series of moves for a unique play, the players can gain an advantage in a game. If a jazz musician can sound a unique expression, he or she can make an improvised solo more engaging. When something is distinctive, it is easily differentiated from similar offerings. That can be important when trying to attract consumers. It also has application within a team. When jazz musicians are repeatedly navigating a musical form, a drummer often signals the beginning of a new section by playing a short fill or a strongly accented hit on a specific drum to help rally the band and keep the members together. When a jazz musician plays something original, other musicians sometimes nod or vocalize their approval because it excites them to know that such creativity is present in their midst and is forming a part of their collaborative effort. This can have a catalytic effect on other musicians and inspire them to express their own original thoughts.

Another important but rarely discussed benefit of creativity is the way in which it can improve decision making. John Boyd described **destructive deduction** as analysis that proceeds from the general to the specific. This is convergent thinking. He described **creative** or **constructive induction** as synthesis that proceeds from the specific to the general. This is divergent thinking. Boyd noted that effective orientation requires someone to continuously destroy existing mental concepts and replace them with newly constructed concepts that include observations. Doing this requires effective logical and creative capabilities. Quite simply, creativity allows people to be open to possibilities, including those of extreme change. The ability to think creatively is not just for those commonly deemed creative types, but is essential if one is to effectively manage change, especially extreme change that could profoundly affect a situation.

Creativity allows people to be open to possibilities, including those of extreme change.

Enabling Innovation with Collaboration

Being completely and totally original is difficult. Most unique ideas are not conceived in a vacuum. I noted in Chapter 3, "Put the Team First," that we tend to acknowledge only the most visible individuals in a team activity. In the same way, we tend to give all the credit for inventions to singular individuals. Most often, many people contribute directly or indirectly to an idea or its proof or implementation. Sadly, all the mindshare tends to accrue for one person, and sometimes it's not even the right one. Most people think Thomas Edison invented the electric light bulb. Yet Englishman physicist and chemist Joseph Swan received a patent for the incandescent light bulb in 1878, a year before Edison demonstrated his bulb, and countless others demonstrated the technology decades earlier (Friedel, Israel, and Finn, 1986). U.S. President Barack Obama was dead wrong in proclaiming, "I believe the nation that invented the automobile cannot walk away from it," in his 2009 State of the Union address (Healey 2009). Contrary to popular opinion, Henry Ford did not invent the automobile, although he did pioneer its mass production. The U.S. Library of Congress notes that Karl Benz demonstrated the first true automobile powered by gasoline in 1885–86 but also points out that earlier automobiles were powered by electricity and steam, and Leonardo da Vinci was creating designs and models for transport vehicles in the fifteenth century (U.S. Library of Congress 2009). Scott Berkun, author of *The Myths of Innovation,* goes as far as claiming, "Edison, Ford, and countless innovators are recognized as sole inventors for convenience. The histories we know depart from the truth for the simple reason that it makes them easier to remember" (Berkun 2007, 69).

The exchange of ideas is a fundamental principle in the processes of creativity and innovation, even if the exchange is unidirectional, with the thinker observing the work of others or taking inspiration from other sources. Da Vinci was inspired by nature when he examined the flight behavior of birds and proposed mechanisms for flying machines in his *Codex on the Flight of Birds,* circa 1505. Edison's work on the light bulb may well have been based on Swan's research on carbon filament electric lighting, which was published in *Scientific American.* Swan subsequently sued Edison for patent infringement in the British courts and won. Even in America, the U.S. Patent Office had ruled in 1883 that Edison's patents were invalid because they were based on the work of William Sawyer. According to the courts, Edison's work was obviously based on the efforts of others.

The myth of individual creativity applies not just to invention, but also to other forms of creativity. Ask people who painted the famous ceiling in the Sistine Chapel in the Vatican in Rome, Italy, and they will undoubtedly answer, "Michelangelo." Writing for *The New York Times,* William E. Wallace wrote (Wallace 1994):

> *The romantic myth that Michelangelo worked by himself fits our notion of the lonely, self-sacrificing genius—conditions that presumably are necessary for creating art. Actually, he was never alone. He lived with two male assistants and always had a female housekeeper. Thirteen people helped him paint the Sistine ceiling; about 20 helped carve the marble tombs in the Medici Chapel in Florence, with its allegories of Day and Night, Dawn and Dusk. And to build the Laurentian Library in Florence, he supervised a crew of at least 200.*

Berkun points out that nobody knows the names of the individuals who designed the Egyptian pyramids, the Roman Coliseum, or the Great Wall of China: "It wasn't until the 1500s and the rise of the Renaissance that Western cultures grew comfortable acknowledging people's creative abilities and individual achievements." Even when that time came, Berkun notes, "not everyone was allowed in the special 'creative' club. The only people with creative license were geniuses, the Michelangelos and da Vincis, whose talents seemed to stretch beyond human limitations" (Berkun 2007, 75). The reality is that most geniuses are inspired and assisted by others.

Enabling Innovation with Diversity

The myth of the lone inventor was further debunked by recent research in which Jasjit Singh of INSEAD and Lee Fleming of Harvard Business School studied the success of lone inventors using U.S. patent inventorship and citation data. The researchers analyzed more than half a million patented inventions and observed collaboration in two forms:

1. Diversity in technical experience.
2. Extended social networks consisting of indirect collaborators who work with one or more members of the innovating team but are not part of its project. Such people likely have similar skills and experiences to those on the innovating team and, therefore, don't increase its diversity but may contribute fresh perspectives.

They concluded that lone inventors are less likely to generate exceptional solutions, or what they referred to as "breakthroughs." More specifically, they found that "diversity has a relatively and significantly greater effect in trimming poor outcomes than fostering breakthroughs. In contrast, extended social networks also appear to be more beneficial to the invention of breakthroughs than to the trimming of poor outcomes" (Singh and Fleming 2009, 24).

Singh and Fleming's observations are examples of how diversity can improve the success of innovation. Although the precise effects may vary, diversity almost certainly improves success in innovation, whether it happens at the top end, in generating more unique solutions, or the bottom end, in rejecting poor ones. Figure 13.1 illustrates these possibilities.

In a technical environment, logical convergent thinking is likely more dominant than divergent thinking. Consequently, as Singh and Fleming observed, an increase in the diversity of technical experience likely has the greatest effect on increasing the success of rejecting poor solutions. Truly novel technical solutions may take a long time to develop. Rejecting a technical idea usually takes less time and effort than developing a new one.

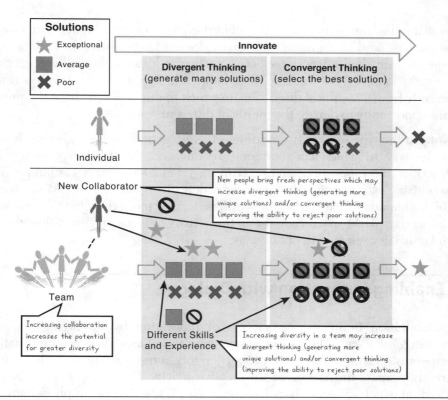

Figure 13.1 *Effects of diversity on the success of innovation*

In contrast, consider an artistic activity such as a jazz performance. Most jazz musicians are not content to always play with the same musicians. They constantly search for new collaborators, inviting them to perform as guest artists with their existing ensembles or engaging with them in new ensembles. The most creative jazz musicians tend to collaborate with musicians who have instruments, playing styles, and musical approaches that differ from their own. They even collaborate with artists in other disciplines, such as dance and the visual arts. In this way, they increase the diversity within the ensemble. How does diversity affect creativity in a jazz performance? At any point when a jazz musician is improvising, he or she individually navigates through a process of divergent and then convergent thinking to generate or recall ideas and then selects one to express. The divergent thinking is affected greatly by the presence of other musicians because jazz musicians constantly feed off one another, exchanging ideas and reacting to what others in the ensemble are doing. An increase in diversity increases the pool of ideas that can be drawn from and the set of possible actions that may trigger a reaction from another musician. The convergent thinking, however, is largely an individual task, and an increase in diversity doesn't have much of an effect on how an individual musician selects a particular idea. Additionally, the jazz musician's convergent thinking must happen in a split second. It works differently from a technical discussion, in which multiple people have the time and opportunity to debate the merits of different solutions.

Not just the type of activity determines the effect of diversity—also involved is the way in which collaborators are engaged. In the Introduction, I described the InnovationJam that IBM staged in 2006. This is an example of harnessing extreme diversity to power widely divergent thinking: More than 150,000 minds spread across the world generated more than 46,000 ideas in just six days. IBM specifically set up the activity to focus on generating ideas and only later selected the best ideas.

Enabling Innovation with Dialogue

Collaboration improves the success of innovation by leveraging a free exchange of ideas. This is not always easy to achieve. When appropriate respect is given to intellectual property rights, a free exchange of ideas can greatly increase the success of any creative activity. This is not simply a free-for-all in which ideas are bandied about. Nor is it a case of simply debating which idea is the best. Instead, it's a controlled dialogue in which conversation takes place with open ears, open hearts, open minds, and honest intentions to share and develop new ideas and solutions.

William Isaacs, a lecturer at the Massachusetts Institute of Technology Sloan School of Management, founded the Dialogue Project at MIT. He refers to dialogue as "the art of thinking together" and writes (Isaacs 1999, 395):

> The willingness to give one's ideas freely, without the sense of having to draw close boundaries to protect or preserve them, generates a common mind and common pool of meaning out of which much can be done.

Isaacs defines four practices of dialogue: listening, respecting, suspending, and voicing. If you think about the principles we've discussed in this book, you'll recognize a lot of overlap:

- **Listening**—Listen for change
- **Respecting**—Build trust and respect

- **Suspending**—Reduce friction and orientation in an execution loop
- **Voicing**—Make contributions count

Before even stepping into a group performance situation, every good jazz musician has listened to and absorbed what the jazz greats have had to say. This begins with studying the masters of a musician's specific instrument. Trumpet players, for example, listen to what Buddy Bolden, King Oliver, Louis Armstrong, Bix Beiderbecke, Roy Eldridge, Dizzy Gillespie, Clifford Brown, Harry James, Miles Davis, and so many others said through their instruments. They are also taught that they shouldn't just confine themselves to those masters, but should listen to the greats on any instrument. Listen to Davis for his economy of notes, Johnny Hodges for his luscious tone and control of pitch, Thelonious Monk for his dissonance and angular melodic lines, John Coltrane for his complexity and intensity, Frank Sinatra for his phrasing on the standards, Chet Baker for his lyricism, Zoot Sims for his sense of swing, and so forth. Jazz musicians learn about both the evolution of playing styles and the evolution of the music. Modern jazz musicians learn about the further evolution of the music by studying today's great musicians. All this study consists of activities such as listening to live performances and recordings, transcribing solos, reading, and playing transcriptions. Although it is all very much one sided, jazz musicians acquire the critically important skills of open listening, appreciating, selecting the ideas and expressions that appeal to them, and synthesizing those ideas with their own. You can't be original without knowing what has already been said. This is particularly true in the business world, where innovators use patents to keep others from exploiting their novel inventions. Novelty of a patent is determined by searching for prior art, the body of knowledge relevant to the patent's claims of originality, including other patents and publicly accessible descriptions or demonstrations of other inventions. If a patent is granted and it turns out that prior art was overlooked, the patent may be invalidated or reduced in scope. In some countries, inventors even have a duty to disclose pertinent prior art with the relevant patent office.

> *You can't be original without knowing*
> *what has already been said.*

In performance, jazz musicians are continually engaged in dialogues. These are not simply functional conversations consisting of perfunctory contributions, much like the musical equivalents of "Hi, how are you?" and "Very well, thanks, and how are you doing?" They are conversations in which each person offers up his or her best ideas for feedback and development. The roots for such musical conversation were laid long before jazz was even born. Listen to the counterpoint of Bach, and you'll hear themes and counterthemes passed around and developed through the parts. The same is true in most classical music, right through to the twentieth century. The musical term for these snippets is *motif.* You're probably familiar with the opening of Beethoven's *Symphony No. 5.* Those first four notes are called the "fate motif." Beethoven developed it and used it throughout each movement of the symphony. In the opening to Davis's *So What,* the horns play a simple but catchy two-note riff as a response to the "call" riff played by the bass. **Call and response** is a musical device in which two phrases are played or sung by two different musicians, with the second phrase acting as a commentary or a response to the first phrase. It's found in all styles of music: Indian classical music, Cuban music, many forms of religious music (can you say "Amen?"), African music, and, hence African-American music, including gospel, blues, and jazz. Improvisation, as we've discussed previously, is instant real-time composition, so it's not surprising that even when they are improvising, jazz musicians engage in musical exchanges. A musician may quote something heard on a recording. Or you might hear one musician finish a solo with a phrase that the next soloist uses as the basis for beginning his or her solo. The most obvious exchanges occur when musicians engage in **trading**. This is a practice in which the musicians take turns improvising over short sections of a tune's harmony, usually taking four bars at a time. Call and response is often employed in trading. These and other practices form part of a performance protocol that helps jazz musicians engage in creative dialogues that can create stronger and more unique performances.

Fostering Innovation

We have established that collaboration, diversity, and an exchange of ideas are all important enablers of innovation. We also know from previous discussions that it's absolutely necessary to take risks in the pursuit of innovation and that trust can enable people to take those risks. How can you bring all this together to create a culture that fosters innovation?

People must feel that there is actually room for innovation. In many organizations, the vast majority of people's time is already fully committed to doing the things that absolutely must be done. They help the organization continue its trajectory by maintaining existing offerings, retaining existing business, and growing and developing incrementally using methods and approaches that have worked in the past. When pushed to innovate with the goal of producing the kinds of ideas that can truly disrupt competitors, they often feel that they have neither the available time nor the freedom to do so. Having recognized this problem, many organizations are mandating that employee work schedules include time for innovation. Google engineers are encouraged to allocate 20 percent of their time (one day per week) to any company-related project that interests them (Mediratta and Bick 2007). Similarly, IBM has Think Fridays, to encourage employees to spend Fridays brainstorming new projects unrelated to their current work (Jana, n.d.).

Innovation may lead to failures, so people must feel that there is room for them to make mistakes within the context of their innovation explorations. Google's culture of innovation accepts mistakes as a normal part of the research and development process. According to Eric Schmidt, Google's chairman and CEO, "The way you say this is: 'Please fail very quickly—so that you can try again.'" ("The Rise and Fall of Corporate R&D" 2007). Larry Page, president and cofounder of Products, said to one employee upon hearing from her that she had cost the company several million dollars, "I'm so glad you made this mistake. Because I want to run a company where we are moving too quickly and doing too much, not being too cautious and doing too little. If we don't have any of these mistakes, we're just not taking enough risk" (Lashinsky 2006). Google hired ex-McKinsey consultant Shona Brown as its Senior Vice-President of Business Operations. Brown is known to some as the company's "Chief Chaos Officer." She coauthored *Competing on the Edge: Strategy as Structured Chaos* with Kathleen M. Eisenhardt, Professor of Strategy and Organization at Stanford University. To quote: "Mistakes occur because systems at the edge of chaos often slip off the edge. But there is also quick recovery and, like jazz musicians who play the wrong note, there is the chance to turn mistakes into advantages" (Brown and Eisenhardt 1998, 28).

Because innovation is best pursued collaboratively, innovators must have the ability to work with others who share their passion for an idea. Google encourages "grouplets," which are groups of people working on a common goal in their "20 percent time." Although they have no budget or decision-making authority, this grassroots approach allows ideas and movements to grow from the bottom up instead of from the top down. This example of decentralized leadership can enable great ideas to gain momentum. In many organizations, top-heavy approaches to idea selection may stifle innovation. This is especially probable when executives aren't really tuned in or simply don't have the time and become a bottleneck. Great ideas backed by the momentum of many internal supporters, even if they are no more senior than middle management, have more chance of bubbling up to the top and receiving a favorable review.

If diversity improves innovation, such informal collaboration as Google's grouplets must be allowed to cross disciplines, teams, and organizational boundaries. Furthermore, if organizations truly understand and believe that diversity is essential to successful innovation, it must be reflected in their hiring and organizational practices. Diversity in culture, experience, skills, leadership styles, and appetite for risk are all necessary to build teams that not only are well-rounded, but have the potential to include the kinds of individual outliers who might just make a huge difference.

Recapitulation

- Creativity, the process of creating new ideas, can be thought of as a subset of innovation, the process of creating new ideas and applying them to a specific situation. Necessity is not necessarily the mother of creativity. One can be creative simply for its own sake. Innovation, on the other hand, is usually undertaken to solve a specific problem.

- Psychologist J. P. Guilford identified two important thinking styles in his study of creativity. Convergent thinking, generally associated with mathematics and science, is the process of selecting a single solution to a problem. Divergent thinking, generally associated with the humanities and the arts, is the process of generating many possible solutions to a problem. If pure creativity can be thought of as mostly divergent thinking, then innovation is the combination of divergent and convergent thought in which new ideas are generated and then tested for suitability and success.

- John Boyd noted that effective orientation requires people to continuously destroy existing mental concepts and replace them with newly constructed concepts that include observations. Doing this requires both logical and creative capabilities. Creativity allows people to be open to possibilities, including those of extreme change.

- The grand success of individual creativity and the concept of the lone inventor is largely a fallacy. Most creativity and innovation is the result of an exchange of ideas, even if the exchange is unidirectional, with the thinker observing the work of others or taking inspiration from other sources.

- Diversity of skills and experience within a team can improve the success of innovation by generating a greater number of unique solutions and increasing the likelihood of rejecting poor ones.

- Collaboration improves the success of innovation by leveraging a free exchange of ideas. This begins with knowing what has already been said in the past. This is why jazz musicians study recordings and live performances of past and present jazz greats.

- A culture that fosters innovation should give people the necessary time, support, and freedom to make mistakes. People should have the ability to collaborate with others who share a passion for their ideas and build momentum at a grassroots level. Hiring and organization practices should help generate diversity in culture, experience, skills, leadership styles, and appetite for risk.

CHAPTER 14

Take Measured Risks

"Progress always involves risks.
You can't steal second base and keep your foot on first."
—Frederick B. Wilcox

Managing Risk

A risk is an event that may impact your operation if it actually happens. Some risks are unavoidable; others are assumed because they are associated with a benefit. To manage risks, you must first identify the risks and then measure them. Every risk has a likelihood or probability of occurring and an impact if the risk is realized. If you can quantify these two aspects of a risk and weigh them against associated benefits, you can make an informed decision to manage the risk. These basic options exist for managing any risk:

- **Avoid the risk** by deciding not to take the path that presents the risk. Of course, any potential gains associated with the risk will be lost.

- **Transfer the risk** to another party. If you cannot avoid the risk, perhaps another party can assume the risk. In this case, the other party usually become the recipient of any potential gains associated with the risk.

- **Share the risk** with another party. This usually involves compensating the other party by either sharing part of the potential gains associated with the risk or paying a fee. Insurance is often thought of as transferring risk, but if anything, it is sharing risk. Insurance rarely covers all risks. There are usually exceptions, such as events classified as *force majeure,* or acts of God. If you purchase personal injury insurance, it doesn't reduce your risk of injury, but if you are injured, the insurer will compensate you. The cost of the risk, not the risk itself, is shared.

- **Reduce or mitigate the risk** by taking specific steps to reduce the likelihood of the risk or its consequences.
- **Accept the risk** after making an informed decision.
- **Ignore the risk** if you don't have the time or ability to assess the risk and you have no choice but to accept it. This is obviously not a desirable way to operate and brings to mind the analogy of an ostrich putting its head in the sand.
- **Exploit the risk** by accepting the risk with the intention of gaining potential benefit. The idea is to actively seek out risk to gain the associated benefits.

Risk management should be an essential skill for all high-performers. Although it makes sense to undertake only tasks that are free of risk, it's not really practical. The reality is that few things are truly risk-free—and your competitors will likely exploit anything that *is* risk-free, thereby reducing the likelihood that it could give you a competitive advantage. If you want to remain competitive, you must identify or create opportunities with benefits while managing associated risks.

Risks of Failing to Diversify

In the book's preface, I identified diversity as one of the themes that runs throughout this book. Diversity is a powerful and essential force for building and maintaining robust, high-performance systems. In agriculture, biodiversity increases the stability and productivity of crops. Monoculture, the dependency on a single crop or a small number of crops, has led to many disasters, such as the collapse of the European wine industry in the late 1800s, the Irish potato blight in 1846, and the U.S. Southern Corn Leaf Blight epidemic in 1970. Diversification is a proven technique for mitigating risk in financial investment by reducing the exposure to any single investment. In marketing, diversification can access new markets and increase sales. When a lack of diversity in thought occurs, people may look at situations primarily through their own filter and fail to consider other possibilities. In 2007, the American College of Physicians and the American Pain Society produced clinical guidelines for the diagnosis and treatment of low-back pain. They noted that "there has been little consensus, either within or between specialties, on appropriate clinical evaluation and management of low back pain" (Chou, et al. 2007). Seth Godin suggests that one reason back pain is frequently misdiagnosed is that specialists tend to apply what they know:

"One study found that when confronted with a patient with back pain, surgeons prescribed surgery, physical therapists thought that therapy was indicated and yes, acupuncturists were sure needles were the answer. Across the entire universe of patients, the single largest indicator of treatment wasn't symptoms or patient background, it was the background of the doctor" (Godin 2009).

Let's recap some of the ways we've previously identified the importance of diversity:

- Synergy is more likely to be present when people combine complementary skills.
- The tendency to resort to groupthink can be exacerbated by a team's tendency to self-select people of like-mindedness and rid itself of people who don't think like the rest of the team.
- Diversity of skills and experience can increase the success of innovation by improving a team's ability to both generate and select great ideas or solutions.
- A balance is needed between people who tend to rush in and others who tend to hold back.
- A balance is needed between people who are good at getting things started and those who are good at finishing.
- A balance is needed between people who readily initiate change or respond to it and those who care about the stability of an activity.

Unfortunately, exploiting diversity is not as simple as inserting people with different skills and experience into a team. Multiculturalism is an example of how diversity can help enrich the culture of societies, build tolerance and understanding, and improve foreign relations. However, multiculturalism can also be met with prejudice, bigotry, and racism from some people's social identity biases. In the quest to benefit from diversity, it's important to realize that people are often scared of the unknown and may feel that it threatens what they are used to.

Risks of Applying Best Practices

At the beginning of this book, I wrote that you must develop practices that enable you to apply the Jazz Process to your own teams and their activities.

The Jazz Process defines a set of 14 best principles, but practices that support these principles should not necessarily be considered best practices. Why is this? The problem is that the adjective *best* is really a misnomer because it implies that something can't get any better. Mary Poppendieck, an authority in the world of agile and lean software development, quotes Taiichi Ohno, originator of the Toyota Production System, on this point (Poppendieck 2007). Ohno writes (Ohno 2007):

> *There is something called standard work, but standards should be changed constantly. Instead, if you think of the standard as the best you can do, it's all over. The standard work is only a baseline for doing further kaizen. It is kai-aku [change for the worse] if things get worse than now, and it is kaizen [change for the better] if things get better than now. Standards are set arbitrarily by humans, so how can they not change?*

Best practices are usually defined when they are found to be effective in a particular circumstance. The danger is that some people assume that these practices should be applied equally in all circumstances. Every situation is different. Most activities are sufficiently complex that there are myriad constantly changing factors. Not only must any set of best practices be applied uniquely to each activity, but their effect must be monitored over time. To do otherwise may lead to degrading performance as circumstances change and people fail to respond appropriately, taking false comfort in practices that might have been the best choice at one time but now require reconsideration. This risk needs to be considered across different activities and companies, as well as within companies. Does the application of corporate-wide policies always make sense?

The more detailed a practice is, the greater the risk that applying it naively will lead to problems. Fundamental principles such as those of the Jazz Process are more likely to hold true in a variety of situations. However, heeding such principles requires that you define concrete practices. If you choose to apply any of the principles outlined in this book, I sincerely hope that you will do so in a way that makes sense for you and your specific situation. I believe that far too many people are overly zealous about the application of processes and methodologies. Proponents often tout the benefits but don't mention the costs of particular methods.

Taking Risks

"Take measured risks," the final principle in the Jazz Process, is important for a number of reasons. It serves as a reminder that taking risks is often necessary in the pursuit of excellence. It's also an open and transparent declaration that the benefits of each Jazz Process principle don't come for free. Principles such as "Employ top talent," "Put the team first," "Build trust and respect," "Commit with passion," "Listen for change," "Act transparently," and "Exchange ideas" appear to be all upside, but risks are definitely associated with them, especially when the principles are applied mindlessly or in the extreme. Principles such as "Use just enough rules," "Lead on demand," and "Reduce friction" carry the greatest risk because applying these principles in the quest for higher performance may introduce instability into an operation. On the other hand, a different risk is of playing it too safe by adhering too strictly to principles that promote stability, such as "Make contributions count," "Maintain momentum," and "Stay healthy."

Let's focus on the specific risks of the Jazz Process principles, looking at each principle in the order in which we've covered them so far. The risks presented for each principle are not intended to be exhaustive and complete but should serve as a good starting point.

Risks of Using Just Enough Rules

The risk of minimizing process is that it can result in a loss of control. Be particularly careful when reducing rules. Although an overabundance of rules can impede productivity, limit creativity, and create frustration, rules also reduce the room for error, assuming that the rules are flexible enough to account for all situations. They also help achieve consistency when it is needed. If you remove the wrong rules, you may end up with a lot of problems. Most rules have a benefit and a cost. You can avoid the cost by dropping the rule, but you must carefully consider the benefit you will lose. In large companies, many rules are related to business controls such as intellectual property, licensing and other legal issues, security, confidentiality, and finance. Such rules are in place to mitigate risks such as theft, breach of privacy, litigation, and fraud. Smaller companies usually have these risks, but in small measures. Rules guard against the possibility of mistakes or other unwanted behavior. If you remove such rules, you must compensate with people who have the skills, experience, and integrity to make the right decisions in any situation. When removing or relaxing rules, proceed with caution and measure the impact of the changes. Consider how the rules affect factors such as speed, quality, employee morale, and customer satisfaction.

If you remove rules that mitigate risk, you must compensate with people who have the skills, experience, and integrity to make the right decisions in any situation.

Risks of Employing Top Talent

Every use of top talent creates risk. We have already determined that excessive individualism may have a negative impact on group efforts. That's a reason to focus on the rule "Put the team first." However, managing top talent involves other, more fundamental risks. Consider the problem of recruiting the best individuals. Some say that the pool of top talent is diminishing and that finding good people is increasingly getting harder. McKinsey Co. conducted a yearlong study involving 77 companies and almost 6,000 executives and managers. The company concluded that most companies have no idea just how critical the problem has become. The aptly titled report, *The War for Talent* (Fishman 2007), underscored that the search for top talent can be a costly battle.

It is becoming harder to find and replace exceptional people. They can cost more, whether they are paid directly or compensated in some other way. High-performers are more likely to be lured away and are also more likely to grow dissatisfied with problems that affect their ability to operate. Customers can become attached to highly talented people in service organizations. If a customer realizes he or she is retaining the services of a company because of the skills and experience of a single person, the customer may try to lure that person away, effectively cutting out the middle man. This is why employee agreements are often structured to prevent people from seeking employment with customer organizations. When companies become dependent on highly talented people, their departure can create a lot of chaos and may even lead to the failure of the organization. Maintaining momentum can be important in this respect. For many years, people riffed on the question of whether Microsoft could survive without Bill Gates. Microsoft has built up a tremendous amount of momentum. Even if Gates's departure from day-to-day operations resulted in a downward slide in performance, Microsoft wouldn't completely fail immediately. The same concerns now surround the dependency of Apple on Steve Jobs.

Another risk of employing top talent is becoming overconfident. Top talent helps facilitate victory but doesn't guarantee it. Harvard Business School professor Rosabeth Moss Kanter notes, "Teams that have stars don't necessarily win" (Kanter, n.d.). In her book *Confidence: How Winning Streaks and Losing Streaks Begin and End,* Kanter notes, "Overconfidence leads people to overshoot, to overbuild, to become irrationally exuberant or delusionally optimistic, and to assume they are invulnerable" (Kanter 2006, 8).

Understand when and why you are creating dependencies on top talent, and use such people sensibly. Most of the time, it doesn't make sense to put your best people on routine tasks. Doing so often creates problems for everyone. Securing and retaining top talent is a huge topic in itself, and any general rules need to be applied specifically. McKinsey's report determined that talent will be the most important corporate resource in the next 20 years. It's already the resource in shortest supply. Such a critical resource deserves a lot of attention. You must know your firm and your people intimately, and that can be especially difficult in a large organization.

Risks of Putting the Team First

The most obvious risk of exclusively focusing on the team is the potential to suffocate the individualism that powers excellence and innovation. A less obvious but more dangerous risk is the potential of amplifying behavior or thinking that can lead to trouble. We've discussed how extreme cases of group decision making can lead to groupthink and group polarization. Group dynamics also play a role in a team's mental outlook and morale. Kanter writes (Kanter 2006, 6):

> On the way up, success creates positive momentum. People who believe they are likely to win are also likely to put in the extra effort at difficult moments to ensure that victory. On the way down, failure feeds on itself. As performance starts running on a positive or a negative path, the momentum can be hard to stop. Growth cycles produce optimism, decline cycles produce pessimism.

If you recognized such winning and losing streaks as positive feedback loops, you're absolutely right. Of course, individuals can also fall prey to outlooks of optimism and pessimism, but it's often much easier for them to break out of such patterns. As we know, when it comes to maintaining momentum, it can be more difficult to reverse the momentum of a large group than to change the momentum of a small one. Encourage the positive aspects of putting the team first, while discouraging the negative possibilities before they get out of control.

Risks of Building Trust and Respect

The most extreme cases of dangerous positive feedback loops in groups can be found in herd behavior, also known as pack mentality or mob mentality. This is the phenomenon that causes rioting and mass panic. Fortunately, such extreme behavior is usually seen only in groups that lack cohesion and structure, such as random crowds. Yet this is precisely where the risk lies because trust and respect increase the cohesion of a group. People who place unfailing trust and respect in leaders can be led down the wrong path.

Extreme examples include James Warren "Jim" Jones, who coerced 900 people to commit suicide in Jonestown, Guyana, in 1978. Thirty-nine members of the Heaven's Gate cult also committed suicide in 1997 in California. They reportedly believed this would enable them to reach an alien spaceship traveling in the tail of the Comet Hale-Bopp (Purdum 1997). News sources frequently inform us of less bizarre but equally disturbing stories of people who went off on tangents and took down entire organizations or groups of people with them. Such people are often, but not always, senior leaders. Rogue trader Nick Leeson was trusted with huge trading positions for Barings Bank, the oldest merchant bank in London until the time he brought on its collapse. It should be pointed out that Leeson was able commit his fraud as a result of a deficiency in auditing and risk management practices. In other words, not enough rules were in place.

These examples demonstrate that trust should always be measured, and only rarely should we place complete and unfettered trust in people. The need for measuring trust should be proportional to the risk that the trust might turn out to be misplaced. Measured trust begins in small degrees and increases as people do things to earn more trust. You should always have a plan for extraction or a backup plan, just in case things don't work out. Above all, always exercise caution and vigilance, and don't be afraid to question things (Kramer 2009).

Risks of Committing with Passion

When we commit with passion, we promise all necessary time and resources to a task or the pursuit of a goal. We're not afraid to advertise that commitment to others in the hope that it will motivate them to similarly commit to the same task or goal. The associated risk is overcommitting. Individuals may overcommit to their teams. Teams and organizations may overcommit to customers. In situations of overcommitment, something must give. Commitments may need to be dropped. Deliverables may have to be completed late. Quality may suffer. Calling in extra help may be costly. People may work extended hours, which can be stressful and harmful to health. Overcommitment can be particularly dangerous in the context of lean operations or any kind of cost cutting as a result of economic conditions, low revenue, or a multitude of other factors. In these situations, commitments are not necessarily scaled back accordingly, and teams may be left trying to deliver with reduced resources. Other resource constraints, such as a failure to obtain credit or the unavailability of materials, can also lead to overcommitment. The key to avoiding overcommitment is careful planning and risk management. Employ buffers, slack time, spare capacity, and other methods to allow for the possibility of the unforeseen. Be willing to make sacrifices. Most projects are constrained by time, cost, scope, and quality. For example, when teams work in a timebox, they usually sacrifice scope by decommitting on lower-priority deliverables. If reducing scope doesn't produce an acceptable solution, one or more other constraints must be compromised.

Risks of Listening for Change

You may recall that the rule "Listen for change" has a bearing on observation and orientation in the context of an execution loop. These steps are vital. You can't make good decisions and act on them without acquiring the right data and making sense of it. Imagine a company that is performing poorly and is on the brink of total failure. Sales are down, and management doesn't know why. The manufacturing process is slow, and the number of defective products is higher than the industry standard; the managers can't seem to figure out the problems. The firm doesn't have great relationships with its partners and suppliers, who prefer to deal with the company's competitors. To top it all off, the productivity of most employees is only satisfactory, and morale is at an all-time low. Management has tried to improve the situation with corporate functions, motivational speeches from senior management, team-building exercises, and extra vacation days, but it hasn't helped much. In fact, employee attrition in the last six months has actually increased.

Management is desperate to turn things around. The CEO consults an advisor and finds that he is unable to answer many of the questions thrown at him. The fundamental problem is that he knows that things are bad but can't explain why. The advisor tells the CEO that he needs to get more data. The company needs to start speaking to its customers, partners, suppliers, and employees to gain perspective on the situation and find out what would make everybody happier. The CEO and his senior vice presidents implement a new series of feedback programs to gather data. Their slogan is, "Your feedback is valuable to us."

Now, how does this story end? There are so many ways to do this incorrectly, and each one presents a risk of not only destroying the quantity and quality of the feedback, but of frustrating or upsetting people. If the company doesn't have suitable skills and experience, it should hire human resource or management consultants to help them. Management should clearly state their motivation for soliciting feedback. Most people are only too glad to help out, especially if it will benefit someone or something they care about—and even more so if it benefits them. The company should use mechanisms such as anonymous surveys and confidential focus groups run by independent facilitators. After the executives have analyzed the information, they should let the subjects of feedback know about specific results privately. For example, leaders need to know what people in their teams have to say about their leadership. Results should always be provided in a way that ensures the anonymity of those who provided feedback. Executives should then release the findings to all those who provided feedback and to other interested stakeholders. Most important, they should act on the findings and do so in a visible way, embracing critical feedback instead of dismissing it.

Other methods of soliciting feedback provide the opportunity to gain more detailed, specific comments. These include entirely voluntary one-on-one discussions and completely open and transparent group discussions such as online forums and town hall meetings. Of course, a much greater risk is associated with such efforts because they are not as controlled and may veer into unforeseen territory. Listening for change is fraught with risks, but the benefits are substantial because feedback is critical to mitigating other risks. The good news is that the risks drop dramatically after you have established appropriate processes and a good reputation for obtaining and acting on feedback. It's important to continually evolve feedback mechanisms in the quest for more relevant and accurate data.

Not all feedback comes from people. Much of what we observe is also readily available. Organizations in competitive situations must keep tabs on the competition, competitive offerings, customers, and environment. *Competitive intelligence* is the discipline of acquiring, analyzing, and making available such information using ethical legal means. Industrial espionage is its evil twin, using illegal methods. In any observational effort, acquiring the wrong data is always a risk. Another risk is misinterpreting that data or failing to turn it into useful information. Ultimately, unless the data collected can be used in strategic decision making, it is of little use.

Risks of Leading on Demand

Clear risks are involved in encouraging everyone to take the initiative and lead. The obvious risk is that chaos may ensue if multiple people give conflicting direction. This is mitigated by ensuring that leadership is granted only to those who understand the importance of stabilizing principles such as "Put the team first," "Stay healthy," and "Maintain momentum." It's also important to define protocols for delegating, transferring, and initiating leadership. Jazz musicians accomplish a lot of this through the notes they play and through eye contact, hand signals, or a quick word. Consider some examples of this:

- Saying "head" or pointing to one's head to signal that everyone should play the head, which is usually the form with the melody
- Saying "bridge" to signal that everyone should jump to the bridge or middle section, in a form such as AABA
- Saying "top" or pointing up to signal that everyone should jump to the top of the form
- Saying "fours," or showing four fingers or pointing to oneself and then another person to indicate trading fours

Such signs may vary, and it doesn't matter what conventions are used, as long as they work. Another less obvious risk with on-demand leadership is that no one will lead. Again, mindful of the need to stay healthy, jazz musicians always seem to appoint a default leader to give direction if no one else cares to.

Risks of Acting Transparently

Some people view transparency as one of the riskiest principles to employ. Sometimes organizations have no choice but to adopt transparency mandated by legal or regulatory compliance. De facto standards may have the same effect. It doesn't look good if all your competitors have chosen to be transparent but you are still operating opaquely. As we've noted previously, although transparency provides benefits to customers and other stakeholders, it also allows competitors to gain insight into your plans and progress. If you are truly transparent, you can't hide inefficiencies, mistakes, suspicious activities, or wrongdoing. People are sometimes motivated to increase transparency for the purpose of creating buzz or interest about something. Early releases, design or concept documents, movie trailers, and behind-the-scenes interviews can all help, but if people don't like what they see, they may discount the offering and never give it a second chance. Transparency can be damaging, annoying, and even boring if you are transparent about the wrong things. Business or operational transparency is about adding value for consumers, partners, employees, and other stakeholders. Anything else may only be entertaining or interesting for the curious. The signal-to-noise ratio in social networking varies greatly, depending on the medium. One 2009 study estimated that more than 40 percent of tweets on Twitter were pointless babble, with conversational tweets at 37 percent, retweets or forwards at 8.7 percent, promotional tweets at 5.85 percent, and spam and news at 3 percent each (Leahul 2009). On the other hand, many blogs focused on specific topics have a significantly higher signal-to-noise ratio, and many bloggers seek to always provide at least one useful piece of information in each post.

Transparency is not an excuse to bypass fundamental rules of privacy, confidentiality, or ethics. If a consultant is working on a client site and sees something clearly internal to the client's operations, blogging about it is not being transparent. Being open about yourself or your company's processes or offerings is the kind of transparency people want. Providing intimate details about other parties without their consent is not.

Transparency is often defined in terms of what companies must do. They must be open, authentic, clear, and consistent. Yet transparency is not a one-way conversation. The most successful transparency is a dialogue that gives consumers and other interested parties the opportunity to provide feedback and engage in conversation. Companies must enable such dialogue and should never discourage it. In 2006, Chevrolet created a marketing campaign around the Chevy 2007 Tahoe sport utility vehicle (SUV). People were encouraged to create ads for the new Tahoe in a contest that allowed them to supply text captions to stock video clips. At first, the campaign appeared to be a disaster, with hundreds of people submitting ads that accused General Motors and Tahoe owners of contributing to global warming and criticized the Tahoe's quality and gas consumption. General Motors chose to keep the contest running, and although the company did screen the ads for offensive and inflammatory content, it stated that no material would be removed based solely on a negative tone toward the company. The contest polarized a long-standing argument about SUVs, but the resulting free dialogue between consumers was decidedly in favor of the Tahoe. General Motors trusted that Tahoe owners and other SUV owners would defend their purchases, and they did, with more than 80 percent of the 21,000 ads casting the Tahoe in a positive light. The dialogue and controversy helped the campaign go viral, with more than 2.4 million page views (Sandoval 2006). It had a huge effect on sales: The Tahoe doubled sales of its nearest competitor, the

Ford Expedition, and the length of time Tahoes spent on dealer lots dropped from four months in the previous year to just 46 days (Rose 2006).

Risks of Making Contributions Count

To make contributions count, you must take care in your actions, understanding their cost and impact and the value they will add to an activity. The only real risk is being too reserved and contributing less than you could. In "Essentials of Execution" we discussed the ability of skilled and experienced people to feed-forward and act with little forethought. Having all the fundamentals down pat gives people the confidence to take risks when they need to or want to do so. People who are not equipped with the requisite level of skill and experience, on the other hand, must go through the motions of orienting themselves and then deciding on a course of action.

Risks of Reducing Friction

Any given activity has an optimal amount of friction. Too little is just as bad as too much. The risk of reducing friction is that you may restrict performance. For example, by seeking to minimize social friction in discussions, you remove all sources of opposing thought and dissenting opinion. This allows you to arrive at solutions quickly without bruising egos or offending anyone. But how good are those solutions? As we noted previously, diversity of thought and experience improves the ability to innovate. It's important to understand how each source of friction functions. It may be tempting to immediately remove or cease something that is causing friction, but that may be a mistake. If the source of friction provides benefits, it may make more sense to try to determine how to reduce the friction without eliminating it entirely. When teams try new methods of working, substantial friction may be generated in the beginning, but the degree of friction may be reduced in time as the team becomes more efficient.

Risks of Maintaining Momentum

Momentum is a double-edged sword. Just as positive feedback loops can be both good and bad, momentum depends on the direction in which you're advancing. The concept of financial interest is a helpful example. Money in the bank earns interest, which increases principal, which then earns more interest, and so forth. Unfortunately, interest works the same way when you have a debt. Many people get caught in a "death spiral" of debt, unable to free themselves as the debt and the interest keep ballooning. As the saying goes, the rich get richer, and the poor get poorer. In organizations, people can get stuck in a rut and continue to make the same mistakes. Consequently, systems, people, and processes continue to fail, and the activity marches inevitably toward disaster. Just as it takes foresight and the ability to react in time to maintain constructive momentum, it takes the same powers of long-range observation to avoid establishing destructive momentum. In this regard, it's essential to understand the limits of your agility. The captain of a cargo ship knows that the momentum of his ship is huge. If he is to have any chance of avoiding collisions at sea, he must become aware of potential problems way ahead of time. A small boat can turn or reverse direction much more rapidly because it has less momentum than a large ship.

Risks of Staying Healthy

Staying healthy involves no specific risk, but there is a risk when accepting help to aid recovery. When you're physically sick and certain bacteria are reproducing at a faster rate than your immune system can handle, antibiotic drugs can help fight off the bacteria. One downside of this is that the body's immune system can become weak if antibiotics are used too often. This can occur especially if antibiotics are used for fighting bacteria that the immune system might be able to handle on its own, such as those of the common cold. Worse, the bacteria may mutate and return in a stronger form that the immune system has no chance of fighting alone. Without antibiotics, an immune system is forced to adapt to keep up with mutating bacteria and can become stronger and more able to fight off certain bacteria without the need for drugs.

In a general sense, relying on external assistance can weaken your internal abilities if you are too quick to call for help. In some cases, outside help certainly is the best option, but it's important to remember that handling the situation on your own enables you to learn skills, gain experience, and build robustness that will aid you if the same problem crops up in the future.

Risks of Exchanging Ideas

The exchange of ideas powers innovation. A risk of innovation is that efforts may be misdirected or may lose focus over time. Innovating is hard. For this reason, it's critical that innovative efforts be directed to the right areas and given appropriate priorities. A good proportion of work does not demand innovation. If a team responsible for a software product could pursue innovation as its sole goal, its developers could spend all their time adding their most desired features. In practice, they must ensure that any new features will add value for existing users and attract new users. They must also ensure that new code is bug-free and that it doesn't degrade the overall performance of the product or the performance or function of existing features. Then there's software maintenance, which may account for 40 to 90 percent of total life cycle costs. This involves more routine tasks, such as fixing bugs in existing code and adding support for new platforms. Although exceptions exist, maintenance and other routine tasks should generally avoid fancy footwork and go with what works. **Feature creep** is the term given to the dangerous situation in which the set of features in a product such as a software application continually expands. The desire to add "just one more feature" can lead to schedule and budget overruns.

When innovation can be appropriately directed, the primary concern is the risk of introducing instability. Substantive innovation often requires wholesale revolutionary changes or repeated evolutionary changes that add up to the same degree of change. Such changes introduce risks of sacrificing stability, generating friction, and putting the creative desires of individuals before the team. You can mitigate these risks by giving sufficient consideration to principles such as "Listen for change," "Stay healthy," "Reduce friction," and "Put the team first."

Recapitulation

- A risk is a possible event that may impact an operation if it actually happens. Some risks are unavoidable; others are assumed because they are associated with a benefit. It is often necessary to take risks in the pursuit of excellence.

- To manage risks, you must first identify the risks and then measure them by quantifying the probability that the risk will be realized and determining the subsequent impact. You must then weigh this against the potential benefits associated with it.

- One of the most significant risks in any quest for excellence is failing to diversify. Diversity is a powerful and essential force for building and maintaining robust, high-performance systems.

- It can be dangerous to label any principle or practice as "best" and assume that it can be applied equally in all circumstances. The adjective *best* is really a misnomer because it implies that something can't get any better. When applying any practice or principle, carefully consider the specifics of the situation and be aware that the situation may change over time.

- Proponents often tout the benefits of particular practices or principles but don't discuss the costs. If you choose to apply any of the principles of the Jazz Process, do so in a way that makes sense for you and your specific situation.

Coda

The idea of applying jazz performance principles to other domains is occasionally met with skepticism. Those who discount it are often quick to read too much into the idea. Jazz musicians don't make much money, so how can jazz be a good model for business? That, of course, is an overly literal interpretation of the analogy and an unfortunate dismissal of a potential learning opportunity.

I am not the first to suggest that jazz has more to offer than a listening experience, nor am I the first to have shared the idea in detail. When other people have riffed on the premise that jazz might be a source of inspiration for business teams, they have tended to focus on the more noble qualities of jazz. Jazz is democratic. Jazz is genuine. Jazz is joyful and at times soulful. Jazz is all of these things. However, it's not just the end result that's interesting but the process of making the music. In this book I've been very specific about what I believe to be the key parts of that process. In each case I've then distilled those elements into a general principle. Jazz musicians are not alone in applying these principles. Written from another perspective, this book might have been "The Basketball Process" or "The Warfare Process."

I see these principles applied each day in a multitude of domains and disciplines in commerce and recreation, and even in nature. Every instance of collaboration presents a learning opportunity. I can discover much from the behavior of a pack of wolves, a pride of lions, or a colony of beavers just as I can from other people. Even if I don't identify something new, observing successful or failed collaboration provides me with an opportunity to validate my beliefs or question them. Either way, it's a chance to learn.

Two points merit restatement. The first is that a heightened awareness allows one to identify these valuable learning opportunities. The second point is that being honest about problems and having a desire to correct them can enable improvement. This seems like an obvious point but many people have difficulty being honest with themselves, let alone others.

I hope you found some food for thought and perhaps even a little inspiration in this book. I invite you to join the growing community of those inspired by jazz at jazzprocess.com. Thank you for reading.

Adrian Cho
Ottawa, Canada, April 2010

Works Cited

Abdul-Jabbar, Kareem. *On the Shoulders of Giants: My Journey Through the Harlem Renaissance*. Simon & Schuster, 2007.

Adolph, Steve. "What Lessons Can the Agile Community Learn from a Maverick Fighter Pilot?" Agile Conference, Minneapolis, 2006.

Albrecht, Karl. *Practical Intelligence*. Jossey-Bass, 2007.

Asian Development Bank. "2007 Benchmarking and Data Book of Water Utilities in India." *Asian Development Bank*. Available at www.adb.org/documents/reports/Benchmarking-DataBook/Part1.pdf (accessed January 1, 2010).

Bahmanyar, Mir and Michael Welply. *US Army Ranger 1983–2002*. Osprey Publishing, 2003: 24.

Bailey, Derek. *Improvisation—It's Nature and Practice in Music*. The British Library National Sound Archive, 1992.

Barrett, Frank J. "Creativity and Improvisation in Jazz and Organizations: Implications for Organizational Learning." *Organization Science*, Institute for Operations Research and the Management Sciences (September–October 1998): 605–622.

Bastien, David T. and Todd J. Hostager. "Jazz as a Process of Organizational Innovation." *Organizational Improvisation*. Edited by Ken N. Kamoche, Miguel Pina e Cunha, and João Vieira da Cunha. Routledge, 2001.

Beck, Kent, and Martin Fowler. *Planning Extreme Programming*. Addison-Wesley Professional, 2000.

Beck, Kent, et al. "Manifesto for Agile Software Development." February 13, 2001. www.agilemanifesto.org (accessed September 9, 2009).

Bennis, Warren. "Flight Plan for Leaders, or The Puck, the Plaque, and the Art of Jazz." *USC Business* (Summer 1994).

Bennis, Warren and Patricia Biederman Ward. *Organizing Genius*. Basic Books, 1998.

Bennis, Warren, Daniel Goleman, James O'Toole, and Patricia Ward Biederman. *Transparency: How Leaders Create a Culture of Candor*. Jossey-Bass, 2008.

Berkun, Scott. *The Myths of Innovation*. O'Reilly Media, 2007.

Block, Ned. "The Mind as the Software of the Brain." In *An Invitation to Cognitive Science, 2nd Edition, Vol. 3: Thinking*, by Edward E. Smith and Daniel N. Osherson. (MIT Press, 1995): 377–420.

Blumenfeld, Larry. "Links Between Basketball and Jazz Run Deep." *The Times-Picayune*, February 17, 2008.

Board of Directors of the Global Reporting Initiative. "The Amsterdam Declaration on Transparency and Reporting." *Global Reporting Initiative* (March 2009). www.globalreporting.org/CurrentPriorities/AmsterdamDeclaration/ (accessed August 23, 2009).

Bogle, John C. *Enough: True Measures of Money, Business and Life*. Wiley, 2008.

Boyd, John R. "Destruction and Creation." *Goal Systems International*. September 3, 1976. www.goalsys.com/books/documents/DESTRUCTION_AND_CREATION.pdf (accessed October 4, 2009).

Brown, Shona L. and Kathleen M. Eisenhardt. *Competing on the Edge: Strategy as Structured Chaos*. McGraw-Hill Ryerson Agency, 1998.

Buffett, Warren. "Chairman's Letter." In *2008 Annual Report*, by Inc. Berkshire Hathaway, 2008: 3–23.

Buxton, William. "Less Is More (More or Less)." In *The Invisible Future: The Seamless Integration of Technology into Everyday Life*, by Peter J. Denning (McGraw Hill, 2001): 145–179.

Carroll, J. E. and Dr. William R. Taggart. "Cockpit Resource Management: A Tool for Improved Flight Safety." Edited by Harry W. Orlady and H. Clayton Foushee. *Proceedings of the NASA/MAC Workshop on Cockpit Resource Management (NASA Conference Publication 2455)* (Moffett Field, CA: NASA, Ames Research Center, 1987): 40–46.

Chatain, Olivier and Peter B. Zemsky. "Value Creation and Value Capture with Frictions." *Social Science Research Network* (June 16, 2009). http://papers.ssrn.com/sol3/papers.cfm?abstract_id=1424950 (accessed September 8, 2009).

Chou, Roger, et al. "Diagnosis and Treatment of Low Back Pain: A Joint Clinical Practice Guideline from the American College of Physicians and the American Pain Society." *Annals of Internal Medicine* 147, no. 7 (October 2, 2007): 478–491.

Citino, Robert M. *The Path to Blitzkrieg: Doctrine and Training in the German Army*, 1920–1939. Lynne Rienner Publishers, 1999.

Coolman, Todd. "Liner Notes for Six CD Boxed Set, Miles Davis Quintet 1965–1968." Columbia, 1997: 58.

Cooper, Alan. *The Inmates Are Running the Asylum: Why High Tech Products Drive Us Crazy and How to Restore the Sanity*. Sams, 2004.

Coram, Robert. *Boyd: The Fighter Pilot Who Changed the Art of War*. Little, Brown and Company, 2002.

Cosner, Sgt. Kyle J. "Unlawful Orders? Rangers' 'Standing Orders' Historically Inaccurate." United States Army Special Operations Command, May 15, 2003.

Coutu, Diane. "How Resilience Works." *Harvard Business Review* 80, no. 5 (May 2002).

Couzin, I. D. and N. R. Franks. "Self-Organized Lane Formation and Optimized Traffic Flow in Army Ants." *Proceedings of the Royal Society (Biological Sciences)* 270, no. 1,511 (January 2003): 139–146.

Covey, Stephen M.R. *The Speed of Trust*. Free Press, 2006.

Covey, Stephen R. *The 8th Habit*. Free Press, 2004.

"Creaking, Groaning: Infrastructure Is India's Biggest Handicap." *The Economist,* December 11, 2008. Available at www.economist.com/specialreports/displaystory.cfm?story_id=12749787 (accessed January 1, 2010).

Davis, Miles and Quincy Troupe. *Miles.* Simon & Schuster, 1990.

Deming, W. Edwards. *Out of the Crisis.* MIT Press, 2000.

Downing, Wayne A., Richard H. Schultz, Robert L. Pfaltzgraff, and W. Bradley Stock. *Special Operations Forces: Roles and Missions in the Aftermath of the Cold War.* Diane Publishing Co., 1996: 3

Epstein, Keith. "Cybersecurity's New Guard." *BusinessWeek* (March 21, 2008). Available at www.businessweek.com/technology/content/mar2008/tc 20080320_011308.htm.

Fishman, Charles. "The War for Talent." *Fast Company* (December 18, 2007). www.fastcompany.com/magazine/16/mckinsey.html (accessed October 5, 2009).

Friedel, Robert D., Paul Israel, and Bernard S. Finn. *Edison's Electric Light: Biography of an Invention.* Rutgers University Press, 1986.

G-20. "The Global Plan for Recovery and Reform." *G-20.* April 2, 2009. Available at www.g20.org/Documents/final-communique.pdf (accessed August 22, 2009).

Gabor, Andrea. *The Capitalist Philosophers: The Geniuses of Modern Business—Their Lives, Times, and Ideas.* Three Rivers Press, 2002.

George, Michael L. and Stephen A. Wilson. *Conquering Complexity in Your Business: How Wal-Mart, Toyota, and Other Top Companies Are Breaking Through the Ceiling on Profits and Growth.* McGraw-Hill, 2004.

Gilmore, James H. and B. Joseph Pine II. *Authenticity: What Consumers Really Want.* Harvard Business School Press, 2007.

Gitler, Ira. "Trane on the Track." *Downbeat* (October 16, 1958).

Gladwell, Malcolm. *The Tipping Point: How Little Things Make a Big Difference.* Little Brown, 2000: 33

Godin, Seth. "Hammer Time." Seth Godin's Blog, November 13, 2009. http://sethgodin.typepad.com/seths_blog/2009/11/hammer-time.html (accessed November 13, 2009).

Godin, Seth. *Linchpin: Are You Indispensable?* Portfolio Hardcover, 2010.

Green, Joshua. "The Front-Runner's Fall." *The Atlantic* (September 2008). Available at www.theatlantic.com/doc/200809/hillary-clinton-campaign (accessed August 9, 2009).

Greenwald, John, William McWhirter, and Joseph R. Szczesny. "What Went Wrong? Everything at Once." *Time* (November 9, 1992).

Healey, James R. "Obama's Auto Faux Pas Leads to History Lesson." *USA Today,* February 25, 2009. Available at www.usatoday.com/money/autos/2009-02-25-obama-claim-daimler-differs_N.htm (accessed September 27, 2009).

Hesselbein, Frances, Marshall Goldsmith, and Richard Beckhard. *The Leader of the Future: New Visions, Strategies and Practices for the Next Era.* Jossey-Bass, 1997.

Hillaker, Harry. "Tribute to John R. Boyd." *Code One*, Lockheed Martin Aeronautics Company (July 1997).

Holusha, John. "W. Edwards Deming, Expert on Business Management, Dies at 93." *The New York Times,* December 21, 1993, 7.

Isaacs, William. *Dialogue: The Art Of Thinking Together.* Broadway Business, 1999.

Jackson, Julian. *The Fall of France: The Nazi Invasion of 1940.* Oxford University Press, 2004.

Jackson, Phil. Sacred Hoops: Spiritual Lessons of a Hardwood Warrior. Hyperion, 1995.

Jana, Reena. "India's Next Global Export: Innovation." *BusinessWeek* (December 2, 2009). Available at www.businessweek.com/innovate/content/dec2009/id2009121_864965.htm (accessed January 1, 2009).

Jana, Reena. "Trend: Structuring Unstructured Time." *BusinessWeek*. Available at http://images.businessweek.com/ss/07/05/0530_inshort/source/7.htm (accessed November 29, 2009).

Jones, Del. "Can Small Business Help Win the War?" *USA Today,* January 3, 2007. Available at www.usatoday.com/money/2007-01-02-terror-war-business-usat_x.htm.

Judicial Watch. "New Judicial Watch/Zogby Poll: 81.7% of Americans Say Political Corruption Played a 'Major Role' in Financial Crisis." *Judicial Watch* (October 21, 2008). Available at www.judicialwatch.org/news/2008/oct/new-judicial-watch-zogby-poll-82-7-american-say-political-corruption-played-major-role (accessed August 23, 2009).

Kahn, Ashley. *Kind of Blue: The Making of the Miles Davis Masterpiece.* Da Capo Press, 2000.

Kahn, David. *Seizing the Enigma: The Race to Break the German U-Boat Codes*, 1939–1943. Barnes & Noble, 1998.

Kanter, Rosabeth Moss. *Confidence: How Winning Streaks and Losing Streaks Begin and End*. Three Rivers Press, 2006.

Kanter, Rosabeth Moss. "Winners Learn to Face Up to Problems." *Businessworld*. Available at www.businessworld.in/index.php/Winners-learn-to-face-up-to-problems.html (accessed October 5, 2009).

Katzenbach, Jon R. and Douglas K. Smith. *The Wisdom of Teams.* Harvard Business School Press, 1993.

Kaufman, James C. *Creativity 101.* Springer Publishing Co., 2009.

Kelleher, James B. "ANALYSIS–Six Sigma Mystique Takes Beating in Downturn." *Reuters UK,* April 29, 2009. Available at http://uk.reuters.com/article/idUKIndia-39310120090429?pageNumber=5&virtualBrandChannel=0&sp=true (accessed July 5, 2009).

Kelling, George L. and James Q. Wilson. "Broken Windows." *The Atlantic* (March 1982). Available at www.theatlantic.com/doc/198203/broken-windows (accessed September 24, 2009).

Keyes, Maj. Ricky J. *Cockpit Resource Management: A New Approach to Aircrew Coordination Training.* Maxwell Airforce Base, Ala.: Air University Press, 1990.

Kirchner, Bill. *Introduction to Kind of Blue transcriptions.* Hal Leonard Corporation, 2001.

Kramer, Roderick A. "Rethinking Trust." *Harvard Business Review* (June 2009): 69–77.

Lashinsky, Adam. "Chaos by Design: The Inside Story of Disorder, Disarray, and Uncertainty at Google. And Why It's All Part of the Plan. (They hope.)" *Fortune* (October 2, 2006). Available at http://money.cnn.com/magazines/fortune/fortune_archive/2006/10/02/8387489/index.htm (accessed December 14, 2009).

Leahul, Dan. "Twitter Mostly 'Pointless Babble' Says Study." *Brand Republic* (August 13, 2009). Available at www.brandrepublic.com/news/index.cfm?fuseaction=BR.News.DigitalAMBulletin.Article&nNewsID=926942&sHashCode=& (accessed October 6, 2009).

Levin, Floyd. *Classic Jazz: A Personal View of the Music and the Musicians.* University of California Press, 2000.

Martin, Roger L. *Opposable Mind: Winning Through Integrative Thinking.* Harvard Business Press, 2009.

Maxwell, John C. *The 21 Irrefutable Laws of Leadership: Follow Them and People Will Follow You.* Thomas Nelson, 1998.

Mediratta, Bharat, and Julie Bick. "The Google Way: Give Engineers Room." *The New York Times,* October 21, 2007. Available at www.nytimes.com/2007/10/21/jobs/21pre.html?_r=1 (accessed December 1, 2009).

Michaelson, Gerald. *Sun Tzu: The Art of War for Managers—50 Strategic Rules*. Adams Media, 2001.

Miller, Saul L. *Why Teams Win: Keys to Success in Business, Sport and Beyond*. John Wiley & Sons Canada, 2009.

Mitchell, Houston. "How Many Has Michael Made?" National Basketball Association. 2001. Available at www.nba.com/jordan/game_winners.html (accessed September 20, 2009).

Monson, Ingrid. *Saying Something: Jazz Improvisation and Interaction*. University of Chicago Press, 1996.

Moore, Stephen. *It's Getting Better All the Time: 100 Greatest Trends of the Last 100 Years*. Cato Institute, 2001.

Morris, Michael, Janice Nadler, Terri Kurtzberg, and Leigh Thompson. "Schmooze or Lose: Social Friction and Lubrication in E-mail Negotiations." *Group Dynamics, Theory, Research & Practice* 6, no. 1 (May 2002): 89–100.

Ohno, Taiichi. *Taiichi Ohno's Workplace Management*. Edited by Jon Miller. Gemba Press, 2007.

Osinga, Frans P. *Science, Strategy and War: The Strategic Theory of John Boyd*. Eburon Academic Publishers, 2005.

Peters, Tom. *Re-Imagine! Business Excellence in a Disruptive Age*. DK Publishing, 2003.

Pink, Daniel. *A Whole New Mind*. Riverhead, 2005.

Pistole, John S. "Congressional Testimony, Statement Before the Senate Judiciary Committee." Federal Bureau of Investigation, February 11, 2009. Available at www.fbi.gov/congress/congress09/pistole021109.htm (accessed August 23, 2009).

Poppendieck, Mary. "Lean and Software Project Management." *Lean Software Development* (October 6, 2007). Available at http://tech.groups.yahoo.com/group/leandevelopment/message/2111 (accessed November 12, 2009).

Porter, Lewis. *John Coltrane: His Life and Music*. University of Michigan Press, 2000.

Portfolio.com. "Portfolio's Worst American CEOs of All Time." CNBC.com, April 30, 2009. Available at www.cnbc.com/id/30502091?slide=9 (accessed July 4, 2009).

Purdum, Todd S. "In Serene Setting in California, a Suicide Investigation Unfolds." *New York Times,* March 30, 1997. Available at www.nytimes.com/1997/03/30/us/in-serene-setting-in-california-a-suicide-investigation-unfolds.html (accessed October 5, 2009).

Rarick, Charles A. "Ancient Chinese Advice for Modern Business Strategists." *Society for the Advancement of Management Advanced Management Journal* (1996): 38–43.

Ratcliff, Rebecca Ann. *Delusions of Intelligence: Enigma, Ultra, and the End of Secure Ciphers.* Cambridge University Press, 2006.

Raymond, Eric S. "The Cathedral and the Bazaar." *The Cathedral and the Bazaar.* May 21, 1997. Available at www.catb.org/~esr/writings/cathedral-bazaar/cathedral-bazaar/ (accessed July 26, 2009).

Rheingold, Howard. Tools for Thought: The History and Future of Mind-Expanding Technology. MIT Press, 2000.

Richards, Chet. *Certain to Win: The Strategy of John Boyd, Applied to Business.* Xlibris Corporation, 2004.

Safranski, Mark "The Origins of John Boyd's A Discourse on Winning and Losing." In *The John Boyd Roundtable: Debating Science, Strategy, and War,* 6–10. Nimble Books, 2008.

Riley, James C. *Rising Life Expectancy: A Global History.* Cambridge University Press, 2001.

"The Rise and Fall of Corporate R&D: Out of the Dusty Labs." *The Economist,* March 1, 2007. Available at http://globaltechforum.eiu.com/index.asp?layout=rich_story&doc_id=10225&title=The+rise+and+fall+of+corporate+R%26D&categoryid=15&channelid=5 (accessed December 14, 2009).

Robinson, Linda. *Masters of Chaos: The Secret History of the Special Forces.* PublicAffairs, 2004: 114

Rose, Frank. "Commercial Break." *Wired* (December 2006). Available at www.wired.com/wired/archive/14.12/tahoe.html (accessed October 7, 2009).

Ross, Alex. "Absolutely Final Applause Post." *The Rest Is Noise* (January 24, 2005). Available at www.therestisnoise.com/2005/01/mozart_ignoramu.html (accessed August 2, 2009).

Ross, Alex. "Applause: A Rest is Noise Special Report." *The Rest Is Noise* (February 18, 2005). Available at www.therestisnoise.com/2005/02/applause_ a_rest.html (accessed August 2, 2009).

Sandoval, Greg. "GM Slow to React to Nasty Ads." *CNET News,* April 3, 2006. Available at http://news.cnet.com/2100-1024_3-6057143.html (accessed October 7, 2009).

Sawyer, R. Keith. "Is Baseball Really a Team Sport?" *The Huffington Post,* June 12, 2007. Available at www.huffingtonpost.com/dr-r-keith-sawyer/is-baseball-really-a-team_b_50071.html.

Scherer, Klaus and Hans-Jörg Fahr. "Drag Forces in the Near and Distant Solar System." *Earth Planets Space* 50, nos. 6 and 7 (1998): 545–550.

Schwartz, Peter, and Kevin Kelly. "The Relentless Contrarian." *Wired* 4.08 (1996): 116.

Selby, John and Ahmos Netanel. *Executive Genius.* Career Press, 2008.

Sia, C. L., B. C. Y. Tan, and K. K. Wei. "Group Polarization and Computer-Mediated Communication: Effects of Communication Cues, Social Presence, and Anonymity." *Information Systems Research* 13, no. 1 (March 2002): 70–90.

Singh, Jasjit, and Lee Fleming. "Lone Inventors as Sources of Breakthroughs: Myth or Reality?" Social Science Research Network, July 24, 2009. Available at http://papers.ssrn.com/sol3/papers.cfm?abstract_id= 1299064 (accessed September 20, 2009).

Slavek, John, and Paul Donato. "Fast Times in a Hot Property Market: Frauds Which Contributed to Today's Financial Crisis." *Kroll Global Fraud Report,* January 7, 2009. Available at www.kroll.com/library/fraud/FraudReport_English-US_Jan09.pdf (accessed August 23, 2009).

Sobel, Andrew. "What's So Special about Special Ops?" *Strategy+Business* (November 24, 2009. Available at www.strategy-business.com/article/09403?pg=all (accessed November 25, 2009).

Spinney, Franklin. "Genghis John (Boyd)." *Proceedings of the U.S. Naval Institute.* July 1997: 42–47.

Steed, Brian L. *Piercing the Fog of War: Recognizing Change on the Battlefield.* Zenith Press, 2009.

Steel, Duncan. "Slow-Down in Space." Guardian.co.uk. February 28, 2002. Available at www.guardian.co.uk/science/2002/feb/28/physicalsciences.research.

Taleb, Nassem Nicholas. *The Black Swan: The Impact of the Highly Improbable*. Random House, 2007.

Talukdar, Sudip. "Makeshift Miracles: The Indian Genius for Jugaad." *The Times of India*. Available at http://timesofindia.indiatimes.com/home/opinion/edit-page/LEADER-ARTICLEBRMakeshift-Miracles-The-Indian-Genius-for-Jugaad/articleshow/398740.cms (accessed January 1, 2010).

Task Force on Financial Integrity and Economic Development. "Economic Transparency: Curtailing the Shadow Financial System." July 7, 2009. Available at www.financialtaskforce.org/wp-content/uploads/2009/06/the-case-for-global-financial-transparency-updated.pdf (accessed August 23, 2009).

Thompson, Clive. "The See-Through CEO." *Wired* (March 2007): 135–146.

Transparency International. "Transparency International: Financial Crisis a Betrayal of Public Trust." October 29, 2008. Available at www.transparency.org/news_room/latest_news/press_releases/2008/2008_10_30_amm_financial_crisis (accessed August 23, 2009).

Transparency International India. "India Corruption Study 2007." Available at www.transparencyindia.org/ICS_national_report_2007.pdf (accessed January 1, 2010).

The Universal Mind of Bill Evans. Directed by Louis Carvell. 1966.

U.S. Library of Congress. "Who invented the automobile?" Everyday Mysteries: Fun Science Facts from the Library of Congress. Feburary 12, 2009. Available at www.loc.gov/rr/scitech/mysteries/auto.html (accessed September 27, 2009).

Vandehei, Jim, and David Paul Kuhn. "Clinton Leadership a Study in Missteps." Politico, September 4, 2008. Available at www.politico.com/news/stories/0408/9478.html (accessed August 9, 2009).

von Clausewitz, Carl, Beatrice Heuser, and Michael Howard. *On War.* Oxford University Press, 2007.

Wallace, William E. "Michelangelo, C.E.O." *New York Times,* April 16, 1994. Available at www.nytimes.com/1994/04/16/opinion/michelangelo-ceo.html (accessed October10, 2009).

Warner, Philip. *The SAS: The Official History.* Sphere Books, 1982.

Weisberg, Robert W. *Creativity: Understanding Innovation in Problem Solving, Science, Invention, and the Arts*. Wiley, 2006.

Wesolkowki, Slawo. "The Invention of Enigma and How the Polish Broke It Before the Start of WWII." 2001 IEEE Conference on the History of Telecommunications, 2001.

Wharton School of the University of Pennsylvania. "How a Little 'Friction' Can Change a Competitive Landscape." Knowledge@Wharton, July 22, 2009. Available at http://knowledge.wharton.upenn.edu/article.cfm?articleid=2293 (accessed September 8, 2009).

Wheatley, Margaret J. "Leadership of Self-Organized Networks: Lessons from the War on Terror." *Performance Improvement Quarterly* 20, no. 2 (2007): 59–66.

World Bank. "New Global Poverty Estimates—What It Means for India." Available at http://go.worldbank.org/51QB3OCFU0 (accessed January 1, 2010).

World Health Organization. "The Top 10 Causes of Death." October 2008. Available at www.who.int/mediacentre/factsheets/fs310/en/index.html (accessed September 20, 2009).

Yamamori, Hisaaki. "Optimum Culture in the Cockpit." *Proceedings of the NASA/MAC Workshop on Cockpit Resource Management (NASA Conference Publication 2455).* Moffett Field, Calif.: NASA, Ames Research Center, 1987.

INDEX

Symbols

1-Click, 190
2008 NBA finals, 120

A

A-teams, 142
Abdul-Jabbar, Kareem, 12, 77
accepting
  responsibility, 68
  risk, 252
acknowledging
  efforts and results, 63-65
  efforts of team, 53-54
Adderley, Julian, 76, 136
advocacy, 156
Agile Manifesto, 28
agile methods, 28
agility, organizational agility, 44-45
aircraft, static stability, 222
Albrect, Karl, 43
Allies (WWII), 86
The Amsterdam Declaration on
  Transparency and Reporting, 66
applause rule, 148
Apple, 256
Aravind Eye Care Hospital, 172
Armstrong, B. J., 59
The Art of War, 29
Asian Development Bank, 171
assessment, 200
assimilation bias, 122

authenticity, 150-154
  perception of, 152
auto racing, 220-222
autonomy, 24
avoiding
  groupthink, 51
  risk, 251
  team elitism, 54-55
awareness, teams, 52-53

B

Bailey, Derek, 11
balance of power, 88
Baratto, Gen. David, 35
Barrett, Frank, 47, 103
basketball, 42
  team awareness, 52
  teams, 48
bass players, 62
Bastien, David, 9
bebop, 174
Beck, Kent, 116
Beckstrom, Rod A., 138
Beiderman, Patricia Ward, 39
Below Poverty Line (BPL), 171
Bennis, Warren, 7, 39, 155
  Leadership, 134
Benz, Karl, 240
Berkun, Scott, 240
best practices, risks of
  applying, 254

E

F

G

Gilmore, James, 151
Gladwell, Malcolm, 39
Godin, Seth, 37
Goldsby, John, xvi-xix
Google, 11, 231, 247
  grouplets, 247
Great Wall of China, 1
Gretzky, Wayne, 104
GRI (Global Reporting
  Initiative), 66
Grieg, Edvard, 72
groove, 207-209, 218
group polarization, 123
grouplets, Google, 247
groupthink
  avoiding, 51
  openness, 156
Guilford, Joy Paul, 237-238, 248

H

Hancock, Herbie, 40
  transparency, 148
harmony in jazz, 11, 38
Harris, Barry, xix
Harris, Jerome, 78
health, 219-222
  chronic conditions, 227
  injuries, 223-225
  low-back pain, 252
  monitoring, 231-232
  prevention, 225-226
  recovery, 228-230
  risks of staying healthy, 264
  shock, 231
heel-and-toe, 221
Heisenberg Uncertainty
  Principle, 227
heisenbug, 227
Hillaker, Harry, 94
hindsight bias, 125

Hinton, Milt, 78
Hostager, Todd, 9
human effect
  organizational agility, 44-45
  personal awareness, 40-43
human element, 35-36
  individuality, 37-40
human resources, managing, 45
hunting
  reacting too slowly, 90-91
  trying too hard, 89-90

I

IBM, 16
  Rational Team Concert, 17, 31
ideas, risk of exchanging, 264-265
identifying
  change, 129-131
  noise, 111-113
identity, 153
ignoring
  noise, 111-113
  risk, 252
illusions, 205
implicit theories, 152
improving processes, 32-33
improvising, 8-10, 13
"In the Hall of the Mountain
  King," 72
incestuous amplification, 123
increasing transparency, 147-150
India, poverty, 171-172
individuality, 37-40
  music, 38
information, versus data, 113-115
information bias, 123
information cascade, 88
initiative, 134-135
injuries, 223-225
  prevention, 225-226

M

maintaining momentum, 212, 216
managing
  human resources, 45
  risk, 251-252
mandelbug, 227
Manhattan Project, 39
marketing timing, 179
Martin, Roger, 122
Maxwell, John; leadership, 134
McCain, John, 3
measuring
  contributions, 166, 170-177
  success, 115-119
Michaelson, Gerald, 29
Microsoft, 256
A Midsummer Night's Dream, 74
MiG-15s, 94
Miller, Dr. Saul, 115
mistakes
  absorbing as a team, 49-50
  be willing to make, 74-77
modal jazz, 175
modules, timeliness, 158
momentum, 197
  critical mass, 198
  entrainment, 198
  form, 199-201
  groove, 207-209
  maintaining, 212, 216
  in organizations, 210-212
  pulse, 205-207
  risks of maintaining, 263
  tempo, 202-205
Mona Lisa, 150
monitoring health, 231-232
monoculture, 252
Monson, Ingrid, 62
Most Valuable Player award, 165

Motian, Paul, 62
motivation, 70
Mozart, 148
music, individuality, 38

N

NASA, Ames Research Center
  (pilot-error accidents), 156
navigating teams, 140-141
negative feedback loops, 88
Nelson, Lloyd S., 116
Netanel, Ahmos, 43
NIH (Not Invented Here), 123
noise, 111-113

O

O'Toole, James, 155
Obama, Barack, 3
obfuscation, 161
observation, 103-108
  cognitive biases, 121-123
  listening continuum, 108
  peripheral vision, 105
  sources of data, 107-111
  tunnel vision, 104
ODA (Special Forces Operational
  Detachment Alpha), 4
Ohno, Taiichi, 254
OODA (Observe, Orient, Decide,
  Act), 93
  Jazz Process and, 97-101
OODA Loop, 104, 123
  Boyd, Col. John, 92-95
open source projects, 225
openness, 154-157
optimizing friction, 190-194
orchestras, 177
Organizational Climate for
  Operational Success, 97

organizational restructuring, 32
organizations
    momentum, 210-212
    that lacked transparency, 162
originality, 238
Out of the Crisis, 117-118
overcommitment, 259

P

Page, Larry, 10, 247
Palin, Sarah, 3
Pareto principles, 39
passion
    performing with, 78-80
    risks of committing, 258
Peer Gynt, 72
people, 35-36
    individuality, 37-40
    organizational agility, 44-45
    personal awareness, 40-43
perception of authenticity, 152
perfect competition, 193
performance, 5-6
    learning from jazz, 6-10
performing
    with conviction, 72
    with passion, 78-80
    in social media, 80-81
peripheral vision, 105-106
personal awareness, 40-43
personality, creativity, 238
Peters, Tom, 95
Peterson, Oscar, 52
Peterson, Ralph, 75
pick-and-roll, 178
Pine II, B. Joseph, 151
Pink, Daniel H., 37
Pioneer 10, 119
Pioneer anomaly, 119
Pioneer effect, 119

pitch, determining, 89
planning, 200
political campaigns,
    contributions, 169
politics, synergy, 3
Porter, Lewis, 79
positive feedback loops, breaking
    out of, 91
positive static stability, 222
poverty, India, 171-172
premature termination of search
    for evidence, 123
prevention, 225-226
principles of Jazz Process, 85
processes
    defining, 28-30
    documenting, 30-31
    evolving and improving, 32-33
*Project Decisions: The Art and
    Science*, 123
projects, subprojects, 158
proximity, contributions, 179-181
Public Company Accounting
    Reform and Investor Protection
    Act of 2002, 155
pulse, 205-207, 218
    groove, 207-209
purpose tremor, 87

Q

quality movement, 151

R

rallying, 221
Rangers, 22, 29
Rarick, Charles, 121
Rational Team Concert, 17, 31
    collecting metrics, 63
    data versus information, 114
    observation, 109

FREE Online Edition

Your purchase of *The Jazz Process* includes access to a free online edition for 45 days through the Safari Books Online subscription service. Nearly every Addison-Wesley Professional book is available online through Safari Books Online, along with more than 5,000 other technical books and videos from publishers such as Cisco Press, Exam Cram, IBM Press, O'Reilly, Prentice Hall, Que, and Sams.

SAFARI BOOKS ONLINE allows you to search for a specific answer, cut and paste code, download chapters, and stay current with emerging technologies.

Activate your FREE Online Edition at
www.informit.com/safarifree

> **STEP 1:** Enter the coupon code: TDZSOXA.

> **STEP 2:** New Safari users, complete the brief registration form.
> Safari subscribers, just log in.

If you have difficulty registering on Safari or accessing the online edition, please e-mail customer-service@safaribooksonline.com